RJ Unstead's Book of
Kings & Queens

RJ Unstead's Book of Kings & Queens

Illustrated by Peter Dennis

WARD LOCK LIMITED·LONDON

© R. J. Unstead 1978
Illustrations © Ward Lock Limited 1978

First published in Great Britain in 1978
by Ward Lock Limited, 116 Baker Street,
London W1M 2BB, a member of the Pentos Group.

Text filmset in Baskerville
by Rembrandt Filmsetting Ltd, London

Printed in Great Britain by
Hollen Street Press, Slough.

Bound by Webb Son & Co. Ltd, Ferndale, S. Glamorgan.

British Library Cataloguing in Publication Data

Unstead, Robert John
    Kings and queens in world history.
    1. Kings and rulers – History – Juvenile Literature
    I. Title
    909   D107
    ISBN 0-7063-5550-4

Colour illustrations were kindly supplied by
the following: Werner Forman (p.33);
Scala (p.34); Michael Holford (pp.51, 52);
National Portrait Gallery, London (pp.133,
152); CFL-Giraudon (p.134); Lauros-
Giraudon (p.151). The painting on p.152 is
by Sir James Gunn.

Contents

FOREWORD

In this book are stories of twenty-four men and women who were, I think, among the more remarkable and interesting persons in world history. All of them were kings or queens, even though some might have been called Khan or Emperor or, in the case of William the Silent, merely Stadtholder. Altogether, more than 220 royal persons are mentioned in this book.

They include some whose achievements earned them the title of 'the Great', but others, tragic or ridiculous, were failures, and a few were quite ordinary persons who would not have aroused anyone's notice but for the accident of royalty.

Today, the few monarchs left are mostly regarded by their people with affectionate respect, and there is hardly one anywhere who would dare say, like James I,

> *Kings are justly called gods . . . they make and unmake their subjects . . . they have the power of raising up or casting down of life and death – to make of their subjects like men at chess.*

Nevertheless, although the conqueror's power of Alexander or Napoleon, the autocratic rule of Louis XIV or Frederick the Great and the despotic cruelty of Peter Romanov have dwindled to a mild and limited authority, worship of power has not disappeared. Our own century has seen the rise of dictators with powers even more frightening than those of the emperors. But a King *was* different from ordinary mortals. In ancient times, he was a god or the god's representative on earth; later, anointed and crowned with solemn pomp, he held his authority by divine Will. His subjects therefore regarded him with awe and served him with loyalty amounting to worship. That is why they often put up with kings who were wicked, cruel or mad, for there was no sin worse than treason, no crime so monstrous as to depose or kill God's anointed.

Thus, kingship, in its splendour, loneliness and power for good or evil, is a fascinating subject and, in this collection of stories, I have tried to describe some of the persons who held this godlike power and what they did with it and, perhaps even more interesting, what it did to them.

R. J. Unstead

7

'Here,' cried Akhnaten to his courtiers, 'is the site of Aten's city. It shall be called Akhet-aten, the City of the Horizon.'

AKHNATEN OF EGYPT

'Make way! Make way for Pharaoh!' cried the runners, as they trotted out from the huge gateway of the temple of Amen-Ra.

With their staves, they struck right and left at the people who crowded forward to see the richest king on earth.

Suddenly, the gilded chariot came into view. Above the running footmen and the royal bodyguards, Pharaoh himself could be seen, standing erect in a dazzling white robe, a tall disdainful figure, made taller by the high crown of Egypt.

In a swirl of dust, the chariot and its escort passed rapidly down the avenue of crouching sphinxes and entered the Queen's Palace called The House of Joy.

Pharaoh strode through a dozen lofty rooms until he came to the Queen's glorious apartment. A servant was painting Queen Tiyi's eyelids, while a black maiden rubbed scented oil into the soles of her feet. The servants slid away and the Queen rose:

'Have you prayed for our son, my lord?' she asked.

'I have left Aahmes, the High Priest, at his prayers. I have told him to tell the god that I will eat him in Paradise if he does not make our son well.'

'The boy is sleeping now,' said the Queen. 'Perhaps tomorrow he will be better.'

'Ah, Tiyi, why could not the gods have sent us a son as beautiful as his mother and as strong as I? But come, forget our grief. Let us sail for an hour in your golden pleasure-boat. Tomorrow, I leave for the lion-hunt.'

The lordly Pharaoh never saw his ailing son again. His chariot overturned during the hunt and he was trampled to death by the horsemen following hard behind. Queen Tiyi was left to rule the kingdom until her little son, Amenhotep IV, was considered old enough to take his father's place.

The child was delicate and he grew into an awkward, ugly boy. He shambled along on spindly legs and his head, too big for his thin body, was thrust forward like some puzzled animal. His large, gentle eyes seemed always to be searching for something and his lips were parted as if to speak with trembling eagerness. His tutors reported to the Queen that the boy was clever, though he liked poetry and pet animals better than archery and riding.

When he was nine, Amenhotep was married, since royal Egyptians were given a bride at an early age. Queen Tiyi chose the Princess Nefertiti, a little girl as shy and beautiful as a fawn, who came to live at the Palace and to play in its gardens with her boy-husband.

At fifteen, Amenhotep began to rule Egypt. He sat on his father's jewelled throne to receive ambassadors and governors from the distant parts of his vast Empire. He listened to reports about crops, trade and foreign kingdoms; he rode out to inspect troops, buildings and canals. He was surrounded by counsellors and ministers. The most powerful of all, forever whispering and warning, was Aahmes, the High Priest.

One day, as he walked with Nefertiti in the scented garden, Amenhotep burst out, 'I hate this city of Thebes!'

'You hate the richest and most wonderful city in the world?' cried Nefertiti.

'Rich? Wonderful? Rich with wealth piled up into monstrous temples. Wonderful for the darkness of fear. Aahmes and the priests are strong because everyone fears the gods and only the priests can understand them—or so they say.'

'Hush, lord husband. The gods might hear you.'

'Ah, the gods. There are so many. They say that my ancestor, Amen-Ra, is the greatest, but there is Osiris too, who judges the dead, Nut, goddess of the sky, Bast, the cat-goddess, Anubis, the jackal-headed one. Sebek, the crocodile, Thoth, Neith, Horus and so on and so on to Bes, the little fat dwarf-god. Why, there are thirty-six gods to look after the parts of our bodies!'

'But this is so, husband. There *are* many gods in Egypt.'

'Listen, dearest Queen, and look about you. Look at these feathery leaves, this blossom whose petals are so frail that no court jeweller can match their beauty. Look at these great painted butterflies and that white bird dipping low across the lake. Outside, in the fields, the corn grows tall and the waters of the river nourish the earth.

'Who gives us all this beauty and life? Not those gods in the dim temples. I believe that there is only one god and he is there, Nefertiti, above us.'

'Above us? I do not see a god in the tall trees.'

'Look in the sky. There is Aten, the Shining One, who brings life to the earth. He is our god. He alone.'

Once he had put his belief into words, Amenhotep found the strength to act. He dismissed Aahmes from the Court and began to speak openly of his new religion. He sent heralds through the land with a proclamation:

> *Be it known that Pharaoh, the All-Wise Father of Egypt, hath decreed that Aten, Disk of the Sun, is the true god, the giver of life.*
> *Since his old name is hateful to him, Pharaoh hath taken a new name. Hail Akhn-aten, Spirit of Aten, pleasing to Aten is thy name!*

The priests of Amen-Ra were deeply shocked. They prayed, lectured and threatened. The King was young. He must learn who really ruled Egypt. A weakling could not challenge the power of Amen-Ra and his priests. But in the dreamy eyes of Akhnaten was a new look of determination. He was Akhnaten now. In him dwelt the spirit of the god. Nothing could harm or frighten him.

Instead, it was Aahmes who began to be frightened. He could see his power slipping away. He paid men to whisper against the Pharaoh, so that the people muttered and turned aside when the royal chariot passed. He spoke to nobles who were shocked by Akhnaten's ideas and he held secret talks with generals of the army. Perhaps, he whispered, it would be best to remove Pharaoh; an accident or a revolt might be arranged; poison might find its way into the royal kitchens.

But Pharaoh's spies were not idle. Akhnaten was kept informed about the plots and began to make his plans.

'I shall leave Thebes,' he announced. 'Aten shall not dwell in the same city as Amen-Ra. Let us build a new capital where Aten may be worshipped in temples open to the sacred rays of light.'

So, in the sixth year of his reign, Akhnaten and Nefertiti went aboard the royal barge and were rowed away from Thebes. They took with them their closest friends, some of the loyal ministers and a nobleman named Ay who was now the High Priest of Aten. A great crowd on the quay watched in silence as they left.

For two days, the rowers sweated at the oars. At length, two hundred miles downstream, the glittering barge and its fleet of escorting vessels came to a place where the cliffs curved away into a crescent-shaped plain, eight miles long.

'Here,' cried Akhnaten to his courtiers, 'is the site of Aten's city. It shall be called Akhet-aten, the City of the Horizon.'

At fantastic speed, the new capital of Egypt took shape, as the eager King urged on the overseers of the labour gangs. The delicate youth who had hated hunting and hard exercise found a new energy that astonished his friends. He was out at dawn with the architects, measuring, directing and praising the progress.

The King's House and the Royal Palace rose on either side of a noble avenue. Nearby stood the Great Temple of Aten, two hundred metres in length and open to the sun's rays. Beyond the gardens and lake were mansions of the nobles, built in sumptuous style with courts where fountains tinkled softly among the palm trees.

In a short time, Akhnaten established his Court in the new capital, with Queen Nefertiti, their three little daughters and the officials of the kingdom. He continued to lay out gardens and ornamental lakes. In the Palace grounds, there was a zoo with aviaries, an aquarium and many rare animals.

As the city neared completion, religion became the centre of Akhnaten's life. He ordered Amen-Ra's name to be hacked from every monument and temple in the land and he forbade worship of any god except Aten.

This worship of one god was an entirely new idea to the Egyptians. While, in the new capital, Ay the Priest and the inhabitants obeyed Pharaoh, the rest of the nation continued at heart to reverence the old gods. At Thebes, the priests of Amen-Ra glowered and bided their time.

But Akhnaten was happy. With his beloved Queen, he spent his days making the city beautiful and proclaiming the truth about Aten.

Aten, he said, was all-powerful but he was also loving and kind. He bade people live peaceably, not in fear, but with honesty and kindliness towards one another.

Until this time, artists had always carved and painted the Pharaohs in stiff, dignified poses. But Akhnaten, seeking truth, gave orders that artists must set down exactly what they saw. It was exciting for a sculptor to use his chisel in this way and to be rewarded for carving a statue that revealed the King's podgy stomach, his thick lips and large nose.

On the walls of tombs hewn out of the cliffs near the city, there were scenes showing Akhnaten and Nefertiti in their everyday lives. Those carvings are still there and the royal couple can be seen together, the King kissing his baby daughter while the Queen smilingly nurses a second child. The Queen Mother, Tiyi, can be seen at dinner, passing a titbit to one of the little princesses while her son gnaws a cutlet and Nefertiti eats a whole roasted chicken.

In these pictures, Aten's rays are shining down upon the Royal Family, each ray ending in a little hand that seems to caress them.

To please his master, Ay the Priest had a tomb hewn out for himself and on its walls he had carved the great hymn of praise which Akhnaten wrote to his god. This long poem, not unlike the Psalms of David, is filled with the wonder of a poet who sees beauty all around him and thinks of the god who gave so much to the people of the world.

But while he dreamed and wrote his poems, Akhnaten's empire was crumbling. Letters came to the Palace from governors and from commanders holding out desperately in distant fortresses. They begged Pharaoh to send help. One governor wrote, 'I need men to save the rebellion of this land. . . . Give me soldiers!'

There was no reply. Perhaps Akhnaten put the message on one side and forgot it or perhaps he was never told.

A letter of despair arrived: 'There is no money to buy horses. All is finished. . . . Give me thirty companies of horses with chariots—men! men!'

Was Akhnaten lost in his dream of beauty? Did he care nothing for his kingdom and for the brave men dying at their posts? We cannot tell. We know that parts of the empire were lost and that he made no effort at all to save them.

At Thebes, the people said, 'Amen-Ra is angry. That is why our armies have been defeated. This new god is a weakling and we will not obey Pharaoh.'

The priests began to stir up rebellion, so Akhnaten sent the husband of one of his daughters to rule in Thebes, but he would not go there himself. He could not bear to leave his beautiful city. Seeing her children in danger, Nefertiti tried to rouse the King:

'You must put down the priests,' she cried. 'Place yourself at the head of an army and march to Thebes. The people love you, but they are puzzled and they want a leader. What is more, do not trust Ay the Priest. He still has friends in Thebes. But you must act!'

Akhnaten looked sadly at his beautiful wife. She did not understand. He was Aten's spirit; power meant nothing, bloodshed was useless. His life had to be spent in worshipping the god of beauty.

The quarrel grew deeper and Nefertiti retired to her own palace with one of her daughters who was married to a noble youth named Tutankh-aten.

Heart-broken and alone in the Southern Palace, Akhnaten died in the seventeenth year of his reign. His religion died with him.

Nefertiti had her son-in-law proclaimed Pharaoh. The crafty Ay soon enticed him to Thebes where the priests made the boy change his name to Tutankh-*amen*, so that it ended with Amen's name.

That was not all. The names of Akhnaten and of the hated god were chiselled from all his monuments and temples; they were to be forgotten as if they had never existed. As for the beautiful City of the Horizon, it was deserted. Since the curses of all the gods would fall upon a man who set foot there, it was left to slide into ruins. Gradually, the gracious buildings tumbled and sand covered the broad avenues.

But Akhnaten has not been forgotten. The gentle poet-king was the first ruler to believe in one god and it is thought that Moses may have lived at Akhnaten's Court. Perhaps it was there that he, too, came to believe in one God.

More about Akhnaten (died c. 1350 BC)

Akhnaten, also known as Amenhotep IV and Amenophis IV, came to the throne in about the year 1375 BC when the New Empire was at its peak of power and wealth. Egypt had been civilised for three thousand years before his reign and Akhnaten belonged to the Eighteenth Dynasty or family of rulers whose great Pharaohs had included Thotmes I, Queen Hatshepsut and Thotmes III.

The new sacred capital Akhetaten was built half-way between Thebes and Cairo where the modern town of El-Amarna now stands. Diggings were made there from 1891 to 1937 by British and German archaeologists who uncovered the foundations of vast numbers of brick buildings and they also found clay tablets covered with writing. Among them were the pleas for help sent by governors and military commanders of distant provinces in Syria and Palestine where rebellions had broken out against Egyptian rule. Rock tombs were discovered in nearby cliffs where the wall-carvings can still be seen but, although a boundary stone was found on which Akhnaten recorded his intention to be buried in his beloved city, his tomb has not been identified there. A mummy, discovered in a damaged tomb at another place, has been thought to be Akhnaten's but this is doubtful. It seems however that he was not buried with the magnificent pomp accorded to other Pharaohs.

The beautiful Queen, Nefertiti, did not go back to Thebes with her daughter but she stayed on in the now accursed city until her death.

Akhnaten's son-in-law, the new Pharaoh Tutankhamen, was twelve when Ay the priest took him to Thebes and made him return to the old religion. He died in about 1340 BC when only nineteen, yet, by pure chance, Tutankhamen has become one of the most famous of all the Pharaohs. Grave-robbers always plundered the royal tombs but the entrance to Tutankhamen's tomb was covered by stone chippings from a later tomb and the secret lay hidden for 3,000 years until, in 1922, an Englishman named Howard Carter uncovered a flight of stone steps leading downwards. The tomb was opened and its astounding riches were so great that Carter spent ten years in examining and cataloguing them. Most of them are now to be seen in Cairo Museum, whilst the stone sarcophagus and one of the gold coffins it contained still lie in the tomb in the Valley of the Kings.

There is one last twist to Akhnaten's strange story. Tutankhamen left no son, so the divine blood of kingship was now possessed only by his widow, Akhnaten's daughter, and the priests therefore decreed that she must take another husband who would become Pharaoh. This proved to be none other than the rascally priest Ay. The young Queen did her utmost to find someone else, but in vain. Ay's corrupt reign was soon brought to an end by Hor-em-heb, an Egyptian general who was able to become Pharaoh because he was married to a royal princess, Nefertiti's sister. The Eighteenth Dynasty was over and the new family of kings that succeeded it included two of the greatest Pharaohs, Seti I and Rameses II.

Alexander treated them nobly. 'I am not here to fight against women,' he said. 'I have come to master the empire of Asia.'

ALEXANDER THE GREAT

'Look! Look at the King's new horse! What a splendid creature! See how he kicks. No one will ever stay on his back!'

The cries of the excited boys could be heard across the dusty parade-ground where, in the presence of the King and his attendants, half a dozen grooms were trying to subdue a magnificent horse that reared and plunged with terrifying strength.

One of the boys, fair-haired and taller than the rest, suddenly ran across to the leader of the struggling grooms and spoke to him sharply.

'Give me the rope, Amyntas. I will ride him!'

The startled man let go the bridle and before even the King himself could act, the boy had turned the horse's head and had led him away from the noisy crowd of onlookers. Patting the horse's neck with his free hand, speaking to him softly and, above all, making sure that the animal could no longer see his own shadow which had been the cause of his terrified behaviour, the boy quickly brought the horse under control. Then he leapt upon his back and rode across to where the King was watching from the shade of the cypress trees.

The King, no longer anxious, roared with laughter. 'Keep him, he is yours!' he shouted. 'You conquered him so easily, you must ride him to conquer kingdoms!'

The boy was Alexander, son of King Philip of Macedonia, who ruled a half-civilised kingdom to the north of Greece more than three hundred years before the birth of Christ. The horse was Bucephalus, the 'bull-headed one', and he was soon to carry the boy in triumph across the known world.

King Philip was a mighty ruler. By skill and cunning, he had made his little kingdom powerful, for he had not only subdued the lands that lay northwards, but he had made all the city-states of Greece, except Sparta, recognise him as their overlord.

Alexander was brought up in a draughty palace that echoed with the quarrels between his father and his furious-tempered mother, Olympias, but the lad was given an education to fit him for greatness.

He was taught how to ride, hunt and fight like any young noble but his father also summoned from Greece the great scholar Aristotle to act as tutor. From Aristotle, Alexander learned about science and mathematics; he grew to love Greek ideas and, above all, the stories of the Greek heroes who had fought at Troy. He knew Homer's long poem, 'The Iliad', by heart and he carried the book with him wherever he went.

Alexander was certain that he was more than a Macedonian. His father had the head of Heracles (Hercules) stamped on his coins, so the boy felt sure that he was descended from that legendary figure, half-god, half-man, and, on his mother's side, from Achilles, the hero of the Siege of Troy.

At sixteen, Alexander was left in charge of the kingdom while his father was on campaign. At eighteen, he commanded a wing of the army that defeated the Greeks and made them obey Philip. But soon afterwards, the family quarrels grew worse and Alexander and his mother had to take refuge in an uncle's kingdom.

Just when it seemed as if Alexander would never inherit his father's throne, for Philip had taken a second wife and had a baby son, he suddenly became King of Macedonia.

Philip was stabbed to death at a marriage feast by a discontented noble and, in the confusion, Alexander seized his chance with the speed for which he was soon to be famous. He won over the army with fiery promises, crushed the Greek cities that had jeered at the idea of taking orders from a mere boy of twenty, and announced that he would raise a force of Greeks and Macedonians to conquer the mighty Persians whose empire stretched from the Mediterranean to the frontiers of India.

In 334 BC, Alexander left Greece with an army of 30,000 foot-soldiers and 5,000 horsemen. It was a small force to challenge the numberless hordes of Persia, but although the archers and the cavalry were splendidly trained, the strength lay in the Macedonian way of fighting under the brilliant commander. The soldiers formed up in dense squares armed with pikes of enormous length, so that an attacker could not pierce the wall of spears; when the square, known as the 'phalanx', charged, no army in the world could stand against it.

Having prayed to his heroic ancestors at the site of ancient Troy, Alexander advanced to meet the army sent against him by Darius III, ruler of the Persian empire. He found the enemy drawn up on the far bank of a river. The Greeks hesitated, but Alexander plunged into the water with reckless bravery calling them to follow. The white plume was slashed from his helmet, his pike broke and he had just seized another, when he was narrowly saved from death by his friend Clitus. After a furious battle, the Persians broke and fled.

Alexander sent some of the captured gold vessels and rare Persian cloth to his mother. To Athens, in honour of the goddess Athene, he sent 300 Persian shields with these words engraved upon them:

Alexander and the Greeks (except the Spartans)
won these from the barbarians of Asia.

With furious energy, Alexander now marched through Asia Minor, capturing city after city, but Darius himself soon advanced with an enormous army to put an end to this upstart conqueror. So confident was Darius that he brought his family with him, living in the camp in silk-lined tents with luxuries and slaves.

Again, the Greeks were victorious and Darius fled, leaving behind immense treasure and his wife, mother and young children who cowered trembling in the tent, awaiting the fate of royal captives. But Alexander treated them nobly. 'I am not here to fight against women,' he said. 'And my contest with Darius is not undertaken out of hatred. I have come to master the empire of Asia.'

But when Darius sent a letter asking for peace and friendship between equals, Alexander was scornful to the man who had run away. 'I have defeated your generals and now yourself,' he wrote back. 'Come without fear and you shall receive back your mother and wife and anything else you please. But do not write to me as an equal, address me as Lord of Asia and of all that belongs to you.'

The conqueror turned south. Syria was taken, Tyre was captured, Jerusalem was entered to the songs of the welcoming priests and then the great land of Egypt was reached. Here, Alexander founded a city at the mouth of the Nile and named it, like many others, Alexandria, in his own honour.

From Egypt, the Greeks marched back into Persia to fight Darius for the third and last time. His army was said to number a million men but it was routed and Darius fled once more. Eventually he was slain by his own bodyguards who hoped that Alexander would reward them, but he put them to death for their treachery.

The hardbitten Greek and Macedonian soldiers now entered the cities of Persia behind their god-like leader. The treasures of Babylon and Susa filled them with amazed greed, but Persepolis, the capital, was more magnificent still. After a great feast, Alexander himself set fire to the beautiful city and utterly destroyed its temples and avenues of statues; he did this to show that Persia had been laid low, though he was afterwards sorry for the deed.

The truth was that the character of Alexander was changing. The noble youth was becoming suspicious and cruel. He still loved knowledge; he was as generous and brave as ever, but he began to behave like an Eastern tyrant, surrounding himself with slaves and Asiatic attendants, making even his generals bow themselves to the ground when they approached him,. He had his trustiest old general put to death and, in a fit of temper, he stabbed his friend Clitus who had once saved his life.

Alexander soon became bored with all the feasting and athletic games that followed his victory. He told his soldiers to destroy their plunder, for he would lead them to fresh triumphs. Mounted on Bucephalus, he led them eastwards, conquering every tribe and kingdom that stood in his path until he reached the foothills of India.

The invincible army broke into the Punjab and defeated King Porus with his immense force of cavalry and elephants, for even these great creatures could not daunt the men who followed Alexander. As usual he treated his foe generously, and leaving Porus to rule for him, he planned to go to the end of the world where, the Greeks believed, he would find the uncrossable river called Ocean.

First, however, Bucephalus, the marvellous horse who had died from old age, had to be given a splendid burial at a place where a city was to be built in his honour. Then a greater sorrow came to Alexander. His troops refused to march. He pleaded and threatened, but in vain. The men would not go on. 'I have known defeat only from my own soldiers!' cried Alexander when he gave the order to turn westwards.

On the way back, the soldiers suffered terrible hardships; half the army died of thirst in a desert but the survivors struggled on to Babylon. Here, Alexander set up a sumptuous court and busied himself with endless plans for his vast empire which he would bind together by means of the Greek language and Greek culture. He was planning cities, harbours and voyages of exploration when he caught a fever in the marshes of the River Euphrates. He was still only thirty-two when he died at Babylon.

Near the end, his Macedonian veterans, eager to see their beloved leader once more, broke into the Palace and filed past the couch of the dying man.

'There will be splendid Games at my funeral,' he joked as they came slowly by, and then, almost to himself, 'It is sweet to have lived with courage and after death to leave behind immortal fame.'

More about Alexander the Great (356–323 BC)

Alexander the Great was the son of Philip II of Macedon (382–336 BC), a soldier-king who trained his army so skilfully that, by 338 BC, he had subdued the city-states of Greece. Jealousy and the long war between Athens and Sparta had weakened Greece since the Golden Age of Pericles, Rome was still a struggling little town fighting for its life against the local tribes, and the great empires of the past, Egypt, Babylon and Assyria, had fallen under the rule of Persia.

Alexander was only twenty when he crossed into Asia Minor with an army of Macedonians and Greeks but his brilliance as a general and the discipline of his troops enabled him to defeat the vast Persian armies at the battles of Granicus, Issus and Arbela (331 BC). Leaving Macedonian governors to rule the conquered territories and the new towns which he founded, Alexander pushed into the wild regions south of the Caspian Sea, defeated the tribes, overcame an army revolt and married Roxana, daughter of a chieftain. The successful invasion of India was an incredible feat by a small army consisting mostly of foot-soldiers armed with pikes, bows and swords.

Though he was vain and cruel, Alexander was far more than a mere conqueror. His brilliant mind planned to unite his conquests into one great family of Greek-speaking people with Babylon as their capital. No one can tell what the course of history might have been if he had lived longer; as it was, his empire was divided into separate kingdoms and most of them, 300 years later, became provinces of Rome.

JULIUS CAESAR

The pirate galley swept alongside the merchant ship and, with cries of triumph, the pirates leapt aboard and forced the crew at dagger-point to hand over everything of value in the cargo. The passengers were lined up on deck.

In Roman times, piracy in the Mediterranean was a well organized business and the pirates gleefully noticed that their captives included a young nobleman with his ten slaves:

'We shall hold you until your servants bring us a ransom of twenty talents of silver!' they cried.

'Am I worth no more than that?' answered the scornful Roman. 'My men will bring you fifty talents! Then, when I am freed, I shall come back and hang the lot of you!'

Delighted with the young man's boldness, the pirates carried him off to an island, while his servants were dispatched to raise the large ransom. By the time it arrived, the pirates and the young man were firm friends, for the nobleman's wit and athletic skill won the admiration of his rascally companions.

Released from captivity, the Roman acted swiftly. He ordered the authorities at a Greek port to provide him with ships and volunteers with whom he sailed back to the island. There he surprised the pirates and captured the entire band. True to his promise, he ordered that the criminals should be crucified, but, as a mark of his friendship, their throats were to be cut to shorten their sufferings.

The young man was Gaius Julius Caesar, and the adventure with the pirates showed that he was already brave and ruthless. Born into one of the noblest families in Rome, so ancient that he claimed descent from the early kings and even from a goddess, young Caesar had been on his way to Rhodes to study the art of making speeches, since he intended to be a politician.

But politics was a dangerous game in Rome. Two rival parties were engaged in a bloodthirsty struggle. On one side was the Senate party, composed of rich nobles, and, on the other side, was the Popular party of the common people, with a sprinkling of aristocrats and ambitious young men.

Young Caesar was in a tricky position. By birth, he was a noble, but his uncle by marriage had been the great Marius, a famous general who had cared about the poor and humble folk. Since the people still remembered Marius as a hero, the Senate looked on his nephew with suspicion. That was why Caesar had taken the voyage to Rhodes. He had been warned that it would be safer for him to leave the city for a while.

Presently, Caesar returned to Rome to live as a smart young man-about-town. He was handsome and charming, and although his family was not wealthy, he spent money like water, so that his parties and entertainments became a by-word. Generous to the poor, he provided shows for the crowds of unemployed who lounged about the streets and made trouble unless they were given free food and amusements.

No one knew where Caesar got his money from. Once, he put on a show in which 320 pairs of gladiators appeared in silver armour. The mob loved him for this showmanship and for the glamour that surrounded an elegant aristocrat who would chat to a workman in the streets. People whispered that his money came from Crassus, the richest man in Rome. Crassus had his own reasons for assisting the brilliant young man.

Eventually, with the help of Crassus, who paid his debts, Caesar became Governor of Spain, where he had his first experience of real fighting against rebellious mountain tribes. In less than two years, he was back in Rome with plans to climb even higher.

The famous general, Pompey, had returned from his victorious wars in Asia, but the Senate feared his popularity and would not give him the plots of land he had promised to his soldiers. So Pompey looked round for support and, since he disliked Crassus, he turned to Caesar. The Senate was alarmed at this partnership and Caesar used all his charm to bring Pompey and Crassus together. The three friends soon became the real rulers of Rome.

After a year as Consul, Caesar received the reward he had been longing for— the Governorship of Gaul. In March 58 BC, at the age of forty-one, he left Rome and it was nine years before he saw the city again.

During those nine years, Caesar astonished everyone. He had made his name as a playboy politician who could make speeches, but no one imagined he could command armies. Yet, given the chance, he immediately proved himself a master of war.

We often think of Gaul as the old name for France, but to the Romans it was a much larger area. It included Northern Italy and a strip of Southern France, both civilised and peaceful by this time but, inland, Gaul was a wild, little-known land, making up what is now France, Belgium, Holland and parts of Switzerland and Germany.

When Caesar arrived in his new province, he found that the Helvetii, a sturdy race inhabiting Switzerland, were preparing to invade southern Gaul. The new Governor surprised everyone with the speed with which he defeated the tribesmen and hurled them back into their mountains. Then he pushed into Gaul itself.

It was a hard and risky task to attempt conquest. Gaul had none of the treasures that could be won in the fabulous East, for it was a land of woods, plains and swamps, with a bitter climate for men from the Mediterranean lands. There were no sumptuous palaces or cities, no highways tramped out by centuries of conquest and trade, only earth-walled settlements and grassy tracks, defended by proud tribesmen whom the Romans had dreaded for hundreds of years.

Nor were there any obvious advantages for the Roman legions. The Roman soldier was not better-armed than the Gaul; he was a swordsman, trained to fight with a short sword and a large square shield; he carried no spear, but two javelins which he hurled at the last moment, before closing in on the enemy. The legionary was a professional soldier, who served for pay and for the loot that he could win, and his oath of loyalty was not to Rome, but to his commander. His sole advantage in war was discipline and training in absolute obedience.

With men like this, Caesar fought battle after battle, nearly always against superior numbers and almost always victoriously. By this time, the pleasure-loving gallant of Rome was as hard as nails. He was an excellent swordsman and horseman, though he usually led his armies on foot, bareheaded to the rain and sun. He always travelled fast and shared the same hardships as his men. Like them, he could swim an unfordable river, scramble over an enemy rampart or force his way across a swampland; then, at the end of each day, he would supervise the building of the fortified camp that the Romans always constructed. He was tireless and thorough, taking as much care in protecting his forces from sudden attack as in questioning spies to find out the enemy's plans.

Knowing that his strength lay in the discipline of his troops, Caesar treated them all alike and kept them forever on the alert. He would reward bravery, but often he ordered his men to turn out needlessly at night or, on a rest-day, he would suddenly dart off and expect them to follow. Once, he rallied his men in battle by seizing the precious Standard from a legionary who had lost his nerve. On another occasion, when the Twelfth Legion was hard-pressed by the Belgians, he snatched up a fallen shield and led a charge on foot. As a result, the legions adored him and when civil war came, hardly a man deserted him.

After two years of hard campaigning, Caesar could claim that he had conquered the whole of Gaul, from the Alps to the Atlantic. The Senate had to order a festival of thanksgiving in Rome that lasted fifteen days.

There was still much to be done. The Gauls had been defeated but they had not really been conquered, and were still longing to throw off the hated rule of Rome. Caesar proved to be a terrible foe, for he did not hesitate to massacre a defeated army or to sell whole tribes into slavery. Yet, once the Gauls had submitted, he treated them justly, for he admired them and knew that they would soon make good Roman citizens.

By the fourth year of war, the legions had reached the Rhine and Caesar decided that the German tribes must be taught to keep out of Gaul. He defeated them with horrible slaughter and then ordered his soldiers to build a bridge across the river. They did so in no more than ten days and the army marched into Germany to overawe the tribesmen.

Next, Rome was agog with excitement to learn that Caesar was about to invade Britain, the remote island that was supposed to be the Land of the Dead. It was also thought to be rich in gold and tin.

With only two legions, numbering about 8,000 men, carried in eighty ships, Caesar crossed the English Channel and coasted along the Kent cliffs until he came to a sloping beach, where the heavy ships drove their prows into the pebbles several yards from shore.

The Britons had gathered in force to repel the invaders. Their ferocious appearance, the war-chariots wheeling to the water's edge, the rain of spears, the surge of the waves and the confusion of the ships as they canted over with sails flapping, filled the Roman soldiers with dismay. The hardened legionaries hated the sea and, for a moment, they hesitated. 'Then,' wrote Caesar in his 'History' 'the Standard-bearer of the Tenth, calling on the gods to bless the legion, shouted, "Come on, men! Jump, unless you want to betray your Standard to the enemy!"'

The disgrace of losing a Standard was unthinkable, so with hoarse shouts, the legionaries leapt after their comrade and struggled ashore through the surf.

The fight on the beach was bitter, but once they were on land, the Romans formed their ranks and pressed the painted warriors back until they retreated to the woods. The ships carrying the cavalry had not arrived, so Caesar could not follow up his hard-won advantage.

A camp was built and the British chiefs had come in with offers to pay tribute, when a disaster almost overwhelmed the invasion force. The Romans knew little about ocean tides and were horrified to awake one morning to find that some of their ships had floated off the beach, while those at anchor had broken their cables and drifted away. It looked as if the expedition would be stranded and, naturally, the Britons saw their opportunity to attack.

While an outer ring of defenders beat off the tribesmen, the rest of the soldiers broke up the wrecked vessels to obtain nails and planks to repair those that were less damaged. It was close work and, after a stay of only three weeks, the Roman force managed to return to Gaul.

It had been anything but a glorious expedition and Caesar was not the man to sit down under a defeat. All that winter, he kept his men hard at work building a new fleet of ships, many of them specially designed by himself.

In 54 BC, a much larger expedition sailed for Britain. Again, the Britons offered fierce resistance and were defeated; again, the fleet was damaged and speedily repaired. This time, however, Caesar advanced inland, forced his way across the Thames and sacked the British stronghold near St Albans.

The Britons asked for peace, offering hostages and promises of grain and tin, which Caesar gladly accepted, for the news from Gaul was bad. He was forced to leave the island in order to deal with a full-scale rebellion that had broken out in his absence.

The Gauls had rallied under the leadership of a chief named Vercingetorix, who scorned to lose his freedom for the sake of Roman peace and fine towns. He laid waste the land so that the Romans were almost starving, then he attacked the garrisons and forced some of his enemies to retreat. A legion was cut to pieces on the march; Roman troops holding a fort killed themselves rather than be captured. One major defeat could have turned the legions into a rabble, had not Caesar returned to rally the troops.

Relentlessly, he crushed the rebellion and hunted down the leaders, putting most of them to death, though he spared Vercingetorix in order to parade him in chains through the streets of Rome. Men said that by the time Gaul was finally conquered, a million Gauls had died and another million had been sold into slavery.

After nine years, Caesar settled his province. He imposed fair taxes and insisted that they were collected honestly; he founded law courts and opened the ranks of the legions to Gallic volunteers. The Gauls mourned their dead heroes, but the country became quiet and prosperous.

What was Caesar to do next? His thoughts turned to Rome where the party struggle was as bitter as ever: Crassus was dead and Pompey had gone over to the side of the Senate, who still hated Caesar and feared his power. Suddenly, he received an order to quit his legions and return to Rome as a private citizen. He knew that if he obeyed, he was ruined, so he decided to meet the threat in his own way.

At the head of his army, Caesar marched to Italy and reached the Rubicon, a stream that marked the limit of his territory. No commander was allowed to bring troops beyond this point, but, after a short hesitation, Caesar gave the order to cross the Rubicon and march on Rome. Pompey and many of the Senators fled to Greece and Caesar entered the city in triumph.

In a whirlwind campaign, he crushed Pompey's legions in Spain and then crossed into Greece and defeated Pompey himself, who escaped from the battle and made his way to Egypt. Caesar pursued his rival through Asia Minor and boldly shipped his exhausted troops to Alexandria where he learned that Pompey had been murdered.

For a time, the conqueror lingered in Egypt, where he is said to have fallen in love with Queen Cleopatra. Soon, he was back in Asia to defeat an Asiatic king so swiftly that, in his despatch to Rome, he described his victory in three words, 'Veni, Vidi, Vici', meaning 'I came, I saw, I conquered'. Finally, he crossed to North Africa to crush the last forces of the Senate.

Ten years after he had first taken command of an army, Caesar was master of the Roman Empire. The people made him Dictator, a king in all but name.

During the short time left to him, Caesar showed his true greatness. Unlike previous conquerors, he did not massacre the citizens of Rome but he tried instead to bring peace to the troubled Empire.

He settled many soldiers on farms in Italy and encouraged others to settle in the lands they had conquered, for the Romans always preferred town life and where there were towns, civilisation could grow. Roads were built and plans were made for new ports, canals and aqueducts; Rome was to be beautified with splendid buildings, the government was to be reformed and the laws were to be strengthened, but before Caesar could complete his plans, he was murdered.

Many Senators still hated the all-powerful ruler and they won over some of his friends by pointing to his golden throne, to his statue placed among those of the ancient kings and to his air of being greater than mortal men:

'Caesar is ambitious,' they murmured. 'He means to be a king. See how he always wears that laurel wreath like a crown, see how he encourages the mob to hail him and to strew the streets with flowers whenever he appears!'

Friends warned him of plots, but the man who had survived twenty battles was not frightened of a pack of discontented Senators. Once, a soothsayer touched his arm as he passed and muttered, 'Beware the Ides of March, Great Caesar.'

When that day came, the fifteenth day of the month, Caesar left his house as usual to take his place in the Senate, though his wife tearfully begged him to remain at home. As he neared the Theatre of Pompey, where the Senate met since a mob had burned down the Senate House, he caught sight of the soothsayer among the crowd of idlers that thronged the street:

'Ah, old man,' he called, 'the Ides of March are come!'

'Yes,' replied the soothsayer, 'but they have not passed.'

Caesar went in smiling and was at once approached by a Senator who had a formal request to make. As usual, a group collected round the great man, but this time all were conspirators, holding daggers under their robes.

Suddenly, Casca drew his dagger and struck at his old enemy. Caesar, soldier-like, turned to defend himself, holding his toga over his left arm like a shield. A dozen daggers faced him and it is said that when he saw Brutus, one of his oldest friends, among those that were pressing in to kill him, he put his arm across his face and died, murmuring, 'And you, too, Brutus!'

He lay at the foot of Pompey's statue with more than twenty dagger wounds in his body, as the conspirators ran out into the Forum, crying 'Liberty! Liberty!'

More about Julius Caesar (c. 102–44 BC)

Gaius Julius Caesar was undoubtedly ruthless, extravagant and ambitious, but he was a brilliant success at everything that he attempted. By conquering Gaul and turning it into a rich, peaceful province, he delayed for over 200 years the invasions of the barbaric German tribes.

During the struggle with Pompey, Caesar conquered Italy, Spain, Sicily, Sardinia, Greece and Asia Minor; he made Cleopatra Queen of Egypt and became ruler of the Roman world.

After Caesar's murder, his friend Mark Antony, his nephew Octavian and a general named Lepidus defeated Brutus. Then came a struggle for power between Antony and Octavian. Antony went to Egypt where he too fell in love with Cleopatra, but both committed suicide after their forces had been beaten in a naval battle at Actium.

Thus in 31 BC, Caesar's nephew became the Emperor Augustus whose long reign was probably the most glorious period of Rome's history. In the time of the ten emperors who followed him it became customary for the name 'Caesar' to be used as a title.

All his finest knights lay dead and in the midst of the slain was Roland.

CHARLEMAGNE

A throng of monks and nobles came out from the abbey gateway to meet the cavalcade that was winding up the mountain road towards them. Presently, both parties halted and there stepped from a litter, a little old man in gorgeous vestments of blue and gold.

As the monks sang and the nobles pressed forward to gain a better view, the Abbot Fulrad laid his hand on the fair head of an eleven-year-old boy standing beside him:

'Go, Charles, my son,' he said. 'Greet his Holiness in the name of your royal father.'

The boy advanced and knelt reverently before Pope Stephen, who presently allowed himself to be escorted into the Abbey of Saint Maurice in Switzerland.

Charles was the son of Pepin the Short, King of the Franks, who had sent his heir to meet the Pope at the borders of Frankland. The life and lands of Pope Stephen were threatened by the Lombards of Northern Italy, and his Holiness had fled for help to the Franks.

After Stephen had rested for several months in Frankland, King Pepin took him back to Italy, where he defeated the Lombards and restored the Pope to the Church of Saint Peter. We do not know if young Charles accompanied his father to Rome or if he remained at his lessons with the Abbot Fulrad, but it is certain that the meeting on the mountain pass made a deep impression on the boy. All his life, he was to regard himself as the protector of the Pope and guardian of the Christian Church.

Some years later, when King Pepin died, he left his kingdom to be divided between Charles and his younger brother, Carloman. Their mother was to keep peace between the brothers but the joint kingdom was on the brink of civil war when Carloman died. In 771, Charles became sole ruler of Frankland, a kingdom that included most of modern France and Western Germany.

Soon after his brother's death, Charles led an expedition against the Saxons. He did this to punish the heathen tribesmen for their constant raids, and also to unite the Frankish nobles. On the march and in battle, they marvelled at his prowess and rejoiced in the loot of victory, even if the northern plains produced little except horses, cattle and slaves.

The son of Pepin had grown into a magnificent leader. He was a blond giant, six feet four inches tall and so strong that he could straighten four horseshoes clamped together or lift with one hand a mailed knight as high as his shoulder. But the barrel-chested hero, with his piercing eyes and strangely high-pitched voice, was jovial and friendly. He welcomed people with wide-flung arms and won their loyalty through his boyish generosity.

But besides being a man of gigantic energy and appetite, Charles had a sharp and inquisitive brain. In the crowd of courtiers, womenfolk and children who accompanied him on his travels, there were always scholars. Nothing pleased him better than a long discussion about religion or Latin grammar and he would often be deep in talk with a scholar, far into the night, while his nobles dropped asleep or rolled in drunken stupor under the table.

Having taught the Saxons a sharp lesson, Charles led his army across the Alps to deal with the Lombards. When he was younger, his mother had chosen the daughter of the Lombard King for his bride, but Charles had not liked the girl and had sent her back in order to marry the gentle Hildegard who bore him four sons and five daughters. The Lombards had avenged this insult by supporting Charles's enemies, but they proved no match for the Franks who drove them back across the Plain of Lombardy and captured Pavia, their chief city.

Meanwhile, Charles himself went on to Rome. The city had fallen on evil times since its days of glory, but it was still the most wonderful city in the world. The Frankish giant, in his fur-lined cloak and sea-green tunic, gazed with awe at the vast monuments and the numberless stone buildings, but to him the greatest wonder was the Church of Saint Peter, built upon the apostle's bones.

Charles knelt in front of the great church and kissed each step as he ascended to where the Pope stood waiting to greet him. The Pope was now Hadrian I, who became Charles's friend, but, even in this solemn moment, Charles showed that he had no intention of playing second fiddle to any man on earth. In the sight of the cheering crowds, he took Hadrian's arm in an easy gesture of friendship and led him into his own church, as if to say:

'I am the master here.'

In these times, no king could leave his realm without inviting trouble, and messengers soon arrived in Rome with news that the Saxons had recovered from their drubbing and were over the borders of Frankland, killing and burning. Charles marched back across the Alps and slaughtered every Saxon who failed to escape into the woods and swamps of his wild native land. But the position troubled him. There could be no happiness in the northern part of the kingdom while these raids and counter-raids went on. The Saxons must be made to give up their heathen ways. He would give them a simple choice: Christian baptism or death.

For thirty years, Charles carried out his policy of forcing Christianity on the stubborn Saxons. He defeated them in battle and then sent missionaries into their midst to build churches and monasteries. But as soon as he turned his back, the Saxons broke their oaths. Again and again, the tribes burst into rebellion, until Charles lost all patience and took a terrible vengeance.

After an uprising, he summoned over four thousand Saxon nobles to a meeting where he angrily upbraided them for the treachery of their people; then, refusing to listen to their pleas of innocence, he had them all beheaded in a single day. When this murderous punishment still failed to break the Saxon spirit, Charles ordered the removal of whole tribes. Men, women and children were driven from their homes and forced to settle hundreds of miles away in the remoter parts of Frankland.

The stern defender of Christianity invaded Spain with a huge army in order to attack the Saracens who had long been a menace to the kingdoms of the West. He captured several cities but the Moslem fortresses were too strong to take without siege machinery, so Charles decided to retire. He had already re-crossed the Pyrenees when he sustained one of the most famous defeats in history.

According to legend, the heroes of the battle were Roland, the nephew of Charles, and his friend Oliver, who were two of the famous group of knights called Paladins. After many deeds of glory against the Saracens, Roland and Oliver were commanding the rear guard, while Charles pushed on with the main army. He had, however, given Roland a hunting-horn which he was to blow if he required assistance. In the narrow pass of Roncesvalles, the Paladins realised that they were trapped by a huge force of Moorish soldiers.

'Sound the horn and call the king,' said Oliver.

'Nay, friend,' replied Roland, fingering the blade of his famous sword, Durandal, 'God forbid that I should lose my good name. Let us rest and then do our duty.'

For hours, the Frankish knights fought valiantly, but the odds were too great. When Oliver was dead and only a handful of weary men were left, the warriors begged Roland to blow the horn. Roland sounded a blast that echoed through the valley and was borne on the wind to Charles, in camp eight miles away.

'I hear the horn of Roland!' he cried.

The nobles laughed, for they were jealous of the King's favourite:

'Nay, Sire, it is only the moaning of the wind.'

An hour later, the King again heard the faint sound of a horn and, this time, he called his men to arms and rode back to the pass.

He found a scene of disaster. The enemy had vanished but all his finest knights lay dead and in the midst of the slain was Roland, his sword broken in his hand.

Charles was deeply grieved by the loss of his best knights and he never again attempted an invasion of Spain but was content with a fortified border and a strip of territory known as the Spanish March.

By this time, the King of the Franks had a great reputation and his name alone was often enough to scatter his enemies. A poet called him the 'Man of Iron', for his great body and his iron spirit never grew weary. He was determined to bring order and Christianity to Europe.

When Bavaria was added to his domains, Charles was ruler of all the Germanic tribes, except the Anglo-Saxons who had settled in Britain. He even thought of picking a quarrel with King Offa of Mercia to add Britain to his empire. But he had no fleet and, in any case, events on the continent demanded all his energy.

There were the Saracen pirates along the Mediterranean coast; the Eastern Emperor threatened to invade Italy; the Danes were restive and the terrible Avars of Hungary were robbing and killing on his borders. These Mongolians, with their flowing hair and swift horses, had long terrorised eastern Europe, and even the Emperors at Constantinople regularly bought them off with gold which they stored in a huge fortification, known as the Ring from its nine circles of walls.

Charles invaded the land of the Avars and, after three years of savage warfare, wiped out the pagan tribesmen and brought back the robber-hoard from the Ring. With kingly generosity, he gave away wagon-loads of treasure so that Byzantine gold, jewels, silver cups and eastern silks found their way into abbeys and churches all over Western Europe. The choicest treasures went, of course, to the Pope, but even King Offa, now a friend, received a jewelled sword and silken cloaks.

The ruthless conqueror had a kindly, lovable side to his nature. He was never happier than when, accompanied by a noisy, cheerful Court, he could tour his kingdom and put everything to rights. Charles had the Roman roads repaired and new bridges built, with tolls to pay for the cost, but he gave orders that the charges were not to be too heavy and if a man preferred to cross a river by wading across a ford, he need not pay the toll.

Like every medieval king, Charles adored hunting but he did not rate deer higher than men, for he encouraged the peasants to drain and cultivate their land in peace. With his stewards, he would ride about an estate to find out for himself how things were done. Nothing was too trivial for his eager gaze; the manner of salting meat and treading grapes, of bee-keeping and dairy management interested him as much as the breeding of fine horses. The King was forever issuing homely commands about the proper way to farm.

Charles loved children and treated everyone in his kingdom as though they were children who needed a wise father's care. If, like the Saxons, they misbehaved, he punished them severely, but he believed that it was only for their good. He lectured everyone—the peasants for their foolish superstitions, the nobles for their love of finery and strong drink, the churchmen for their laziness. But, if he was forever scolding them, they knew that he worked ceaselessly to bring order and justice to the realm and they called him Charlemagne or, in Latin, Carolus Magnus—Charles the Great.

Naturally, the nobles did not like losing their right to bully and rob the weak, and when Charles was away at the wars, the old evils would creep back. But he hit upon a brilliant idea. He divided his empire into 'counties', each under a Count of the palace, but to make sure that the Counts ruled justly, he also appointed a number of special envoys, known as 'missi', because they were sent round the kingdom on missions of inspection.

Four times a year, the missi set out on their tours, travelling in pairs, each to keep an eye on the other and each with his special tasks. When they returned, the missi made their reports to the King who thus learned how the Counts and the bishops were performing their duties.

As the years went by, Charlemagne was able to spend more time guiding his realm, for his generals could defend the frontiers and his sons were old enough to take on the tasks for which he had educated them since babyhood. Louis, the youngest, a spiritless lad for all his father's training, was given Aquitaine and the Spanish March to govern; Pepin, a much more robust character, was King of Italy, and Charles, the eldest, the image of his father, was everywhere, leading armies in Saxony, Bavaria and in the lands of the heathen.

More and more, Charlemagne longed for a settled home. He was over fifty, with a mane of white hair and a vast stomach, but he was as vigorous as ever and he wanted to build a capital worthy of the empire he had forged.

Like Louis XIV, nine hundred years later, Charlemagne made a city where there had been only a hunting-lodge and, like Louis, he gathered the best craftsmen and artists of the day whom he directed with jovial enthusiasm. He chose a site in the green country between the Rhine and the Meuse, in the heart of his ancestors' estates, but not too far from the troublesome Saxons. The place, called Aachen or Aix-la-Chapelle, was near to the busy Rhine where there were medicinal springs and an ample water-supply for the huge marble swimming-bath that he intended to build. The King was a magnificent swimmer and, on his tours, he would often stop by a river or lake and order the entire Court to join him in a bathe.

The palace was built on a hill and from its roof, a great bronze eagle proudly surveyed the countryside. In addition to an assembly hall, treasury, library and royal apartments, there were bathrooms and, of course, the swimming-pool. Attached to this palace, decorated with mosaics and marbles from Italy, was the cathedral where Charlemagne worshipped three times every day, and around these two buildings grew up a busy town with its market-square, churches and taverns.

Here, at Aachen, Charlemagne could lead the life he loved best. He was a family man, devoted to his daughters and grandchildren; indeed, it was said that he loved his daughters so much that he could not bear to see them go away as brides; they had to remain single or marry a Frankish nobleman and continue to live at the Court. Fond as he was of bustle and gaiety, he saw to it that there were always minstrels, jugglers, tumblers and story-tellers to amuse the company. Best of all, he could now invite scholars to come and live at his Court.

Some years before, during his second visit to Italy, Charlemagne had chanced to meet Alcuin, an English monk who was returning from Rome to Northumbria, where he directed the Cathedral School at York. At this time, English scholars were the best in Europe and Charlemagne promptly invited Alcuin to join his wandering Court in order to spread learning throughout Frankland.

The two men, so different in their characters, became lifelong friends, for each admired the other's good qualities and together they founded a system of education that lasted for centuries. Alcuin brought with him a rare knowledge of books and he also introduced the art of illuminating manuscripts at which the English monks excelled.

Alcuin soon discovered that the Frankish nobles despised learning and that even the monks were sadly ignorant, for many could barely read their books and these, through bad copying, were full of mistakes. With the King's eager support, he started abbey schools where boys, especially the sons of nobles, were taught reading, singing, arithmetic and grammar. The Palace School at Aachen became one of the most famous centres of medieval learning.

In the year 800, Charlemagne made his fourth and last visit to Rome. The Pope was now Leo III, whose enemies had actually beaten him and put him in prison only a year before. Like Stephen in years gone by, Leo had fled for help to Frankland and Charlemagne had honoured him and restored him to his Holy Church. Now, to let the world know that he was God's champion and the Pope's protector, Charlemagne came to worship at St Peter's on Christmas Day.

The great church was filled with priests, worshippers and pilgrims from all over the Christian world when Charlemagne knelt in prayer before the High Altar. According to custom, he had taken off his crown, sword and outer tunic, and, as he prayed, the chanting of the monks gradually ceased and the church fell silent. At last, the King rose and stood deep in thought. At that moment, the Pope lifted a golden crown from the altar and placed it upon the head of Charlemagne, as the congregation shouted three times:

'To Charles Augustus, crowned by God, the great and peaceful Emperor of the Romans, long life and victory!'

Charlemagne was taken by surprise and, for a moment, he was angry. Leo's action made it seem that crowns were given by the Pope, whereas he regarded himself as King by the grace of God. However, nothing could undo the ceremony and the West had once again an emperor who, for centuries, was known as the Holy Roman Emperor.

Greater than ever in authority, though he refused to use the new title for more than a year, Charlemagne returned to Frankland to pass his remaining years touring his kingdom and enjoying the company of his scholars at Aachen. One Christmas, the King's three sons came to visit him with their families and they celebrated, we are told, 'with joy and exultation', for it seemed as if the long years of effort had brought peace at last.

Beaming with gladness, Charlemagne made lavish gifts to all his family and then, in accordance with Frankish custom, he made his will, dividing his empire into three parts. Each son appeared to be content with his share and each promised to follow in his father's footsteps.

Alas, for Charlemagne's hopes. His good friend Alcuin died, the seafaring Northmen spread terror along the coasts and war broke out with the Danes. The old King strapped on his body-armour and rode into battle again, but there were no triumphant victories. Plague broke out in the army and spread across Frankland. A favourite sister and daughter died and then came the news of Pepin's death in Italy.

The King mastered his sorrow and rearranged the kingdom. He still had two sons left and there was always the hope that pious Louis would enter a monastery, so that Charles, the well-beloved, could rule alone as he himself had done. But, in that same year, Charles died and the old king was left to mourn at Aachen.

He did not give up hope and, throughout the last year of his life, he kept Louis at his side, pouring out advice about the way to rule a kingdom. In his heart,

Opposite *Akhnaten and Nefertiti with two of their daughters*

however, he must have known that advice could never turn a weakling into a great man. Nevertheless, he himself crowned Louis in the great cathedral at Aachen and he named Pepin's son as King of Italy.

Three months later, in January 814, Charlemagne died and was buried in his own church. Almost at once, the empire began to fall to pieces.

Louis the Pious was quite unable to control the nobles. Fighting broke out and, in Italy, Pepin's son was captured and put to death. Soon, the sons of Louis were battling against each other for their grandfather's realm, the Norse raids grew worse and, as Frank fought against Frank, the empire broke into fragments.

Yet, Charlemagne's work had not been in vain. He left behind schools and monasteries, the memory of a great monarch and a vision of a united Europe.

More about Charlemagne (742–814)

Most of the barbaric tribes which destroyed the Roman Empire vanished from history, but the Franks settled in Gaul, which became known as Frankland. The founder of the kingdom was King Clovis (481–511) who made Paris his capital and turned his pagan subjects into Christians.

The descendants of Clovis, known as the Merovingians, were violent ruffians whose authority grew so weak that the kingdom came to be ruled by nobles called 'mayors of the palace'. The last of the Merovingians were mere puppets but, with their long beards and flowing hair, they filled a place in the people's minds as priest-kings.

Charles Martel ('The Hammer'), who drove the Saracens out of Gaul by his victory at Tours in 732, was a 'mayor of the palace', but his son, Pepin the Short, finally thrust the King on one side in 751 and took the crown for himself when Charlemagne was nine years old.

The Lombards mentioned in the story were, like the Franks, a Germanic tribe. They had settled in Northern Italy and also in lands lying south of the Pope's territory round Rome. When Charlemagne destroyed Lombardy as a separate kingdom, the Lombards turned their attention to trade and, by the Middle Ages, they were the leading merchants and bankers of Europe. Some of them settled in London (where Lombard Street, the banking centre of the City, still bears their name) and were well known as money-lenders, especially to kings like Edward III who needed money for the French wars.

The Holy Roman Empire, which Charlemagne founded, lasted a thousand years, until 1806, when it was abolished by Napoleon. In its later stages, the Empire consisted mostly of German states and Austria and the Emperors were chosen from the House of Hapsburg.

Opposite *Alexander in battle against Darius*

Alfred was forced to take refuge in the swamps of Somerset with his family and household bodyguard.

ALFRED THE GREAT

A small boy, wearing a scarlet cloak fastened by a gold brooch, glanced eagerly about him at the tall buildings, the archways and fallen pillars; 'Look father,' he cried, 'across the river; there lies the palace of the Pope.'

His father nodded, patting the boy's head, as he turned to speak to the thanes and monks in his company. A couple of porters carrying wine-jars, paused for a moment, 'Foreigners,' said one. 'Franks or Saxons, I dare say, by their cloaks and fair beards.'

The year was 855, and the boy was Alfred, youngest son of Aethelwulf, King of Wessex, who was visiting Rome, where he presented His Holiness the Pope with splendid gifts wrought with the skill for which Saxon craftsmen were famous. Wessex was the strongest of the English kingdoms, and the Pope looked with favour upon Aethelwulf because he had recently won a stirring victory over the heathen Northmen.

Alfred and his father stayed a year in Rome and the boy never forgot the great city with its churches and stone walls. Its paved streets and air of learning were so different from his native land of woods and chalk hills, with little towns of wooden-walled houses surrounded by earth banks.

Back home again, Alfred's brothers saw to it that he was taught to ride and to use weapons like every nobleman's son but they soon realised that the sharp inquisitive boy was going to be the cleverest one of the family. There was a story that his mother gave him a beautiful book because he learnt to read it before his older brothers. Whether or not this was true, Alfred said afterwards that his boyhood lessons were all too few, with so much moving about during the troubles that came upon the kingdom.

His father found that the Northmen, who were also called Vikings or Danes or simply 'the heathen host', were raiding again. They came across the North Sea in their dragon-ships, made up the rivers and went ashore to fan out over the countryside. Far and wide they ranged on stolen horses, to plunder and kill with such terrible ferocity that the people prayed nightly, 'From the fury of the Northmen, Good Lord, deliver us'.

King Aethelwulf died when Alfred was nine and soon it seemed as if a curse lay on the royal house of Wessex. The eldest son died within two years and the next son, Ethelbert, only five or six years later. Ethelred, the third brother, became king with seventeen-year-old Alfred as his devoted helper, but men shook their heads gloomily, for the boy suffered from a strange illness that brought bouts of sickness and pain. However, his spirit was so courageous that he refused to be ill when every fighting man of Wessex had to stand ready to meet the enemy.

One winter's day, a messenger from Mercia rode into Ethelred's camp and asked to be taken to the King:

'What tidings from my sister's husband, messenger?' asked Ethelred.

'Evil news, Sire. The host has taken York with great slaughter. The King of Northumbria is slain with his bishops and the kingdom is lost.'

Worse followed, for the Danes overran East Anglia and spread into Mercia, where they set up their winter quarters at Nottingham, building a stronghold near the river from which they could raid the country as they pleased.

The King of Mercia asked Ethelred for help, so the Wessex 'fyrd' or army marched to Nottingham where Alfred had his first glimpse of the terrible Northmen, with their horned helmets, mail-shirts and huge battle axes. By this time, the Mercians were too frightened to attack the enemy camp, saying that no one had ever captured a Danish stronghold, so they gave them gold to go away, and the men of Wessex returned to their homes.

Naturally, the Danes came back, and Mercia fell. Wessex, the last Christian kingdom in Britain, seemed to be doomed.

In 871, when Alfred fought in nine battles, Wessex was attacked by land and sea. Raiding parties harried the south coast, but the main assault came down the ridge of hills to the Thames. At Reading, Ethelred and Alfred led an attack against the Danish stockade, but they quickly learned what the Mercians had feared, for, as a monk wrote:

> *The heathens fought with valour, and rushing out of all the gates like wolves, joined battle with all their might. Alas! the Christians at last turned their backs and the heathen gained the victory.*

The Wessex army retreated, but when fresh troops came up to join them, Ethelred made a stand at Ashdown. After a feast of triumph, the Danes followed and took up a position on a hill opposite. Confident that they would wait to be attacked, Ethelred went into his tent for Holy Mass. Suddenly, the Danes charged and Alfred was forced to take command. 'Fighting like a wild boar', as his friend Bishop Asser wrote, he led a counter-charge with such skill that, for once, the enemy was defeated and forced to retreat.

The Northmen soon came back; Ethelred died and Alfred was hurriedly elected king by the Witan. He was only twenty-two and his kingdom was collapsing around him. By the end of the year, his men were so exhausted that he had to scrape together all the gold in his Treasury to buy a breathing-space from the enemy. Both sides were glad of the truce, for the Danes were settling in Northumbria and Mercia, while Alfred had to work desperately to rebuild his army, and to bring some order to his suffering people.

Four or five years passed before the Danes were ready to swallow Wessex. Under an able leader, Guthrum, their main army drove into Dorset, while another force prepared to strike from the West and a large fleet appeared off the coast. Exeter was captured, but Alfred hung on stubbornly at the enemy's heels until a great storm wrecked more than a hundred longships and drowned thousands of Vikings who were closing in for the kill. Trapped in Exeter, without supplies or reinforcements, Guthrum had to make a truce and retreat to Gloucester.

It was Christmas time and the people of Wessex drew a sigh of relief, for the enemy would not march again until the Spring, since, in winter, the land was too flooded and short of food to support armies. But Guthrum was no ordinary leader. On Twelfth Night, when the season of feasting was at its height, he pounced on Chippenham, stockaded his main army and sent his savage horsemen to ravage the countryside. Caught off guard, Wessex collapsed. The army was scattered, many thanes fled and Alfred was forced to take refuge in the swamps of Somerset with his family and household bodyguard.

Despite the old tale of the fugitive king being scolded by a peasant woman for burning the cakes, Alfred was not alone. Saxons came to join him in the reedy wastes of Sedgemoor until he had a force that could threaten Guthrum's flank. On a patch of higher ground, he built the Athelney fort, from which raiding parties went out to harass the enemy, while messengers threaded their way across the marshland with secret plans to rally the men of Wiltshire, Dorset and Hampshire.

By Whitsuntide, the fighting-men of Wessex were trudging across the hills to meet at Egbert's Stone, high up on the downs, and when thousands had gathered there, with their spears and cooking-pots, their sons and rough-coated horses, a shout went up,

'The King! The King! Alfred comes with the men of Somerset!'

Cheers of unspeakable joy burst out at the sight of their own king moving amongst them again with the calm assurance of a true leader.

Without delay, the Wessex army marched. They found the Danish host on the chalk slopes of Wiltshire above Eddington, where, locking their shields together, they tore upon the foe with the fury of men who remembered their savaged homes and slaughtered children. The Danes broke and made for their stronghold at Chippenham, but Alfred allowed no pause for victory feasts. Following hard, his men cut down the stragglers, captured vast amounts of booty and shut Guthrum in his fortress. Two weeks later, 'terrified by hunger and cold', the Danes surrendered.

When custom cried out for revenge, Alfred showed noble generosity. He fed his enemies and spared their lives. Awed by this spirit of true Christianity, Guthrum gave up his heathen gods and was baptised into the Christian faith, while agreeing to withdraw all the Danes behind a line drawn roughly from London to Chester.

Although this victory and the Peace of Wedmore allowed Alfred to rebuild his devastated kingdom, the Danes did not suddenly become law-abiding. Even Guthrum had to be given another sharp lesson and fresh bands of raiders had constantly to be driven off. The Danes of East Anglia were particularly troublesome, so Alfred captured London and brought Mercia under his control.

First and foremost, Wessex had to be made safe; the defenders must never again be caught napping. Alfred therefore organised the army so that some fighting-men remained on service whilst others tended the fields and afterwards took their turn in the ranks. To prevent hhe Danes from sweeping across a defenceless land, the King ordered his thanes to fortify towns qith ßitches, earthworks and palisades. Meanwhile, he sent abroad for shipwrights to help build a fleet big enough and swift enough to defeat the sea-wolves before they could set foot ashore.

But Alfred's true greatness lay in peace. His country was ruined, its churches and monasteries gutted by fire, its homes and schools destroyed. Trade had ceased, the people were hungry and lawless, the nobles too ignorant to know what to do. Alfred himself said: 'Hardly a man in my kingdom can read his prayer-book—or write a letter. I would have you set all the boys now in England to learning.'

He set a matchless example. Not only did he take a hand in the actual work of building churches and towns, but he designed houses, worked alongside craftsmen, founded schools and compelled even the nobles and eldermen to take lessons.

'It was a strange sight', wrote a bishop of the time, 'to see eldermen and officials, ignorant from boyhood, learning with difficulty to read.'

The best pupils learned Latin, the language of educated people everywhere, but there were few English books for the others to read, so Alfred himself polished up what Latin he remembered from boyhood. Then he translated parts of the Bible, books on history and geography, and Bede's famous 'History'.

Everything interested this amazing man. He never wasted a minute, but divided up the day into periods for business, study, prayer, building and translating.

He was always on the move in the kingdom, distributing justice and visting the twenty-five towns he founded or rebuilt. Yet he found time to have the old Saxon laws gathered together, with some new ones, to provide a written Code of Law. He encouraged trade and loved to talk to merchants and sea captains to find out about strange lands, astronomy and new ideas; he kept in touch with Rome, brought scholars and teachers from abroad, cared for the orphans and the homeless, and taught his nobles that a kingdom should be ruled with justice and mercy.

Worn out by his labours and illness, Alfred died when he was only about fifty, but he left behind a free country and the ideal of the perfect king, brave, diligent and just.

'I have striven,' he said, 'to live worthily and to leave to the men who come after me, the memory of good works.'

In his lifetime, the people called him 'England's Shepherd' and 'The Truth Teller'; they said 'in him the poor could look for help.' Afterwards, the English gave him a title which they have given to no other monarch in their history—'the Great'.

More about Alfred (849–899/900)

Alfred was born at Wantage in Berkshire, the fifth son of King Aethelwulf. It was his grandfather, King Egbert (802–839), who made Wessex supreme over the other five or six kingdoms into which England had been divided for more than two centuries.

Towards the end of Egbert's reign, the Danes began to attack the coasts of England, at first as plunderers and afterwards as settlers.

Egbert's son, Aethelwulf, defeated the Danes and went on a pilgrimage to Rome, but his four sons, each of whom in turn became King of Wessex, had to defend the kingdom against the heathen invaders who had overrun the north and the east.

From 871, when he became king, to the Peace of Wedmore in 878, Alfred was engaged in a desperate struggle against Guthrum and other Danish leaders but, after his victory, Wessex consisted of about half of England, separated from the Danelaw by a line running from London to Chester. This was the kingdom which he ruled so well and which he again had to defend during his last years.

Fortunately, Alfred founded a line of splendid kings. His son, Edward the Elder, conquered the Danes and became ruler of the whole country; his grandson, Athelstan (925–940), added southern Scotland to his dominions and two more capable grandsons were followed by Edgar (954–975) whose peaceful reign and good government recalled the days of Alfred, his great-grandfather.

Beneath was not a table but a chest containing the bones of a saint.

HAROLD, THE LAST OF THE ENGLISH

Count Guy of Ponthieu was supping with his knights in the rush-strewn hall of his castle when, above the gale outside, the clatter of men and arms was heard from the courtyard.

The knights grasped their weapons, but a serving-man hurried to the high table and spoke to the Count. Then the oak doors were flung open to admit a crowd of villagers and fishermen, armed with cudgels and flaring torches.

'A wreck, Sir Count!' cried their leader. 'An English ship fast on the rocks below Saint Catherine's Point. We took the crew as they came ashore through the surf.'

Count Guy glowered at the exhausted, dripping strangers who were thrust forward, some with their arms bound by ropes.

'Who are you?' he asked. 'Know you that what the sea casts up upon this coast is mine by right.'

One of the strangers, whose torn silken shirt and fair hair matted with blood did not disguise his magnificent presence, answered curtly in French,

'I am Harold Godwinson, Earl of Wessex, counsellor and kinsman to Edward, King of the English. Is this a Christian welcome to men who have suffered shipwreck? In the name of Saint Christopher, I ask for food and shelter and a safe return to England.'

The Count's eyes narrowed as he thought of the ransom for such a prisoner.

'Bold words, stranger or spy,' he replied. 'A dog barks loud when he cannot bite. But even an English dog may be worth a price to his master. We will find out if you speak truth. Till then, you stay here at my pleasure.'

Earl Harold and his men were forced to stifle their anger while they endured several days of inhospitable treatment from the French count, but although they cursed the storm that had wrecked their ship on an unfriendly coast, not a man blamed the Earl for his whim to sail in the Channel on an autumn day. Like every man in Wessex, they loved Harold and asked only to serve him.

News of the wreck soon leaked out and, within days, a crop-headed knight rode to the castle with an order:

> *William, Duke of Normandy, bids Guy, his vassal, to send the Earl of Wessex to his Court with an escort and due honour. The Earl and his men are to be clothed and furnished with all things necessary.*

The Count blustered about a ransom, but when the Norman knight grimly reminded him of the fate that would befall a vassal who bandied words with Duke William, he freed the prisoners with an ill grace and produced food and wine, the vestments and horses that his overlord demanded.

With a splendid company, Duke William rode to meet the English Earl, embraced him and led him to the high seat in his castle, while he smiled with a warmth that astonished the Norman knights. They knew the Duke for a hard man, grim and ruthless from his earliest years, but now he laughed.

It was strange to see William's pleasure in his handsome guest. Gifts were showered upon the Englishmen; tournaments, games and hunting-parties were held in their honour; feasts and dancing took place at night. The two nobles were well matched; with horse and hawk, in wrestling and sword-play, men deemed them equal. Both were mightly warriors, one dark, the other fair; one hard and skilful yet determined to deal gallantly with his guest; the other so generous in his wondrous strength that even the Normans gave him praise.

The winter passed and there was no talk of going home. The festivities and tournaments were enlivened by a real battle against some of the Duke's rebellious subjects when Harold fought manfully beside his host. There seemed to be nothing but trust and affection between the two.

One day, in spring, Harold's brother, Wulfnoth, found the Earl alone.

'Brother,' he began, 'the men would go home. Must we dally here so long?'

'Why, Wulfnoth,' laughed Harold. 'Are you tired of living like a prince?'

'My brother, we long for Wessex and, to speak truth, we fear this black-browed Duke with whom you pass the days. All men know that he covets England's throne and gives out that it was promised him by King Edward. Why do you stay?'

'For my own reasons, lad.'

'What reasons can there be? Edward has no son and—God forgive me—he is more monk than king. The Atheling, last of Alfred's line, is but a child. You will be King when Edward dies.'

'Hush, boy. The Witan and the word of God choose England's king.'

'Harold,' insisted Wulfnoth, 'for the love we bear you, take us home. Edward is old, the Earls and our brother Tostig make trouble while you are away. The people long for you, let us go.'

Harold absently pulled at the ears of a hunting-dog. There was a long silence and then he said,

'Come close, lad. I will tell you a secret that brought a curse upon our House. Years ago, our father, Earl Godwin, was accused of betraying King Edward's brother to the Danes. It was never proved but before he died, he told me it was true. He committed that crime for the sake of the realm, to keep the peace. It weighed heavy on our father's soul and he bade me make amends. I, too, must serve England, not by treachery but by winning the friendship of this Norman Duke. I would not have my country torn by war, so I have won William as my brother. Soon we shall part as brothers—he to remain in his own land and I to serve England as God would have me serve.'

Earl Harold asked the Duke for a ship to carry him home, but William avoided an answer. Presently, the Duke spoke of King Edward's promise of the crown; he insisted Harold must swear to support his claim in return for half the kingdom and his daughter Agatha to wife. Until the promise was given, the guests could not go.

Harold was trapped. Word came that King Edward was ill and the Earls were quarrelling; he must go home but he dare not swear. Old Garth, his father's steward, spoke at last,

'A forced oath, my Lord, is not binding in the sight of God. Swear, and our English priests will absolve you from the oath.'

So, before the nobles and bishops of Normandy, Harold laid his hand upon a table covered with a cloth of gold and swore to be Duke William's man and to serve him faithfully in all things. Then, two priests stepped forward and removed the cloth. Beneath was not a table but a chest containing the bones of a saint. Harold and his men were horror-struck, for an oath sworn upon holy bones was no ordinary oath—forced or not, it was now a promise that filled them all with dread.

The Englishmen sailed home with heavy hearts and the story of the forced oath spread across the land. There were many who shook their heads to think that Harold had sworn away the kingdom and some remembered the curse upon his House. Yet there was no one else to rule England, for King Edward wept and babbled in his weakness; the Earls were at each other's throats and Tostig had to be exiled for his misdeeds in the North. Harold governed the kingdom well, restoring order and justice, so that men spoke of him as a second Alfred.

Towards the end of 1065, King Edward was too ill to attend the hallowing of the Abbey at Westminster which he had spent half his life in building. In January, he died and at the end, he murmured,

'To Harold, my brother-in-law, I commit the kingdom.'

At once, the Great Council chose Harold to be King, overruling the claim of Edgar Atheling because he was a child, and giving no heed to the Norman Duke. But when the news reached Normandy, the Duke burst out in rage,

'Harold has wronged me,' he cried. 'The kingdom was mine, granted and promised as he himself has sworn. By God and the holy bones, I will take my right by war.'

All through the spring of 1066, Duke William made ready to invade, gathering stores and arms, empressing shipwrights, enrolling knights and men-at-arms to serve him for what they might win across the narrow sea. Nor did William forget the power of the Church. He had friends in Rome, and the Pope was persuaded to bless the expedition and to send a banner. The Norman brigands felt themselves to be the knights of God.

So far, however, King Harold had little to fear. Though he had no priests to speak for him in Rome, he had the hearts of the people of England and the strong arms of the men of Wessex. His kingdom was immensely bigger and richer than Normandy. Its people had repelled many an invasion in the past and he himself, Harold the Fearless, was as great a warrior as the Duke and far superior on the sea. All that summer, Harold kept troops and ships ready to meet the invader, while he pacified the North and saw to all things with dignity and strength. Rumours came in that his brother Tostig was in Norway where Harold Hardrada, the mighty sea-robber, was fitting out his longships. What if two attacks fell upon the kingdom at the same time?

'Never fear,' Harold told his thanes. 'The same wind cannot bring both foes. If they come, we shall drub them one at a time.'

In September, the wind blew from the north; it brought the fleet of Harold Hardrada and Tostig into the Humber, where the Northmen came ashore, defeated the Earls and ravaged the countryside like wolves. King Harold marched up from the south, and, seven miles from York, at Stamford Bridge, he attacked the Norwegian host and destroyed it utterly. Among the slain were Tostig and Harold Hardrada, victor of fifty battles; but half the Huscarls and many of the best fighting-men of England died as well.

While the priests sang a Victory Thanksgiving in York Minster, the wind changed in Duke William's favour. On September 28th 1066, only three days after the battle at Stamford Bridge, the Norman fleet beached at Pevensey without so much as a fishing-boat to oppose them.

Hardly able to believe his luck, the Duke landed his horses and stores with ridiculous ease and soon the Normans were plundering Kent and Sussex to their hearts' content. Messengers fled north to Harold who lay at York, tending the wounded and resting his exhausted men.

In fury, Harold gathered all who were fit to march, and he made south at tremendous speed, outdistancing his foot-soldiers and the Northern Earls who, saying they had done enough, came only at a laggard's pace.

Once he was across the Thames, Harold had no thought but to meet his enemy and hurl him into the sea. His brothers urged caution; the King should burn the land to deny food to the invaders. Then, as soon as his footsore troops were rested, and reinforcements had come in from the West and the North, he could attack with overwhelming strength. But Harold refused to listen.

'God's Splendour!' he roared. 'Shall I burn my people's land when I promised them peace? I have whipped a pack of wolves and now will thrash these Norman dogs.'

He led his army into Sussex and set his Standard on Senlac Hill, inviting the Normans to attack. As usual, the English dismounted and ranged themselves for battle on foot. It was a strong position and Harold had his men in close order behind their shield-wall, telling them to stand firm and let the Normans exhaust themselves in uphill charges.

The royal troops, the giant Huscarls, held the middle, guarding the Standards and the King; on either flank were the thanes and the trained men of the shires, with a sprinkling of ill-armed levies hastily raised to fill the places of men who had died in the North. But many, far too many, of England's warriors had not arrived.

The Duke attacked with archers and foot-soldiers, then with a charge by his mailed knights. The English stood firm, letting fly with javelins, stones and hand-axes, meeting the charge with level spears, while axes swung and crashed, and bowmen picked off the horses and the wounded. A second attack broke against the shield-wall, a third foundered among the piles of dead and dying. By afternoon, the Normans were almost spent.

One last charge surged up the hill and reached the shields, when a cry went up, 'The Duke is slain! Fly! Every man to the ships.'

A roar burst from the English and the levies leapt from their ranks and tore after the retreating foe but, in the valley, William checked the flight and sent horsemen from the flanks to ride down the men of the shires.

On the hill, the staunch axe-men still stood beside their King. Then the Duke ordered his bowmen to fire upwards so that their arrows fell in a deadly rain. Harold was struck above the right eye, and the whole line groaned when he fell.

Darkness was coming on when the Norman knights breached the English wall, cutting down those who had not fled. At last, only a knot of Huscarls was left, wielding their axes with matchless courage round the Standard of Wessex and their dying King. They fought on to the last man.

It was night when the Duke's servants pitched his tent where the battle had been fiercest, and the Conqueror, speechless with fatigue, sat down among the slain. Outside, somewhere in the darkness, lay the bodies of Harold, his brothers and the noblest men of England. In a single day, the kingdom had been lost and won.

More about Harold (c. 1022–66)

Harold II was the second son of Earl Godwin, an Englishman who rose to a position of power under Canute, the Danish King of England. Harold's mother was a relative of Canute himself.

When Canute died in 1035, he was followed by his sons Harold I and Hardicanute, neither of whom reigned for long and in 1042, Edward (afterwards called 'the Confessor') became King of England. Thus, the royal line of Alfred the Great was restored, for Edward was Ethelred the Unready's son. He had been brought up in Normandy and, although he married Earl Godwin's daughter, his Norman friends became so powerful that Godwin and his sons had to flee abroad. Harold took refuge in Ireland and at this time Duke William of Normandy visited England and received the so-called promise of the English crown.

Soon afterwards, Godwin and his sons returned to favour and, during the latter part of the Confessor's reign, Harold practically ruled the kingdom. His brothers held important positions and one of them, Tostig, Earl of Northumbria, was a particular favourite of the King.

Harold's victorious campaigns against the Welsh had already earned him a great reputation as a warrior when he was unluckily wrecked on the French coast and so became the prisoner of Duke William.

After his return to England, Harold was obliged to agree to expel Tostig from the kingdom because of his misrule in Northumbria. This fatal quarrel was the real cause of the disaster at Hastings because not only did Tostig try to recover the earldom with foreign aid, but Morcar, the new Earl of Northumbria, and his brother Edwin of Mercia were naturally hostile to all the sons of Godwin and they made no effort to hurry south to help Harold against William. Chosen by the Witan and named by King Edward on his deathbed, Harold was the rightful King of England in January 1066. Duke William's claim was absurd and he won the crown only by a series of lucky accidents.

Contrary winds prevented William from sailing during the summer when he would have stood little chance against the English fleet and army that were waiting for him. Tostig's treachery not only drew Harold north and cost him some of his best troops, but it allowed William to land unopposed. Even so, Harold would not have been defeated if he had waited to build up his forces instead of trusting everything to a single battle.

She knew that she was beautiful and, from his glances, that this serious young man was deeply in love with her.

ELEANOR OF AQUITAINE

On a summer's day in 1137, in the hall of the ducal palace at Poitiers, barons and knights from a hundred distant fiefs and manors sat at table with their ladies, while minstrels played in an upper gallery and the voices of troubadours rose above the hubbub as they sang of courtly love and heroic deeds.

From time to time, the eyes of the guests were drawn to the top table where in the centre of a velvet-covered dais, were seated the youth and the girl in whose honour these nobles of France and Aquitaine had assembled. Louis, heir to the throne of France, was sixteen years old, a pale serious young man, ill at ease in this jubilant company, except that when he glanced at his companion, his eyes lit with adoration.

She was Eleanor of Aquitaine, at fifteen, Duchess of Aquitaine, for her father, Duke William, had died three months earlier. Dying, he had sent messengers to his overlord, King Louis VI of France, commending his unbetrothed daughter to his protection and suggesting her marriage to the heir to the throne.

The King of France, who was himself ill of the 'flux of the belly', immediately saw the importance of the match. At this time, the kingdom of France consisted of little more than the district around Paris, for the lands that lay between Flanders and the Pyrenees, were ruled by semi-independent lords who paid homage to the King of France, but precious little else. They seldom sent warriors to his musters and he dared not demand taxes. But the marriage would join the lands of France to the far wider domains of Aquitaine—Poitou, Gascony and a score of rich fiefs, Lusignan, Berry, Turenne, Astarac, Armagnac, Auvergne, Limoges and others.

So, without losing an unnecessary day, the marriage took place. Louis VI, too ill to travel, put the matter into the hands of his trusted adviser, Abbot Suger, a shrewd little monk, who quickly assembled an escort of five hundred knights and set out with the Prince Louis to Bordeaux. There, on July 25th, in the ancient cathedral, he married Eleanor of Aquitaine and, now, after a second ceremony at Poitiers, the Prince was seated beside his bride at a banquet.

Royal marriages were arranged like treaties; they had to do with great possessions and alliances; love and the wishes of the young couple were of no account. So Louis could hardly believe his good fortune. Eleanor was beautiful, with features and bearing so perfect that, even in old age, her beauty never faded. Moreover, she was witty, high-spirited and clever. She sang, composed verses, spoke several languages, could read and, a rarer accomplishment with the nobility, could write as well. She knew, of course, that she was beautiful and, from his glances, that this serious young man was deeply in love with her. His solemn manner amused her and, saying goodbye to her household at Bordeaux, she had whispered to her sister, 'I think I have married a monk, not a prince!'

Suddenly, a man in riding garb entered the banquet hall and whispered urgently into the ear of Abbot Suger; the churchman crossed himself and rose from the table. He knelt before young Louis and said, 'Sire, your royal father is dead. Long live Louis the Seventh, King of France!'

The death of one parent had made Eleanor a duchess at fifteen and, now, through the death of another, she was a queen. As she rode into Paris at her husband's side, she wondered what lay ahead for them in this shabby city so different from the sun-drenched towns of her own land. She soon found much to occupy her in affairs of state, feudal duties and debates by scholars and men of letters at Court. Her marriage was serene enough, for Louis loved her ardently and they shared an interest in books, though he lacked her passion for music.

Naturally a scholar, Louis nevertheless was determined to be a resolute king and it was to assert his royal authority that he led his army against a rebellious vassal and captured a little town called Vitry. As his soldiers burst in, the terrified populace took refuge in the church but, deliberately or by accident, the building was set on fire and over a thousand men, women and children perished.

Louis never recovered from the shock of this hideous crime; clad in sackcloth, he did public penance and thenceforward devoted himself to fasting and prayer. Songs, dancing, poetry-recitals at Court were abolished and he banished the troubadours whom he had allowed Eleanor to summon from Aquitaine. A shadow of discontent came between the young couple and, although, after seven years, their first child, a daughter, Marie, was born, Eleanor was far from happy.

Perhaps the best thing to do would be to join her husband on crusade. In 1144, the Turks had captured Edessa, one of the four Christian states that made up Outremer, the Crusader kingdom. When news reached Europe that Jerusalem itself was threatened, King Louis and Queen Eleanor took the Cross and made preparations to set out for the Holy Land with an army.

The Crusaders travelled through central Europe to Constantinople, a five-month journey of quarrels and hardship, for a German crusade led by the Emperor Conrad had already passed along the route, consuming supplies and putting up the prices of what was left.

In addition, the French grumbled mightily about Eleanor and her ladies, who, regarding the expedition as a gay adventure, had insisted upon bringing along maidservants and wagon-loads of silks, furs, jewellery, toiletries and even suits of feminine armour. Thus, progress was slow and, in Palestine, there would be too many useless mouths to feed and helpless people to protect.

In fact, the Crusade was a disaster. At Constantinople, Eleanor earned black looks because she made it clear that the elegance and gaiety of the Byzantine court

Opposite *Harold wounded at the Battle of Hastings, and his death, depicted in the Bayeux Tapestry*

were much more to her taste than the dour solemnity of Louis' company. On the way across Asia Minor, his army was badly mauled by the Turks in a rocky gorge and the blame was laid upon Eleanor who, riding with the Gascons, was said to have drawn the advance party too far ahead in order to camp in a pleasant valley.

In bad humour, the Crusaders reached Antioch, where they were welcomed by Eleanor's debonair uncle, Raymond of Poitiers, ruler of the city, 'taller, better-built and more handsome than any man of his time'. Gay as a bird, the Queen threw herself into a round of parties, picnics and festivities, in the company of her uncle and his charming companions. Tongues began to wag. The Queen's dress was immodest and her behaviour too light-hearted for a Crusader's wife; worse, it was whispered that she was in love with one of the southerners who had settled in Outremer. To put an end to gossip, Louis suddenly departed, taking with him a sullen wife to pray at the Holy Sepulchre in Jerusalem.

After an attack on Damascus had failed, Louis and Conrad decided to go home as best they could. Sailing in different ships, the King and Queen reached Italy in 1149, by which time, they were barely on speaking terms.

So worried was the Pope by this state of affairs, that he tried to mend the broken marriage, making them his guests and advising them to renew their love for one another. In the following year, Eleanor gave birth to their second child and if it had been the longed-for son, perhaps the Holy Father's wish would have been granted, but the child was another girl, Alice, who would one day marry the Count of Blois.

By the end of 1151, Louis had made up his mind to end his marriage. He and Eleanor had been married for fourteen years and she had produced only two daughters; her conduct on crusade had been disgraceful and had had much to do with the expedition's failure; she was proud, self-willed, over-fond of pleasure and, possibly, unfaithful as well (had she not recently cast eyes upon Geoffrey the Handsome, Count of Anjou, when he visited Paris with his son Henry?). But there was to be no scandal; Louis would put her aside on the grounds that they were cousins, very distant cousins it was true, but the Church would accept the case for the marriage to be ended.

They travelled together to the borders of Aquitaine where they made their farewells and Louis rode back to Paris, while Eleanor, with a small escort, made for her beloved Poitiers. Luckily, she had the good sense to send scouts ahead, for, presently, one came dashing back with startling news.

'My lady, you must turn aside. In the market-place at Blois, it is said that Count Theobald means to kidnap you.'

'God's teeth! He shall pay for his insolence!'

'But, my lady, his troops are already boasting that they will capture a bride for their master.'

The party took a forest track to the river Creuse, where they had to avoid a full-scale ambush laid for her by another suitor. Crossing the river lower down, they came at last to Poitou, where the bells rang and the people came into the streets to welcome their Duchess home. It was April 1152, and on May 18th, Eleanor married again.

Opposite *The effigy of Eleanor of Aquitaine on her tomb in Westminster Abbey*

Her second husband was none other than Henry Plantagenet, son of Geoffrey the Handsome (now dead) with whom Eleanor had flirted in Paris two years ago. Henry was now nineteen, short, thick-set, sandy-haired and bursting with energy and self-confidence. He had already made a name for himself as a warrior and a masterful ruler, for he had inherited Anjou and Normandy from his father and, from his mother, Matilda, daughter of Henry I of England, a claim to the kingdom of England itself. Her cousin Stephen had seized the throne, but she was now at war with him on English soil, while young Henry held the Angevin possessions lying to the north of Aquitaine.

So, it was easy to see why he asked Eleanor to marry him; her domains would bring him lands stretching from the Pyrenees to the English Channel and, if he and his mother triumphed, to the borders of Scotland. More than that, Eleanor, at 29, was still a dazzling beauty and Henry loved beautiful women all his life. As for Eleanor, she seems to have loved this youthful husband who was so much more the virile man of action than Louis and who was, in addition, surprisingly well-educated and cultured.

The first ten years of their marriage were a time of almost uninterrupted triumphs.

Louis, enraged by the marriage, attacked Normandy, but Henry beat him easily and then went campaigning in England so successfully that both sides agreed that he should be regarded as King Stephen's heir. Within a year, Stephen died and Henry became King of England and the most powerful monarch in Europe.

He and Eleanor were crowned in Westminster Abbey on December 19th 1154. In love, confident of each other's ability, they shared the task of ruling their vast possessions, for while Henry travelled ceaselessly about England, restoring law and order, levying taxes and curbing the barons, Eleanor would cross the Channel to tour their domains and administer justice in Anjou, Poitou and Gascony. They would meet in Normandy, still held in the iron grip of old Queen Matilda, and, at Argentan or Rouen, confer together, receive their vassals and delight in their children. They soon had a growing family, for William, born in 1153, was followed by Matilda, Henry and, in 1157, Richard. Next came Geoffrey, then two daughters, Eleanor and Joanna, and last, in 1166, John, known as John Lackland, because his father had already divided his possessions among the other sons.

During these years, Eleanor was frequently in England, where Henry increasingly put affairs into the hands of the Chancellor, Thomas Becket, a brilliant young man who brought off the remarkable feat of arranging a betrothal to link the royal houses of England and France. Louis VII had remarried and his little daughter, Marguerite, was betrothed to the young Prince Henry (William had died), a union that delighted Eleanor since it might well add France itself to the family possessions.

It seemed as if she and Henry could do nothing wrong. England was prosperous and well-governed, the Welsh barons had been subdued, King Malcolm of Scotland had done homage, the turbulent lords of Aquitaine accepted their rulers and, after the death of his brother, Henry had been able to add Brittany to his domains. Yet, just when everything was going so well, a quarrel broke out between the King and Queen so bitter that it was never to be healed.

In the year when John Lackland was born, Henry fell in love with a lady known as Fair Rosamund, the daughter of a Norman knight, Walter de Clifford, and, without regard to Eleanor's feelings, installed her in the royal residence at Woodstock. The Queen was furious. Gone for ever were the love and trust which had bound them together and, in anger, she left England to make her home in her own duchy of Aquitaine. Henceforward, she lived almost continuously at Poitiers, surrounded by her children, her courtiers, poets and troubadours. The Poitevins supported her wholeheartedly in her unending feud with her husband who had betrayed her.

From time to time, it is true, there was a truce between them, as, for instance, in 1167, when Eleanor returned to England for her daughter Matilda's marriage to Henry the Lion, Duke of Saxony, and when, in 1169, she agreed to allow her husband to take their three sons to do homage to Louis VII. She joined him that year at Nantes when he held a magnificent Christmas court and, again, in 1172, at Chinon when the whole family seemed to be reunited. But, all the while, she was relentlessly pursuing her aim to transfer power from her unworthy husband to her sons. For this reason, she toured Aquitaine with her favourite, Richard, presenting him to vassals and investing him with her lands from the Loire to the Pyrenees, and, for this reason too, she rejoiced when King Henry, following the custom of the time, had their eldest son, Young Henry, crowned in London in 1170.

Six months after this ceremony, King Henry was involved in a tragedy from which his reputation never recovered. In his passion for mastery, he quarrelled bitterly with his former Chancellor, Thomas Becket, after Becket became Archbishop of Canterbury and the fearless champion of the Church. The Archbishop was forced to live in exile for several years, but, in 1170, he returned to Canterbury and at once set about punishing those churchmen who had obeyed the King in his absence. On hearing this, Henry burst into such a rage that four knights, thinking that they were doing his bidding, crossed from Normandy to Kent, rode to Canterbury and murdered Becket in his own Cathedral.

No matter what he did afterwards—humbling himself to the Pope and clergy, doing public penance and suffering monks to scourge him, Henry was seen to be a murderer, a man whose authority could be defied.

To weather the storm, he laid low for a couple of years but, in 1172, summoned an assembly of vassals at Limoges to announce the betrothal of his daughter, Joanna, to William of Sicily, and the gift of certain lands and castles to John Lackland, his youngest son. Since Eleanor left him, Henry had tended to pamper John, and let him have his own way, much to the annoyance of the other sons who had never known such kindness. Suddenly, Young Henry, now seventeen, rose up in the assembly and burst out hotly,

'What justice, Sire, is this? Why should I and my brothers Richard and Geoffrey have to forfeit castles which are vital to the defence of our lands? If this spoilt child must have his own domain, let it be found in Ireland or Wales.'

The King angrily bade him to be silent but Young Henry would not sit down.

'Furthermore, is it not time you gave me Normandy and Anjou to rule as my own? Have I not been crowned King? Where, then, is my realm, my sovereignty?'

No one had dared to oppose Henry II's will before and, after the astonished assembly broke up, he compelled his son to accompany him on the journey northwards. They lodged one night at Chinon Castle and, in the morning when the King awoke, the drawbridge was down and Young Henry had gone. He fled to Paris to the protection of Louis VII, who, delighted by the situation, also gave shelter to Richard and Geoffrey. It was soon evident that this was no escapade but a full-scale rebellion, for the whole of Aquitaine declared for Young Henry, together with William of Scotland and many of the English barons, who were sick of the old King's despotic rule.

Only Normandy remained loyal and while his vassals resisted an attack by Louis and the Young King, Henry hired a mercenary army and, with all his old energy, fell upon Poitou with fire and sword. There was no doubt in his mind that Eleanor had plotted the rebellion and had schemed to turn his sons against their father, vassals against their overlord. He laid seige to a castle in which she was known to have taken refuge but, when it fell, she had vanished.

Some days later, a company of Henry's troops encountered a small party of knights riding towards Paris. Since they were Poitevins, they took them prisoner and later, to their astonishment, discovered that one of them, disguised as a man, was Queen Eleanor. They took her to Henry who, without a word to her, ordered her to be detained in the castle at Chinon. She remained there six months, while the rebellion collapsed, and was then transferred to England where, in various castles, she was her husband's prisoner until his death fifteen years later.

How did she pass the time during this long captivity? The King saw to it that her guards were chivalrous knights, who treated her with the courtesy due to a Queen, so she had her own household, her ladies, servants, pages, chaplains and musicians. She read, composed poetry, wrote letters to her children and sent alms to various abbeys and nunneries; she was allowed to ride out for exercise and sometimes to receive visitors, as at Winchester, when her daughter Matilda and Henry the Lion, came to see her.

From time to time, news reached her from the outside world; Fair Rosamund had died and so, too, had her first husband, King Louis. The new King of France was his son Philip Augustus and fighting had broken out again between Henry and *her* sons. Then, when she had been a prisoner for nine years, came the tragic news of Young Henry's death after a short illness during which he asked his friends to plead with his father for Eleanor's release. Although Henry refused, he relented sufficiently to send her two presents, a scarlet dress lined with fur and a saddle ornamented with gold thread. But he was soon at loggerheads with his sons, Richard and Geoffrey, as he tried to wrest Aquitaine from Richard in order to give it to John, his favourite. After Geoffrey died, Eleanor's hopes were pinned on Richard, the renowned warrior who was also a poet and troubadour; in alliance with Philip Augustus, he attacked his father's territories, capturing towns and winning over his vassals, so that the old King was forced to ask for a truce. Deserted and ill, he took to his bed at Chinon Castle, where he asked his Chancellor for a list of the nobles who had joined the rebellion. At its head was the name of John Lackland, the beloved son for whose sake he had suffered so much family strife.

'Read no more', he cried out, 'Ah, John, John. I care no longer for myself or the world.'

Three days later, Henry died and Richard I, his successor, immediately sent a messenger to England to order the release of Queen Eleanor but he found her, he reported, 'at Winchester, already at liberty and more the great lady than ever.'

She was 67, an age which few reached in those days, but with astonishing energy, she toured England at the head of a magnificent cavalcade, visiting towns and castles, releasing prisoners, righting grievances and even reforming the coinage and the weights and measures used for corn, liquids and cloth. Above all, she prepared the way for her son's coronation, for she realised that he was hardly known in England and she must safeguard his interests against any plot hatched by his rascally brother John.

She succeeded so well that in September 1189, seated on a throne in Westminster Abbey, she saw Richard, a red-haired giant who towered above the Archbishop and the attendant barons, crowned King of England.

No sooner was the coronation over, than Richard made it clear that his sole interest in the country was to raise money for a crusade to win back Jerusalem from the Turks. A special tax was levied, town charters and feudal rights were sold to the highest bidder;

'I would sell London itself', declared the King, 'If I could find a buyer.'

With remarkable speed, the ships, men, horses, weapons and stores were assembled, so that Richard left England in December for Normandy, where Eleanor presently joined him. They had much to discuss, for he was leaving his vast possessions in her charge and she would have to keep a watchful eye on John during his absence.

They said goodbye in June 1190, when Richard marched his army to Marseilles and took ship to Sicily, where they were to spend the winter prior to joining Philip Augustus in the Holy Land. Meanwhile, Eleanor turned southwards, through Aquitaine, across the Pyrenees and into Spain, where, she made for the court of King Sancho of Navarre. She had come, she explained, to seek a wife for her son, Richard of England, and her choice had fallen upon Sancho's daughter, Berengaria.

King Sancho agreed to the match and, with no thought for her age, Eleanor set off with the girl on an immense journey that took them through the Alps, down the entire length of Italy to the port of Brindisi where they embarked for Messina, in Sicily. There, on March 30th, 1191, she embraced her son and introduced him to his Spanish bride whom he married in Cyprus some weeks later.

By that time, Eleanor was back on the road. The tireless old woman had rested for only four days in Sicily before returning to Italy where she visited the Pope in Rome and borrowed 800 marks from money-lenders for her expenses on the journey to Rouen.

At Christmas 1191, she heard some surprising news. In the Holy Land, Richard had covered himself in glory at the siege of Acre, but, in his tactless, arrogant way, had managed to quarrel so bitterly with the French King that Philip had abandoned the crusade and was on his way home.

Eleanor immediately garrisoned the castles along the borders of the Plantagenet possessions and, hearing that John was putting about stories that Richard would never come back from Palestine, hurried to England to call the barons together to swear oaths of fealty to Richard. Eventually, to her great relief, she heard that, having made a truce with Saladin, he had put his wife and his sister Joanna on a ship bound for England and that he would follow in a few days' time.

Anxious weeks followed until, in the spring of 1193, the bombshell fell. Richard the Lionheart was a prisoner in Germany. After being wrecked on the shores of the Adriatic, he had been recognised and captured in the territory of his enemy, Duke Leopold of Austria, who handed him over to the Emperor Henry VI. For a time, no one knew where he was held, but it presently became clear that the Emperor was asking a huge ransom for his release, while Philip Augustus and John were offering as much to keep him in prison, so that they could share his domains.

They reckoned without Eleanor. With indomitable energy, the old Queen put the kingdom's defences in order, sent off innumerable letters to the Emperor, the Pope and her vassals, got into touch with Richard himself and imposed taxes to raise a hundred thousand silver marks for his ransom. When the money had been collected, she herself set sail with the treasure and, accompanied by a great company of barons and churchmen, travelled to Germany, where at Mainz on February 2nd 1194, she was reunited with her famous son.

Hearing of his release, Philip sent an urgent message to his crony, John: 'Look to yourself; the Great Devil himself is unchained!' John fled abroad but Richard forgave him with contemptuous generosity, for his mind was intent upon winning back the lands which his real enemy, Philip, had filched during his absence. London gave him a rapturous welcome but, within weeks, he had raised an army and was back in Normandy preparing for war.

Eleanor crossed the Channel with him and rode to her favourite abbey at Fontevrault where, she told the abbess, she intended to stay for the rest of her days, for she was growing old and could at last leave the kingdom's affairs to her son.

For more than four years, she lived quietly at the abbey, until, in March 1199, a messenger brought word that Richard, fatally wounded by a crossbolt, was asking for her. Making all speed, she reached the little town of Chalus where he died in her arms that evening.

In her grief, she still knew what she must do to save the territories that were so precious to her. She had no illusions about John, her youngest child, and the new King of England. He had always been mean and treacherous, so she could only pray for him and counsel him to try to win the allegiance of the English and Norman barons.

For her part, in order to secure Aquitaine, she made a great tour of the duchy, calling upon her vassals and granting charters of freedom to town after town. Then she journeyed to Tours to meet Philip and pay homage to him for her lands.

During this time, she suffered one sorrow after another, for, in the year when Richard died, she lost three daughters in quick succession, Joanna, her favourite, and Marie and Alice, the two who were born to her when she was Queen of France. Of her ten children, only two were left, John and Eleanor, who lived far away in Spain and it was to Spain that this dauntless old woman set out in the winter of 1200, when she was nearly eighty. One thought, one ambition gave her the strength to endure the hardships of travel along frozen roads and across barren hills: her daughter, Eleanor of Castile, had three young daughters and she would bring one of them to be the bride of Louis, the son and heir of Philip Augustus. By this master-stroke, she would unite the royal families of France and England, thereby preserving the possessions which, she felt certain, John would lose if it came to war.

So, she brought her granddaughter, Blanche to Normandy, where the girl was married to Louis of France, and Eleanor, feeling that her task was done, retired to the abbey of Fontevrault. Alas for her hopes: the war which she dreaded broke out soon enough, and, unable to reach safety at Poitiers, she had to take refuge in the castle of Mirebeau, which was hotly besieged by the enemy. Scorning surrender, Eleanor inspired the garrison with her own courage and, by night, sent off a messenger to her son, John, who lay at Le Mans, 90 miles away.

Capable of brilliant action when he chose to exert himself, John led a lightning dash across country, reached Mirebeau in two days, totally defeated the enemy and rescued his mother. Then, as ever, he showed the other side of his character. Among the prisoners was his own nephew, Arthur of Brittany, whom he almost certainly killed with his own hands, and he treated the other captives with such savage cruelty that many of his vassals refused to fight for him.

After her rescue, Queen Eleanor tried to keep Aquitaine loyal to John but, as the war went badly and Normandy seemed certain to be lost, she retired once more to her prayers at Fontevrault, where she died in 1204 and was buried beside her husband, Henry II.

History has been harsh to her, usually portraying her as a vengeful self-willed woman who defied both her husbands and turned her sons against their father. But, in her own land, she was the greatly loved ruler of the people, beautiful, gifted and, as a chronicler wrote, 'a woman beyond compare'.

More about Eleanor of Aquitaine (c. 1122-1204)

According to legend, Queen Eleanor tracked down Fair Rosamund to her hiding-place at Woodstock, while Henry II was away on the continent, fighting his rebellious sons. In her jealousy, Eleanor was supposed to have offered Rosamund the choice between a dagger and a poisoned cup; Rosamund drank the poison and was buried at Godstow. In fact, Eleanor was a prisoner when Rosamund died in 1176.

The family possessions on which Eleanor set such store were mostly lost by John; his son, Henry III, gave up all claim to Poitou, but English kings did homage for the duchy of Guienne (most of Gascony) for many years. Eleanor's granddaughter, Blanche of Castile, produced twelve children for her husband, Louis VIII, including Louis IX, known as Saint Louis, the greatest of the medieval Kings of France. King John's grandson, Edward I, a warrior of whom the old Queen would have been proud, married Eleanor of Castile, her great-great-granddaughter.

Frederick was 'red, bald and short-sighted,' but with good features and the masterful air of a born despot.

FREDERICK II, STUPOR MUNDI

Stupor Mundi, 'Wonder of the World', was the nickname which men gave to the Holy Roman Emperor, Frederick II of Hohenstaufen, because his character and life-style filled them with amazement.

Frederick, born in Italy in 1194, was the son of the Emperor Henry VI and Constance of Sicily, whose Norman forebears had conquered the island from the Saracens. Through his father and his grandfather, Barbarossa, Frederick belonged to the German house of Hohenstaufen, while, from his mother, he inherited the fabulously rich kingdom of Sicily, which, at that time, included half of Italy. When he was two, his father persuaded the German princes to elect the boy King of the Romans, the title borne by the Emperor-to-be and, at the age of five, after his father's sudden death, he was crowned King of Sicily. In that same year, his mother died at Palermo, leaving her little son in the care of Pope Innocent III.

Without brothers and sisters, without kindly nurses or any knowledge of love and family life, Frederick grew up in the palaces and fortresses of Sicily. His guardians were elderly bishops, while his personal attendants were Court hangers-on, looking to their own interests in the struggle for power between the German and Norman nobles. In this situation, powerful barons managed to seize some of the royal estates and, on one occasion, young Frederick was captured by a group of Germans. He was only seven but, wrote one of the priests to the Pope,

> *When, by treachery, they had penetrated the palace and sought to lay hands on him, the King defended himself with tears and force. Like a ferocious animal, he threw himself upon those who tried to seize him, tearing them with nails and teeth and crying out, 'Dare you touch the body of the Lord's anointed?'*

Throughout these troubled times, Frederick ran wild; he loved to ride, hunt and wrestle, to practise with sword and bow; he was active, strong as a little bull and passionately rebellious against his guardians. Yet his tutors found him a brilliant pupil. No subject seemed too difficult for him; he read history and philosophy far into the night, learned to speak six languages and became so adept at mathematics that he would amuse himself by setting mathematical problems for the Court scholars to solve.

Sicily still possessed the most civilised and luxurious court in Europe; Norman kings had employed Moslems and encouraged Arab and Greek scholars to make translations of ancient works of literature, science and medicine. In the warm climate of the deep south, the northerners adopted oriental ways of life, building themselves palaces with colonnaded courts, fountains and exotic gardens, where poets, musicians and troupes of dancing girls entertained guests dressed in the flowing robes of the East. This was the scene in which Frederick grew up, the land which he loved more than anywhere else in the world. He liked to call himself 'the boy from Apulia', after his favourite province on the mainland, and, once, after he came back from Crusade, he shocked an archbishop by saying:

'God would not have chosen Palestine for His own, if He had seen my Kingdom of Sicily!'

In 1208, when he was fourteen, Frederick was declared of age to rule by the Pope who, a year later, arranged for him to marry Constance of Aragon, widow of the King of Hungary. She was ten years older than Frederick, who was far from keen on the match but, since she brought with her a company of five hundred knights, he felt that this force would give him the striking power he needed to punish the barons who had stolen his domains. As it happened, Constance was a beautiful and cultured woman whose influence transformed an ill-mannered boy into the most polished monarch of his day.

The nobles laughed at the idea of a fifteen year-old asserting his rights, but, when the Count of Tropea insulted Frederick to his face, he and many other barons were suddenly arrested and thrown into prison. The news created a sensation and Frederick followed it up with a circular letter to all the provinces of the realm, describing the crimes of the prisoners and stating his intention to restore order and justice in Sicily. He had made a good beginning but, in 1211, the kingdom was suddenly threatened. Since Henry VI's death, Germany had been devastated by a civil war, from which Otto IV emerged as Emperor and Otto, claiming Italy for the Empire, crossed the Alps with an army and occupied the whole of the mainland part of Frederick's kingdom. In Palermo harbour, galleys rode at anchor, ready to carry Queen Constance and their new-born son, Henry, to safety.

However, the Pope now took a hand. As a great landowner, he had no wish to see the Papal States threatened by a German army, so he excommunicated Otto and sent word to the princes and bishops of Germany that they were freed from their oaths of allegiance. In alarm, Otto struck camp and hurried home but he was too late, for an opposition party had already decided to depose him and offer the imperial crown to Frederick.

At Palermo, he listened to the ambassadors with wonder. A short while ago he seemed likely to be driven out of his kingdom but now, at eighteen, he was offered the Empire itself, with Germany and scores of duchies and lands, including Lombardy in northern Italy. Should he, dare he, accept the glittering offer? Queen Constance and his councillors advised him to refuse: it was too risky and how would they manage in Sicily without him?

Frederick sat silent for a long time. Then he spoke,

'I shall go to Germany', he said, 'And accept my father's crown. For if I refuse, Otto will regain his power and return with an army to attack us again. It is God's will that I should go.'

On his way north, he stopped at Rome to pay homage to Innocent III for the fief of Sicily, which, the Pope insisted, he must swear to make over to his infant son. With bowed head he took the oath but, as he placed his hands between those of the Holy Father, he knew in his heart that he would never give up his beloved kingdom.

Accompanied by only a small band of followers and taking a secret route to avoid the hostile Milanese, Frederick passed through the Alps into Germany to present himself to his new subjects. On the surface, his chances of success were small, for Otto still had a powerful army, but, from the start, everything went miraculously well as Frederick went out of his way to impress the Germans with his charm and generosity. He knew that he needed money to bribe the princes and, though he had little of his own, he borrowed heavily to make lavish gifts to his supporters. Then he was lucky enough to be given twenty thousand marks by the King of France, and, luckier still, the French defeated Otto and reduced the former Emperor to the position of a pathetic fugitive.

It only remained to win over the great princes of the Church, the bishops and archbishops who ruled more than half the land in Germany and this Frederick did by granting them practically all the freedom and privileges they desired.

Hard as it was to give up his rights, Frederick did so because he wanted the goodwill of these powerful churchmen for his chief aim in life—the election of his son Henry as King of the Romans and the union of Germany and Italy into one grandiose Empire which he, like Caesar, would rule from Rome.

In July 1215, at Aix-la-Chapelle, the Archbishop of Mainz placed on his head the silver crown of Germany. In a moment of heady excitement, holding aloft the sword and sceptre of kingship, Frederick rose to his feet and cried:

'We do solemnly swear by Almighty God that, to repay the gifts He has conferred upon us, we will lead a Crusade to win back the Holy Places from the infidel!'

Not long after the coronation, the Pope died and Queen Constance made the long journey from Sicily to join her husband in Germany with their six-year-old son. For the next four years, Frederick plotted and schemed to have the boy elected King of the Romans and when the German princes finally chose him, Frederick took care not to be present, so he could tell the Pope that the election was none of his doing. The new Pope, Honorius III, was not fooled but, passionately desiring the Crusade to be launched, he took no action.

So, in November 1220, in Rome, the Pope embraced Frederick and accompanied him to St Peter's Church where, in solemn pomp, he crowned him Holy Roman Emperor, as his father and grandfather had been before him. Constance was crowned Empress afterwards. Only three days later, they left Rome and, travelling fast, reached the town of Capua, the first sizeable place in the realm of Sicily. After eight years, Frederick had come home.

The Sicilian nobles were well aware that they no longer had to deal with a boy but with a man of twenty-six who, since they last saw him, had proved himself a monarch to be feared. Many hurried to greet him with demonstrations of loyalty, while others promptly handed back castles and lands which they had seized during his absence.

By a mixture of force and cunning, Frederick transformed Sicily into a model kingdom, issuing new laws, reducing the nobles' privileges and crushing those who attempted rebellion. He created a navy, a strong defence force and, in order to educate the laymen who were to replace priests as his civil servants, he founded the University of Naples.

During the troubled years of Frederick's childhood, much of Sicily's wealth had gone into the pockets of merchants from Pisa and Genoa who had established themselves in Syracuse. Although he recognised the danger of making enemies of these powerful states, Frederick expelled the Genoese, confiscated their property and, along with the Pisans, abolished their trading privileges. The Genoese never forgave him, but he had provided himself with the wealth he needed for his dream of making himself the greatest monarch in Europe.

The next task was to subdue the Saracens who had long occupied the western part of the island of Sicily from whose mountain strongholds they constantly raided the fertile plains right to the gates of Palermo. Defeated by the royal army, they returned to their villages, only to resume raiding as soon as Frederick's back was turned. He therefore hit upon the plan of removing the entire Moslem population from the island and, in an all-out campaign that lasted two years, he took some 16,000 prisoners and transported them to the desolate plains of Apulia on the mainland. Settled into communities around the town of Lucera, they took to farming with great skill and many of them later served loyally in Frederick's imperial army.

All this time, the Pope continued to remind the Emperor of his oath to go on Crusade. Frederick made excuses; he had much to do in Sicily, the Saracen war could not be abandoned, his wife, Queen Constance, had died and he was concerned about the upbringing of their son, Henry, in Germany. But the Pope persisted and put forward the idea of Frederick marrying Yolanda, the hereditary Queen of Jerusalem, a child living in Acre, since the Holy City was now in the hands of the Saracens. With a bad grace, Frederick agreed to the match but, by one means and another, he managed to delay matters for another two years until, at last, in 1225, Yolanda, weeping bitterly at leaving her home in Syria, was brought to Brindisi where, with great pomp, they were married. Frederick was thirty-one, 'red, bald and short-sighted', but with good features and the masterful air of a born despot. A scholar, a poet and lover of many women by whom he had several children, he paid scant attention to his young bride but created a scandal by immediately taking the title of King of Jerusalem, and falling in love with her cousin, one of the ladies of the Court. Poor Yolanda; well might she weep, for her husband kept her shut up in one or another of his castles, and she died at Otranto when she was only sixteen, having given birth to their son, Conrad.

This was in May 1228 and still the Crusade had not been launched, so that the new Pope, Gregory IX, lost all patience with the Emperor and actually excommunicated him for failing to keep his vow.

In fact, Frederick had been unlucky. The Crusaders had assembled in Apulia during the previous summer, but, in the blazing heat of southern Italy, a pestilence broke out in the camp, so that hundreds died and many fled northwards. The Emperor ordered the army to sail from Brindisi but when he himself fell ill of the plague, the imperial galley put back to port, while the rest of the expedition continued on its way. It was while he was ashore regaining his health that Frederick learned that the Pope, refusing to believe the story of illness, had pronounced the dire sentence of excommunication. What was he to do? Surely he must humble himself and seek forgiveness? The 'Boy from Apulia' scorned the idea of surrender; as in 1212, when he was offered the Empire, he would take the bold course and go forward, trusting to luck and his own talents. Even as an excommunicate, he still meant to do what Coeur de Lion, Barbarossa, Philip Augustus and so many other Crusaders had failed to do, and win back the city of Jerusalem.

The amazing thing is that he succeeded. His army, consisting of only fifteen hundred knights and ten thousand infantry, with a regiment of Moslem troops from Lucera, was too small to besiege towns and win pitched battles. On the Pope's order, he received no help from the barons and clergy of Outremer, while the Patriarch of Jerusalem and the great Military Orders of the Templars and Hospitallers were bitterly hostile. There was, however, just one ray of hope, for the empire of the great Saladin was now divided between al-Kamil, Sultan of Egypt, and his two brothers, the Sultans of Babylon and Damascus, who hated one another.

Fearing that his brothers might combine against him whilst he was at war with the Crusaders, al-Kamil got into touch with Frederick, sending as his ambassador, the Emir Fakhr, whose cultured mind at once appealed to an Emperor who had known Moslems since childhood. They discussed philosophy, law, poetry and the possibility of coming to some friendly arrangement about Jerusalem. Frederick was in his element, assuring the Emir that he had not come to make war or seize lands; all he wanted was the Holy Places which truly belonged to his son Conrad, child of Yolanda. He despatched princely gifts to al-Kamil who, in return, sent jewels, an elephant, ten of the famous Mehari breed of camels, monkeys, bears and Arab steeds. The Sultan regretted that he could not give Jerusalem to the Emperor, as it would enrage the Moslem world, but something might still be arranged. In truth, both men were anxious to come to terms, for Frederick had had word that the Pope's troops had invaded his kingdom and the Sultan was aware that his Moslem enemies were gathering their forces.

So they made a treaty by which the Christians received Jerusalem, along with Nazareth and the surrounding country. In the Holy City itself, two places sacred to Mohammedans—the Dome of the Rock and the Mosque of al-Aqsa—remained in Moslem hands and their pilgrims were to be free to go there and worship. This clause infuriated the Templars and Christian leaders, while the barons of Outremer felt insulted that Frederick had never sought their assistance. But, from his point of view, he had achieved his aim of getting possession of Jerusalem and could now confront the Pope with the fact that he had kept his word.

On 17th March 1229, the excommunicated Emperor entered Jerusalem to be handed the keys of the city by the Sultan's governor. Next day, he proceeded to the Church of the Holy Sepulchre where, since no Christian priest was present except those in his own company, he took the crown from the altar and placed it on his own head.

After visiting the Moslem Holy Places and making plans to rebuild the city's defences, the new King of Jerusalem rode swiftly to Acre, evading on the way an ambush laid by the Templars. In Acre, where he savagely punished the priests who had preached against him, he appointed barons to rule in his absence and then, pelted with filth and followed by the curses of the population, he went aboard his galley and ordered its master to make all speed for Italy. He landed at Brindisi in June, just one year after he had set out on the Sixth Crusade.

For the next twenty years, the feud between Emperor and Pope continued in all its bitterness. At times, they seemed to make peace but the contest would soon flare up again, in which they hurled insults at one another and, in long letters to the rulers of Europe, each would accuse the other of all kinds of wickedness.

The root of the trouble was that Frederick would not accept the idea of the Pope having authority over kings and princes, let alone the Emperor himself. His aim was to unite Germany and Italy into an empire in which justice would prevail, and art, trade and science would flourish. The Church, purged of its greed and wealth, could look after men's souls but he, the Emperor, would rule their lives and direct their affairs.

No Pope could possibly accept this view. The Church owned vast amounts of land and riches; it told men what they should think and believe; its clergy, from the mighty archbishops down to the humblest clerks, filled practically all the important posts in all the kingdoms of Christendom. Frederick's ideas challenged the power of the Church and therefore the Pope would continue to oppose him to the end.

Refusing to accept that he had taken on an impossible task, Frederick journeyed

incessantly about his domains, issuing laws, building innumerable castles and palaces, encouraging scholars, mathematicians, poets, and scientists, making war on the Lombard cities, quarrelling with his son Henry in Germany and eventually keeping him a prisoner until the wretched young man took his own life by riding his horse over a precipice. The Emperor could be hideously cruel to those who opposed him; prisoners were tortured and executed in public; after his great victory over the Lombards at Cortenuova, he paraded the Milanese governor through the streets of Cremona, manacled with chains and bound by his neck to a chariot; at the siege of Brescia, he had captives tied to his siege-engines so that they would be hit by enemy missiles and, suspecting his faithful servant, Pietro della Vigna, of being involved in a plot to poison him, he had him blinded and threatened with such terrible tortures that Pietro killed himself by dashing his head against a wall.

Frederick travelled his empire like some oriental potentate. When he entered a city, its awed inhabitants, having been ordered to deck their houses and line the streets in his honour, were treated to a spectacle of marvellous pageantry; first came a detachment of Saracen cavalry mounted on Arab steeds and escorting the Mehari camels given by the Sultan of Egypt. There followed a number of palanquins or litters, behind whose gorgeous curtains lay the veiled Eastern ladies of the Emperor's harem, who were guarded by enormous black men of ferocious appearance. Accompanied by armed knights and brilliantly attired courtiers, the Emperor himself rode by, often deep in conversation with one of the scholars who accompanied the Court on its travels. Then, to the spectators' delight, came the imperial menagerie, with the elephant on whose back rode some Saracen archers in a wooden tower, a giraffe, never seen before in Europe, lions, lynxes, hunting leopards and cheetahs, held on leashes by pages, the precious falcons each riding hooded on a falconer's wrist, monkeys, hounds and exotic birds. After the infantry had marched by, with lances on their shoulders, there came a seemingly endless procession of wagons and pack-horses loaded with stores, books, altars, cooking-pots, documents, treasures and bags of gold coins that were needed for the journey.

At the end of 1237, Frederick was at the height of his power. Married now to Isabella, the beautiful sister of Henry III of England, he had secured the friendship of France and England, had put down a rising in Germany, saved the Pope from the rebellious Romans, defeated Frederick the Quarrelsome of Austria and added his territories to the Empire. He secured the election of his son Conrad as German King and defeated the army of the Lombard cities at Cortenuova.

Suddenly his fortunes changed, for, after he failed to capture the key city of Brescia, the Pope gave his support to the Lombards and, accusing him of blasphemy and heresy, excommunicated him for the second time. Just when Frederick was about to lay siege to Rome, Pope Gregory died, as did his successor, soon after his election; however, the new Pope Innocent IV, fled to Lyons in France whence he issued a catalogue of the Emperor's crimes against the Church and renewed the sentence of excommunication. In addition, he sent bands of monks to Italy and Germany to foment rebellion and preach against the Emperor in the streets and market-places. They declared him to be Antichrist, the Great Beast, capable of every crime and guilty of every sin. He oppressed the clergy, loved the Moslem religion and showed friendship to Jews. He had no belief in God, but, once, on seeing a priest give Holy Communion to a dying soldier, had said,

'When will this mumbo-jumbo have an end?' and on another occasion. 'The three greatest imposters in the world were Moses, Christ and Mohammed.'

Frederick reacted by crushing the uprisings with ruthless cruelty and he seemed to be recovering all his power when word reached him that Parma, an imperial stronghold, had been taken by surprise. To win it back, he completely surrounded the city and, as shelter for his troops in the winter, built a wooden town alongside which he called Vittoria. The siege dragged on, but, although the people were starving and Frederick had captives executed daily in front of the walls, the garrison refused to surrender. One day in February, the Emperor went out hunting at dawn. His departure was noticed by a sentry on the wall, whereupon the commander ordered a sally to be made on the other side of the city to attract the attention of the Marquis of Lancia, who had been left in charge of the army. The ruse succeeded. Lancia set off in hot pursuit and the entire population of Parma burst out from the gates and fell upon Vittoria which was practically undefended. As the whole place went up in flames, the crowd seized the imperial treasure—gold, silver, jewels, brocades, robes, books, statues and the Emperor's throne. Even the ladies of his harem were captured and carried back in triumph to the city led by a hunchback beggar, who had jammed the imperial crown on his own head.

Far away in the country, Frederick heard the trumpets and alarm bells and dashed back with his huntsmen to find his army scattered, his treasure lost and Vittoria in smouldering ruins. Barely escaping with his life, he rode hard to Cremona, raised a fresh army and speedily returned to Parma. But the city, re-stocked with supplies, was stronger than ever and he had to abandon the siege and retire southwards.

Frederick never recovered from this disaster. The blow to his prestige gave encouragement to all his enemies and his finances were ruined by the loss of gold needed to pay the mercenaries who formed the imperial army. In these circumstances, the Emperor grew moody and suspicious of even his most trusted companions; his favourite son and most able commander, Enzio, was captured by the Bolognese who swore never to release him and, in his distress, Frederick's health gave out.

Ill and depressed, he made his way back to Sicily where, for a time, he seemed to recover, and actually went hunting again. However, he was taken violently ill with an attack of dysentry at Fiorentino castle in Apulia, where, having made his will leaving the Empire to his son Conrad, he died on 13th December 1250. As he had directed, his body was taken to Palermo Cathedral, and placed in a sarcophagus made of purple stone and mounted on four carved lions. He lies there to this day, Stupor Mundi, the Wonder of the World. But, to the Church, it was the 'Son of Satan' who had died and therefore, wrote Innocent III, 'Let Heaven exult and earth rejoice.'

More about Frederick II of Hohenstaufen (1194–1250)

After Frederick's death, the Hohenstaufen dynasty soon came to an end. His son by Isabella, Henry, died in 1253 at the age of fifteen and, in the following year, Yolanda's son, Conrad, died in Italy, after giving up the hopeless task of trying to rule Germany. His son, Conradin, the last emperor of the line, was captured in battle in 1268 and executed by Charles of Anjou, to whom the Pope had given the kingdom of Sicily.

Frederick had made such an impression on men's minds that for more than a century there were rumours that he was still alive. Many imposters tried to impersonate him and a legend told how he sat in a cavern in Germany before a stone table through which his beard had grown, waiting for the time to awake and restore the Empire to a golden age.

For all his brilliant talents, Frederick was only a moderate general; he preferred diplomacy to war and never had enough troops or siege-engines to totally defeat the Lombard cities. In any case, the power of the Church in the thirteenth century was too great for him to win a permanent victory over the Pope. It is often said that, with his enquiring, cynical mind and his gifts as a poet, scholar and lawgiver, he was a prince of the Renaissance, born two centuries too soon.

The beautiful city of Chung Tu, the capital, was sacked and its palaces continued to burn for weeks.

Genghis Khan and Kublai Khan

Beyond the Great Wall of China lies the Land of Grass, a vast plain inhabited, according to the Chinese, by devils and spirits. As well as limitless pastures, covered in winter by snow and black ice, there is the dreaded Gobi Desert, a waste of grey sand and stones, where demons howl amid the ruins of ancient cities and where, for centuries, travellers followed the route which was marked by whitened bones.

Out of this harsh land, in about the year 1200, poured a race of conquerors known as Mongols or Tartars. They were nomadic tribesmen, nourished on milk and blood, who lived solely for the joy of battle and plunder.

The nomads had no use for permanent dwellings, but their houses were circular tents made of black felt stretched over wooden frames. When a tribe was on the move to fresh grazing lands, the tents were transported on enormous carts drawn by teams of oxen.

The Mongols wintered on the southern steppes and moved in summer to cooler pastures in the north, grazing their herds of horses and cattle as they went. From boyhood, the tribesmen lived almost entirely in the saddle, glorying in their horsemanship and powers of endurance. Often, they would go ten days or more without food, apart from mare's milk and blood, which they obtained by piercing a vein of a horse, afterwards stopping the wound with a pad of mud and dung. Thus, on campaign, they travelled without baggage and their horses, five or six to a man, were as hardy as the riders.

In the year 1162, Yesukai, chief or khan of the Yakka tribe, returned from a successful raid on Temujin's tribe to learn that in his absence a son had been born to his favourite wife. In accordance with custom, the boy was named Temujin after the defeated enemy, and he was brought up in a manner suitable for the heir to the chieftainship of a thousand black tents.

Temujin grew into a tall boy with grey slanting eyes and reddish hair worn in plaits, but when he was only thirteen, his father Yesukai was murdered. The tribesmen would not accept a stripling as their chief, and for several years, Temujin and his brothers lived as fugitives, hunted without pity by their father's enemies. But, in the bitter plains and mountains, Temujin learned to fight.

Gradually, he won back the allegiance of the Yakka warriors and led them to victory against tribe after tribe.

During his perilous youth, Temujin also won Burtai, a chieftain's daughter, who shared his wanderings and was herself captured by his enemies. In a furious raid, Temujin rescued his bride and put her captors to the sword, for he loved Burtai with a steadfastness that was reckoned strange among tribesmen who took as many wives as they pleased.

In 1206, 'the Year of the Leopard', a great gathering of the tribes assembled at Karakorum, the holy place of the Mongols. Here, on the windswept plain, the tribesmen elected Temujin as their Great Khan, 'Lord of Lords', and he took the name of *Chinghiz* which has come down to us as Jenghis or Genghis Khan.

As Marco Polo put it, 'they made up their minds to conquer the whole world', and, in the space of a few years, the name of Genghis Khan was dreaded throughout the immense land mass that stretches from China to Eastern Europe.

The Mongols covered the plains like locusts. A number of good seasons for grass and raiding and the Mongol custom of marrying several wives had led to a terrific increase in the numbers of the tribesmen, so that they poured like a torrent over the settled lands.

The Great Wall of China delayed but could not halt the Mongol hordes. Mounted on their black ponies, they followed the seven-tailed yak Standard of Genghis Khan into Northern China where, for the first time, the blood-drinkers beheld a country that had been civilised for more than a thousand years. Here, in walled towns, amid graceful temples and tall pagodas, an aristocracy of painters, poets and philosophers, with millions of peasant-farmers, served an Emperor called the Son of Heaven.

For a time, the cultivated lands and the ricefields checked the Mongol cavalry, since they could not charge and wheel across land that was ploughed and ditched, nor was there grass for the horses. But Genghis possessed a genius for war and he retired to his native plains to rebuild the strength of his cavalry, and then the hordes swept back to overwhelm the Emperor's armies.

In 1215, the Mongols overcame the forty-foot walls and the triple line of moats and forts that guarded Chung Tu (Peking), the capital. The beautiful city was sacked and its palaces continued to burn for weeks, while the bodies of the slaughtered inhabitants rotted in great mounds outside the walls. But the Mongols did not stay.

With wagon-loads of rich and curious treasures, the tribesmen went back to Karakorum in the grassy plains, where they decked their wives with gold and jade and lined their tents with silk.

Genghis Khan knew that China was no land for the Mongols. Their horses could not live there and the warriors would have grown soft. Nevertheless, he admired the skill and learning of the Chinese and, among his prisoners, was a tall bearded aristocrat named Yeh-lu Chutsai, whose ancestors had been subdued by the Chinese. Yeh-lu was brought into the presence of the Great Khan to be questioned:

'Are you not glad that I have avenged your ancestors?' asked Genghis Khan.

'My father and I served the Chinese faithfully all our lives,' replied Yeh-lu, 'I cannot rejoice in the downfall of a good master.'

Much impressed by such loyalty, Genghis took the captive into his service, bestowing on him the name of 'Long Beard', and in a short while, Yeh-lu became the Khan's Chief Minister.

By patience and honesty, Yeh-lu was able to influence the terrible conqueror and even, on occasion, to persuade him to be merciful. Once, because of a shortage of fodder for the horses, Genghis Khan made up his mind to slaughter the entire population of a province and to turn the fields into pasture. On hearing this, Yeh-lu gently pointed out that the people were hard-working peasants who would pay taxes worth far more than grass and hay, and Genghis, rather to his own surprise, decided to spare them.

Leaving one of his generals as viceroy of China, the Great Khan turned west with his warrior horde to sweep across Afghanistan and Persia. Kings, shahs and emperors were overthrown, their armies destroyed and their cities, many of them ancient centres of trade, reduced to ruins. The slant-eyed horsemen, armed with their deadly bows and curved swords, were victorious everywhere as they swept on towards Europe and the shores of the Black Sea.

Even the Turks, renowned for their fighting qualities, could not stand against these tireless killers, and when Samarkand, with its mosques, aqueducts and walled gardens, fell to the conquerors, thirty thousand Turkish defenders deserted and offered their services to the Khan. For three days, they were rewarded and feasted and then, in one night, every man was slaughtered. The Mongols had no use for traitors.

As Genghis grew older, he gave each of his four sons an army to command, while he himself withdrew to his great tent at Karakorum to devote himself to ruling an empire that stretched for three thousand miles. To keep himself informed and to send out a ceaseless stream of advice and command, he set up a system of staging posts which Marco Polo, in the time of Genghis' grandson, describes as follows:

'When one of the Great Khan's messengers sets out along any of these roads, he has only to go twenty-five miles and he finds a posting-station. These hostelries have splendid beds with rich coverlets of silk. . . . If a king came here he would be well lodged. Here the messengers find no fewer than 400 horses stationed and always kept in readiness . . .'

A code of laws, known as the Yassa, was issued for all men to obey, so that even the fiercest of the tribesmen were bound to their overlord. These laws, some of them hideously cruel and others strangely mild, came to be regarded as sacred and unbreakable, and, for generations after his death, the 'rules of Genghis' were followed in every detail by peoples throughout much of Asia.

Rebellion in China, where the viceroy had died, caused the ageing Khan to march south with an army. Somewhere beyond the Yellow River, sorrowful at news of his eldest son's death in a far-off battle, Genghis Khan died in 1227.

His body was carried back to be buried in the Land of Grass and many legends grew up about the journey to the northern plain. At one place, the cart bearing his coffin stuck in thick mud by a river and no effort by the oxen could move it; at length, the Mongols reproached Genghis' spirit for its unwillingness to go home:

> *O, Lion of Mankind,' they wailed, 'Your palace tent, your golden abode, your realm founded on justice, all are there. Your standard made from the black tails and manes of stallions, your drums, your trumpets, your flutes, the prairies. the place where you mounted your throne as Khan, all are there. Your wife, Burtai, whom you married in your youth, your comrades, all are there. Do you wish to abandon your own country, O Khan?*

At this appeal, the cart moved forward magically of its own accord and went easily all the rest of the way.

It was also said that, in order to provide Genghis' spirit with plenty of servants, the Mongols slaughtered everyone whom they met along the route, crying:

'Go and serve your lord in the next world!'

On his death bed, Genghis had divided his empire between his three surviving sons, with Ogotai as the overlord. For a time, they ruled according to their father's wishes, while his grandson, Batre, led a force of horsemen, the Golden Horde, across the River Volga into Russia.

The city of Kiev was sacked, the armies of the Poles, Russians and Magyars were cut to pieces, most of Austria and Hungary was overrun and it seemed as if all the forces of Christendom could not prevent the Mongols from sweeping into Western Europe. The Pope appealed to all kings and princes to unite against the inhuman Tartars who, he said, had burst out of the depths of Hell to scourge the peoples of the earth. But, at this perilous moment, Ogotai suddenly recalled the Golden Horde to Karakorum and, like the waters of a tidal wave, the Mongols receded into their distant plain, leaving behind a trail of devastation and the memory of unequalled frightfulness.

The jealousy that Genghis had feared was dividing the Mongols' empire into rival kingdoms. Three main lordships emerged, the Lordship of the West, amounting to modern Russia, the Lordship of the Levant, which included Asia Minor and Persia, and the Lordship of Turkestan in central Asia, all of which were nominally under the rule of Ogotai, the Great Khan.

It was at this time, in about 1260, that the merchants Niccolo and Maffeo Polo, set out from Venice on a trading journey. They reached the Black Sea and had joined a caravan that was carrying goods to the capital of the Western Tartars when war broke out between the local Khan and the Khan of the Levant. They were forced to take refuge in the ancient city of Bokhara where they learned several languages and, presumably, made a living as traders.

After a year or so, they joined a mission from the Khan of the Levant to his overlord, the Great Khan, who dwelt in Cathay, or China.

By this time, Ogotai was dead and his son, Kublai Khan, was a very different character from his barbaric forefathers. Brought up in an ancient civilisation, taught by Chinese sages and influenced by the religion of Buddha, Kublai still retained the energy and curiosity of the Mongol. He gave a courteous welcome to the two strangers from the West. Listening attentively to all they had to tell him, he showed particular interest in their religion. Would they petition the Pope to send him a hundred wise men to teach his people the arts and learning of the Western world?

The return journey to Italy took several years and the brothers were dismayed to find that the Pope was dead and that a dispute about his successor prevented them gaining support for a mission to the utmost end of the world. Bravely, they set off again in 1271, accompanied by Marco, the son of Niccolo, and two learned friars.

Alas, the hardships of the journey were too great for the friars who soon found excuses to turn back, but the Polos went doggedly on. They journeyed across mountains and deserts, where travellers suffered tortures from heat and thirst, where some of the camels had to be killed for food and where, in the utter loneliness, it was all too easy to believe in demons that lured men from the route with spirit voices and unearthly music.

But they survived and, after three and a half years on the road, they reached Cathay and bowed themselves to the ground before the Great Khan.

Kublai welcomed his old friends with pleasure and took a great liking to young Marco. During the next seventeen years, he employed him on various missions so that the Venetians collected a vast amount of information about a country that was unknown to Europeans.

Marco was astonished at the size and population of Cathay, at the marvels he saw on every side, the walled towns, paved streets and stone bridges, the waterways and canals crowded with trading vessels.

He was fascinated by the splendour of the Mongol Court at Peking, where

Kublai Khan had built an immense city on the ruins of the old one. Here he feasted his eyes upon the riches and ceremony that surrounded the Khan, the silks, jewels and carpets, the lavish banquets and hunting-parties, the royal parks and aquaria. Here was wealth on a scale that left Marco breathless, though his native Venice was the richest city in Europe.

Above all, Marco admired Kublai Khan. He saw him ride out in his magnificent chariot, accompanied by his nobles, with an escort of elephants and milk-white horses, to make his annual visit to the Summer Capital at Shang Tu (Xanadu) where, fifty miles beyond the Great Wall, he enjoyed the cool air of the steppes. He saw the fabulous gifts that the Khan made to his friends at his Birthday Feast when princes and chieftains bowed to the floor and, after a dignitary cried 'God save our lord and long preserve him in gladness and joy!' they chanted 'God do so! God do so!'

But Kublai's good government was more impressive than his splendour. He appointed governors for each of his thirty-four provinces, with judges, clerks, tax-collectors and civil servants, all answerable to the Khan himself. He cared for the peasants and, at harvest-time, his agents bought up surplus grain and stored it in royal granaries to provide food in times of famine. Officers were appointed to look after the poor and to issue food and clothing which was specially made in a royal factory. The country had order, justice and freedom to worship as men pleased.

But Kublai Khan was a Mongol. He sowed a great courtyard at Peking with grass to remind himself of the northern plains, and he had the Mongol's love of conquest. He overcame the valiant but hopeless resistance of the last Sung Emperor of Southern China and he reunited the country for the first time since the great days of the T'angs, five centuries earlier. He gave his empire the Chinese name of Yüan, meaning 'Greatness', and it is by this name that the Mongol dynasty is known.

Even so, Kublai could not rest. He was still the grandson of Genghis Khan. Korea was added to his dominions and a force of 100,000 troops was sent to punish the Japanese for their piratical raids on his coasts.

Kublai turned south and sent envoys to demand tribute from rulers in South-East Asia. The Burmese insulted the first envoys and killed the next ones, so Kublai's armies invaded Burma.

The states of Indo-China hastened to send envoys loaded with gifts for the Great Khan, Tibet acknowledged him as overlord, but the Malays defied him when their King was addressed as 'Prince of the Second Grade'.

To punish them, Kublai despatched an army and a fleet but, although he won many victories, the jungle and the mountains proved to be unconquerable. He therefore accepted a face-saving offer of tribute and made a sea-borne invasion of Java with a fleet of 1,000 junks. Here too, the Khan was glad to leave with promises of tribute, for he found that, however hard he drove them, he could not turn the Chinese into sailors.

These thrusts into South-East Asia marked the limit of Mongol power which, for a time, stretched from Austria to the Pacific, from India to the Arctic. When Kublai Khan died, in 1294, the seeds of decay had already been sown.

Kublai had abolished the Mongolian custom of electing the Khan by the votes of the chieftains and had put in its place the Chinese practice of succession from father to son. Since Kublai's eldest son was dead, the throne passed to his grandson, but certain princes who would not have dared to murmur when the Great Khan was alive, refused to give their loyalty to a boy.

They plotted against him and the government grew weaker year by year until, under the last Mongol Emperor, a weakling called Sim Ti, 'the Docile', the Chinese people's sufferings became so great that they rose in desperation against their conquerors. In 1368, Sim Ti fled into the desert of his forefathers and the Mongolian Empire of Genghis and Kublai, the two Great Khans, vanished for ever.

More about the Mongol Emperors

The Mongol power over China, India, Persia and Russia lasted for about 200 years. In China itself, where Kublai Khan reached such heights of splendour, the Mongols were succeeded by the Chinese Ming dynasty which was unfriendly to visitors from the West.

Having recovered China, the first Ming emperor sent armies into Mongolia to complete the overthrow of the tribesmen and, although their old vigour sometimes returned and khan still succeeded khan in the royal line, the eastern Mongols became vassals of China and converts to the religion of Buddha.

Farther to the west and south, the numerous tribes that had once been united under Genghis Khan continued to wage perpetual warfare against each other and against their more settled neighbours. Various khans rose to fame, such as Timur or Tamerlane the Great who conquered Persia and southern Russia; various tribes, such as the Kalmuks, the Buriats, the Uzbegs and the Tartars had their moments of glory but gradually Russia subjected the western Mongols and brought them into the empire of the Tsars. The Turks were Mongolians who adopted the Moslem religion and a khan named Baber founded the Mogul Empire in India.

Much of our knowledge of Kublai Khan's China comes from the account of the travels of Marco Polo (1254-1324). Marco was seventeen when he set off to China with his father and uncle. They went by sea to Ormuz on the Persian Gulf and then overland, by the famous Silk Road, across Afghanistan and the Gobi Desert. Although he may have exaggerated his own importance, Marco seems to have travelled widely in the Khan's service.

At length, the Polos began to long for their home in Italy but the Khan was unwilling to let them go. However, in 1292, they obtained permission to join the party chosen to escort a Mongol princess to Persia where she was to marry a prince belonging to Kublai Khan's family. The journey was by sea, via Singapore and India to Persia, then overland to Constantinople and on to Venice, where the merchants astonished their relatives by their appearance and by the precious stones they had brought back sewn into the seams of their clothes.

In 1298, Marco was captured by the Genoese when commanding a Venetian vessel in a war between the rival cities. Whilst in captivity, he dictated the story of his travels to Rusticano of Pisa and, although the book became very popular, it was generally believed that the author was a champion liar. In fact, because he so often said that the Khan's wealth and subjects were numbered in millions, Marco was nicknamed 'Millioni' or 'Mr Millions'. Centuries later, when Europeans were able to visit China, it was found that he had usually described things truthfully.

After his release from captivity, Marco Polo returned to Venice where he lived for the rest of his life as a well-to-do citizen.

He himself was fated to obey Quetzalcoatl. So he put on his gorgeous robes and his plumed crown and went up to the walls.

MONTEZUMA, KING OF THE AZTECS

'I speak truth, your Honour, when I say that with my own eyes I saw a land far richer than this island of Cuba. The people dwell in houses of stone and eat from platters of gold. But, beyond the mountains, they say there is a treasure-city in a land called Mexico, ruled by the Great King Montezuma.'

The speaker paused and Senor Velazquez, Governor of Cuba, answered him, 'You bring great news, Don Pedro,' and his eyes shine. 'In the name of the Holy Virgin and of His Imperial Majesty, we shall send an expedition to discover the riches of this land.'

Velazquez looked round at the Spanish gentlemen who were gathered in the Governor's House; his eye fell upon Hernan Cortes, one of the settlers in Cuba who, it was well known, preferred adventure to the easy life of a slave-run estate. Cortes was the man to lead a search for gold.

The year was 1518. More than twenty-five years had passed since Columbus reached the New World but, so far, Spain had gained only a few islands. Little gold had been discovered and the mainland of America had only been touched here and there by adventurers like Pedro. His news sent hopes soaring again.

By February 1519, Cortes had assembled eleven small ships manned by 100 sailors, with 553 adventurers, mostly gentlemen who contributed money and arms to the expedition. The ships were loaded with stores, armour, gunpowder, crossbows, fourteen cannon, some mastiff dogs and sixteen horses. The Governor and all the aristocracy of Cuba came to see the expedition set sail, but during the high-sounding speeches, it was noticed that Cortes seemed to be occupied with his own thoughts.

Hernan Cortes was thirty-four years old; tall, lean and broad-shouldered, he wore a black beard that partly hid the scar of an old knife wound and, though his manner was courteous, his grey eyes were hard. He had come out to the West Indies from Spain as a lad of nineteen but, although he had done well enough, this was his first real chance to win the fame and riches he longed for with all his soul.

The little fleet sighted the mainland of Central America and sailed along the coast until a suitable place was found for a landing.

A strong army of Maya Indians attacked the Spaniards with ferocious courage, but Cortes made such brilliant use of his cannons and horses, neither of which the Mayas had ever seen before, that the natives surrendered.

Peace gifts were brought, including twenty slave-girls, among whom was an intelligent maiden called Marina. Daughter of an Aztec or Mexican chief, she had been stolen as a child and sold into slavery, but now she was to become the devoted companion of Cortes. Marina learned Spanish, acted as interpreter and adviser and behaved with complete coolness amid the worst dangers because she believed that the gods had chosen her to bring ruin upon her own people.

As the expedition continued along the coast, Cortes asked Marina to tell him about the Aztecs.

'My people are the most powerful race in Mexico,' she said. 'All the surrounding tribes pay taxes to Montezuma, the Great King.'

'What kind of taxes?'

'Cotton cloth, maize, chocolate and honey; incense, tobacco, feathers of every colour, jewels, gold and jade.'

'Are your people brave warriors?'

'O, Captain-General, they never cease from war. War is necessary to obtain prisoners.'

'But why do they need prisoners? For slaves?'

'For slaves, yes. But chiefly for the gods. Unless the gods are fed with human hearts, plucked warm from the bodies of men, disaster would come upon the kingdom.'

The ships anchored off the coast of Mexico and at once two large canoes appeared with messengers who were friendly and strangely respectful. Presently, they hurried away inland to report to King Montezuma, while the Spaniards built a camp on the shore.

Within a week, the envoys returned, accompanied by a string of porters loaded with gifts. There were jewels and masks of solid gold, precious ornaments shaped like jaguars and monkeys, bracelets, necklaces, and gold collars, capes made of brilliant feathers, and two gigantic circles, one of silver, one of gold, covered with carvings and sacred signs. But the envoys said that Montezuma did not wish to see the strangers. They must go away and not attempt to visit his capital.

Cortes pondered. For some reason, the Aztecs feared him and were bribing him to go away, but the gifts proved that this land was richer than anyone had dared to hope. He would certainly go forward, trusting to luck and his own daring.

Montezuma's envoys vanished, but messengers arrived from a neighbouring tribe which had recently been conquered by the Aztecs. These people and their king, known as Fat Lord, were anxious to make friends with the strangers, having already heard about their magic weapons.

Cortes told Fat Lord to arrest Montezuma's tax-gatherers and to send no more people for human sacrifice. Moreover, he ordered his new allies to stop their own horrible sacrifices and boldly threw down the image of the Maize God from the top of a lofty pyramid-temple. The terrified people obeyed him in everything, even setting up a Cross and an image of the Virgin Mary.

Meanwhile in his distant capital, the very thought of the strangers on the coast filled Montezuma with dread. His life, his kingdom and all his riches existed solely to please the gods, especially Humming Bird, the terrible god of war. Unless they were regularly fed with human hearts, the gods would die. Then the Sun would go out, the Rains would cease, the Wind would sweep everything away. But long, long ago, there had been a god named Quetzalcoatl (the Feathered Serpent) who had been driven out by the others; in the year of One Reed, Quetzalcoatl would return to claim his kingdom. He would come from the east on a curious raft; his skin would be white, his beard black; he would not eat human hearts but his coming would bring ruin and great sorrow.

In dread, therefore, Montezuma listened to the bearers of bad news who bowed themselves to the ground and were taken away to be killed. 1519 *was* the year of One Reed and the strangers had landed on the exact day worked out by the wizards of the calendar. The leader was white-skinned, black-bearded; his followers carried rods of lightning whose iron barrels spoke thunder.

Exactly as the sacred books foretold, there had been comets, floods and earthquakes. As expected, the strangers wore hats of iron and were accompanied by four-legged creatures and by smaller animals, as fierce as jaguars, with rolling eyes and lolling tongues.

It was terrifyingly clear that Quetzalcoatl had come.

Montezuma dared not attack a god. It seemed as if Mexico was doomed whatever action he took. Nevertheless, he sent gifts, hoping that the strangers would depart, and he also sent wizards, sorcerers and manwitches, but their magic had no effect whatever on the grey-eyed leader. So Montezuma, wise and gentle in all other ways, tried sacrifice of the most horrible kind, using his own hands to sprinkle blood on the altars of the gods, but there was no answer.

He must await the pleasure of Quetzalcoatl.

Knowing nothing of these dark mysteries, Cortes prepared to advance on the capital. He had the ships run ashore and totally destroyed to convince his men that there was no retreat. Ahead lay riches or death.

Leaving a small garrison at a fort on the coast which he named Vera Cruz, Cortes set off on the 250-mile journey, with 400 men, fifteen horses and the cannons that were carried by porters provided by Fat Lord.

The march took the conquerors through fertile country dotted with neat maize fields, across mountain passes and desert stretches. They were baked by the sun and frozen by icy winds in the mountains. They were often hungry and always thirsty, but their remorseless leader marched on.

Presently, they entered the territory of the fierce Tlaxcalans, the only people in the region whom Montezuma had not conquered. Since they hated the Aztecs, they attacked the strangers who were travelling to Mexico City, but as warriors, they were superstitious and apt to lose heart.

All Mexican warfare aimed at taking prisoners alive so that they could be sacrificed later, but the Spaniards refused to be captured and fought like demons with weapons far superior to slings and wooden swords edged with sharp flakes of stone. Moreover, the Mexicans were badly led, whereas Cortes was a soldier of genius, cool, fearless, and absolutely certain of victory.

Having beaten off an ambush, Cortes boldly attacked the Tlaxcalan main army with such ferocity that all the rumours about him being a god seemed to be true. Since it was useless to fight against gods, the Tlaxcalans gave up the struggle and offered him their help against Montezuma.

So, reinforced by 6,000 allies, the Spaniards marched on to Cholula, a most beautiful city, sacred to Quetzalcoatl himself, whose vast pyramid-temple dominated the countryside. Against the advice of Marina and the Tlaxcalans, Cortes entered the city with only his 400 conquerors, leaving his allies camped outside the walls, but although he was received with friendliness, there were rumours and preparations that made him uneasy. Marina whispered that he had walked into a trap, and, at once, he sent a runner to the camp with a message:

'When I give the signal, attack the city! Break in and kill!'

This was just what the Tlaxcalans wanted and they tore through the streets looting and killing until 6,000 Cholulans had perished and their city was a smoking ruin.

Since all Aztec gods were cruel, this savage deed convinced everyone that Quetzalcoatl had come to take his revenge. At all costs, his anger must be soothed and Montezuma sent slaves loaded with gifts and messages:

'The Great Montezuma sends his loving greetings. He is sorry that the stupid Cholulans offended you, but he offers you his capital. Come, Great One, and rest quietly.'

On to Mexico!

The conquerors crossed a lofty pass between smoking volcanoes and there, below them, lay the fabulous city, its white buildings and gigantic temples reflected in the waters of a lake. Three long roads or causeways connected Mexico City to the mainland, but, for defence, these were broken by several drawbridges and a fleet of war-canoes patrolled the lake.

The Spaniards clattered across the widest causeway, the horsemen riding ahead. Then came the chained mastiffs, the lean, grim swordsmen, the cross-bowmen and the musketeers, all warily fingering their weapons as they passed between rows of citizens who murmured in awe at the sight of such strange beings.

At the city walls, Montezuma himself came forward. Beneath a wondrous canopy, his golden throne was carried by eight lords in magnificent robes and he himself was wearing a jewelled crown topped by green plumes, a feather cloak and vestments that glittered with precious stones; even the soles of his sandals were made of pure gold.

The two men gazed at each other; both were handsome, both held themselves like men born to command. But whereas Montezuma's eyes were troubled by the deep fears of his terrible religion, Cortes showed only the watchful calm of a man who had dared everything to reach his goal.

'Welcome to my capital, Great One,' said Montezuma. 'My father's palace is your resting-place. Come, all things are yours.'

Never, in all their travels, had the Spaniards seen such a city. It was beautiful beyond their dreams; canals criss-crossed the broad avenues and smooth streets, fountains played in noble courtyards where banks of flowers blazed in the warm sunshine; the luxury of the houses astounded men who had seen the cities of Italy and France.

The palace, near to Montezuma's and to the temple of the Humming Bird, was enormous; its one hundred bedrooms each had running water and a stone bath; the ceilings were encrusted with carvings, and the floors gleamed like mirrors. In the throne-room, the walls were decorated with bands of silver and gold inset with precious stones. Cortes noticed that the courtyards were big enough to hold an army or perhaps to trap an army. He was now in a fortress-palace of a lake-city, with a handful of soldiers. What should he do next? What was Montezuma planning?

For several days, the Spaniards toured the city, observing its defences and its vast colourful markets. The two leaders paid each other visits, exchanging courteous conversation, while each tried to read the other's mind. Montezuma was puzzled by talk of an Emperor across the sea and by the Christian religion. Cortes admired the city, but made it clear that he was horrified by the temples with their racks of skulls and hideous images reeking of blood, though the King was quick to see that gold put him into a good humour.

Suddenly, Cortes decided to capture Montezuma, for he could think of no other way out of his difficulties. Boldly he went to the Great King and accused him of ordering an attack on the Spaniards at Vera Cruz. Montezuma gently denied the accusation and immediately sent runners to the coast to make sure that all was well, but Cortes insisted that he must come and live in the Spaniards' palace.

'But my lords would never consent,' pleaded Montezuma. 'What would my people say?'

'You must tell them that it is your own wish. Say the gods have commanded it.'

Montezuma submitted. The god had spoken, he must obey. Perhaps if he pleased him, he might still go away and the people would be saved.

With Montezuma in his power, Cortes began to rule. He put down a rising, had two sloops built and launched on the lake, sent men to inspect the country, especially the gold-mines, and he had a statue of the Virgin placed in one of the temples. Oddly enough, the more the Spaniards saw of Montezuma, the more they loved the sad, noble king. He was so gentle and his generosity was princely compared with Cortes, who was stinginess itself when it came to sharing out treasure.

News from the coast forced Cortes to leave the city with most of his force in order to deal with a rival expedition from Cuba, which he quickly overcame with his usual boldness and cunning. But when he returned, he found that Pedro, his deputy-commander, was in a tight corner, for the townsfolk had broken into rebellion once the god-man had departed. Because of Montezuma's influence, Cortes and his soldiers regained the fortress without difficulty, but the city was seething with rumours that a new King had been elected.

Presently, the Aztecs attacked the palace, firing arrows and spears from the house-tops, hurling stones from slings and primitive machines, leaping from the walls with frenzied courage. There was fierce hand-to-hand fighting in which muskets and cannons were useless, but Cortes retook the walls and made several sorties into the streets.

The Mexicans ignored their losses and kept up the attack until, after five days, Cortes could see that his force would soon be worn down. There was only one thing to do; he would tell Montezuma to stop the fighting so that the white men could depart peacefully.

'It will be of no use,' said Montezuma sadly. 'My people have chosen another King. They will not let you escape.'

He still believed that Cortes was a god, but he knew now that the other gods had won back their power. He himself was fated to obey Quetzalcoatl. So he put on his gorgeous robes and his plumed crown and went up to the walls. At once, the Mexicans ceased to attack when they saw his beloved figure and some fell upon their knees as he began to speak.

Suddenly, a volley of stones was fired by the slingers. Montezuma fell and was carried down to his apartment, where he was found to have a severe head wound but, worse, he clearly had no wish to live.

Next day, Montezuma died, and even as they fought, the hardbitten Spaniards wept for him.

The end of Montezuma was not quite the end of the story. By superhuman efforts, the Spaniards fought their way out of the capital, losing half their men in a desperate night battle along a causeway. Eventually a handful of survivors reached the land of the Tlaxcalans where they were given shelter.

But Cortes was not beaten. He obtained troops and supplies from the Spanish islands, raised a huge army from the tribes and built a fleet of ships to cross the lake. In the following year, after a tremendous struggle, the beautiful city was captured and utterly destroyed, and Cortes claimed Mexico for the Emperor Charles v of Spain.

More about Montezuma (1466–1520)

Montezuma II succeeded his uncle in 1502 as King of Mexico, but although he was a powerful ruler, he seems to have earned the hatred of the neighbouring tribes. This explains why Cortes received so much help from the Tlaxcalans.

The Aztecs were originally a tibe of hunters from the north and they had settled in Mexico about 200 years before the arrival of Cortes. Quickly conquering the surrounding peoples, they had built the wonderful lake-city which they called Tenochtitlan. Theirs was a strange civilisation, for although they were skilful architects and craftsmen who understood trade and mathematics, they had no wheel nor any form of transport except boats; metals were hardly used and iron was quite unknown.

Hernando Cortes (1485–1547) was the son of a poor nobleman; at nineteen, he threw up his law studies and went to seek his fortune in the West Indies. After distinguishing himself during the conquest of Cuba, he had to wait ten years for the chance to win fame and gold. After Mexico had fallen, he was granted a title and estates but he always felt that his great achievements were not fully recognised. He visited Spain and was honoured by Charles v, took part in various voyages and adventures in which he lost much of his wealth and died, sad and neglected, in his own country. Our knowledge of Montezuma and Cortes comes from one of the survivors of the little band of conquerors, who, as an old man, wrote down all that he remembered about the amazing adventure.

Bursting with energy, he took the lead in everything, hunting so furiously that he would exhaust eight or ten horses a day.

KING HENRY VIII

'His Majesty is the handsomest potentate I ever set eyes on: above the usual height, with an extremely fine calf to his leg; his complexion very fair and bright, with auburn hair combed straight and short in the French fashion, and a round face, so very beautiful that it would become a pretty woman, his throat being rather long and thick.' Thus wrote the Venetian ambassador in describing the young King of England.

In 1509, when Henry VIII ascended the throne at the age of eighteen, his delighted subjects must have thought that Heaven had sent them the perfect monarch. Not only handsome and magnificently built, he was also clever and athletic. Few could match him at wrestling, jousting, archery or tennis and no courtier could equal his leaps and twists in the energetic dances of the time. As a boy, his tutors had kept him hard at work, and he proved to be a good linguist, fluent in French and Latin, good at Spanish and Italian; he liked mathematics and was a talented musician who played the lute, recorder and organ, composed songs and sang well in a rather high voice. It was hard to believe that one human being could possess so many talents and there seemed to be no flaw in his make-up, unless it was an over-eagerness to win and a quick temper when something displeased him.

As King he began by ordering the execution of two of his father's ministers who were hated for the heavy taxes they had imposed during the previous reign. His marriage to Catherine of Aragon also pleased the Londoners, for they liked the Spanish princess who had married Henry's brother Arthur and, after his early death, had been a forlorn young widow at Court. She was now twenty-four, six years older than Henry, an attractive intelligent woman, courageous and an especially fine dancer.

Having been kept on a tight rein in his boyhood, the young king was determined to enjoy himself. His grim father had amassed a fortune and Henry at once began to make the money fly in a ceaseless round of banquets, tournaments, hunting, dancing and gambling. Yet he also made time for reading, music and religious services. Bursting with energy, he took the lead in everything, hunting so furiously that he would exhaust eight or ten horses a day, and jousting with such a dash that he sometimes risked his life. Once, he suffered a severe blow on the forehead from his friend, the Duke of Suffolk, and on another occasion, he was knocked unconscious for two hours.

To run the country while he enjoyed himself, Henry chose, not one of the great nobles, but Thomas Wolsey, the son of a butcher, who was a clever young man, had gone to Oxford University and entered the Church. A royal chaplain, he won the attention of the King who raised him to the Council and made him Lord Chancellor. For seventeen years, this brilliant arrogant man practically ruled England, enriching himself in the process and living in a style as magnificent as that of his master.

For, although he shirked business, Henry *was* the master. His quick brain enabled him to grasp affairs, while his domineering character cowed the nobles who detested this low-born favourite. Wolsey was all-powerful only as long as the King allowed him to be.

Their first venture was to go to war. A vain young monarch wanted more realistic action than tournaments and where better than in France? He revived the English claim to the French throne, declaring:

'With God's help, we will recover the realm of France, our very true inheritance, and reduce it to obedience.'

As the ally of Emperor Maximilian and Ferdinand of Spain, he crossed the Channel with an army in 1513. Wolsey organised everything with masterly skill and, in due course, Henry won a victory at Guinegate, where the French bolted from the field so quickly that the engagement became known as the Battle of Spurs. The campaign ended with the capture of Tournai, but, ironically, a far greater victory was won at home. In the King's absence, the Scots invaded the north of England but Queen Catherine, left as Regent, raised an army and sent it north under Thomas Howard, Earl of Surrey, who annihilated the Scots at Flodden. With scores of nobles, James IV was killed and Catherine sent his bloodstained surcoat to Henry, with an exultant message.

'Your Grace may see by this King's coat how I have kept your Kingdom safe.'

Meanwhile, in France, Henry was learning fast. His allies double-crossed him, by coming to terms with the French, whereupon he instructed Wolsey to go one better. Not only would he make peace, but he would send his young sister Mary, aged seventeen, to be the bride of Louis XII, a widower of fifty-two. The Pope blessed the marriage and the King came home in a blaze of glory. No matter that Louis died within eighty days of his wedding, Henry had nevertheless made England a force to reckon with on the continent.

To play a part in Europe, a fleet was needed to guard the Channel, protect the cloth trade with Flanders and also, if need be, to menace the route between the Low Countries and Spain. Henry had inherited a small fleet from his father and he now ordered the building of new warships, including the great *Henry Grâce à Dieu*, a 1000-ton carrack, whose size and cannon-power impressed the world. Considering Portsmouth too exposed to an enemy, Henry founded new dockyards at Dartford and Woolwich in the Thames estuary and he himself loved to go aboard a new vessel, wearing 'a sailor's coat, a thick chain from which hung a large whistle with which he whistled almost as loud as a trumpet'.

In Europe, an intense rivalry had developed between Francis I, the new King of France, and Charles of Spain, who was soon to become the Emperor, Charles V, so that Wolsey's policy was to advance his master's importance by dangling England's support between the rivals. He arranged a meeting near Calais between Francis and Henry, where both monarchs displayed such sumptuous extravagance that the occasion was called the Field of the Cloth of Gold. However, in the same year, 1520, Charles V visited England and made a secret treaty with Henry, for in the war that was about to break out, England was sure to side with Charles, since he was the nephew of Queen Catherine and ruler of Flanders and the wool trade.

Another war with France amounted to little more than a costly marching to and fro, but, in Italy, Charles totally defeated the French and captured Francis I. Hence, he no longer needed England's support and did nothing to fulfil his promise to help Wolsey to become Pope.

By this time, Henry was concerned with a new matter. He had been married to Catherine for many years but of her six children all had died, except a daughter, Mary, born in 1516. 'By the Grace of God,' the King had declared 'a son will follow'. But, as the years passed, there was still no son to continue the Tudor dynasty and Catherine was over 40 and unlikely to have any more children.

Wolsey, intent on an alliance with France, whispered to Henry that the death of Catherine's children might be a sign that his marriage to his brother's widow was not pleasing to God. Could not the Pope be persuaded to set the marriage aside? Henry, who had his own reason for wanting to get rid of his faithful wife, instructed Wolsey to broach the matter with Pope Clement VII and the Cardinal went hopefully ahead, in the belief that, once a divorce was granted, he would arrange a marriage to a French princess.

Wolsey made two mistakes. He totally underestimated Henry's passion for Anne Boleyn, one of the Queen's ladies-in-waiting, and he failed to realise that there was no likelihood of the Pope declaring the marriage null and void. Clement VII was virtually the prisoner of Charles V who naturally supported his aunt, Catherine. So the Pope played for time, giving no definite answer, but sending a Cardinal to London to consider the matter with Wolsey; this only produced further delays and then the case went back to Rome.

In his pent-up rage, Henry turned savagely on Wolsey. For making his master look a fool, the great man was charged with treason but, elderly and ill, he cheated the executioner by dying at Leicester Abbey, murmuring pathetically, 'If I had served God as diligently as I have done the King, He would not have given me over in my grey hairs.'

Still no word came from Rome, so Henry turned next upon the clergy, fining them heavily for having obeyed Wolsey. 'As for the Pope,' he fumed, 'he shall know I am master in my own realm.' Eventually Thomas Cranmer, the new Archbishop of Canterbury, declared that the marriage to Catherine had been illegal and therefore did not exist, at which Henry announced he had already married Anne Boleyn in secret. She was crowned Queen at Whitsun 1533, when the capital was given a gorgeous pageant and the fountains ran with wine.

Even so, the Londoners remained sullen; they had liked Queen Catherine and would not cheer this dark-haired upstart, nor pull off their caps when she rode past, so that her jester yelled at them:

'Ye all have scurvy heads and dare not uncover them!'

Having cast aside his wife and married Anne Boleyn, there was no going back for Henry. Determined to end the Pope's authority, he declared himself Supreme Head of the Church of England and, with Parliament's support, required everyone of any importance to take an oath accepting his supremacy. Hardly anyone refused, for Henry had the knack of carrying his countrymen along with him; they had little respect for Pope and clergy, and relished the idea of being free from control by a foreign bishop. A few brave spirits defied the King and paid the penalty; ten Charterhouse monks were put to death horribly, John Fisher, Bishop of Rochester, was executed and Thomas More, the wise and gentle ex-Chancellor, a former friend of Henry, also went to his death on Tower Hill.

Henry was now at the height of his powers. The athletic youth had grown into an enormous man, barrel-chested and thick-waisted, like some great bull whose unpredictable moods filled everyone with fear. The Court had never been gayer, for the King was in tremendous form, loving company, music, feasting and the heady sense of complete power. Nobles, courtiers and ministers grovelled before him with fascinated awe. In his size and appearance, in his defiance of foreigners, in his selfishness and cruelty, he was obviously everything they thought a king ought to be.

With his new Chancellor, the tireless, immensely able Thomas Cromwell, he now turned his attention to the monasteries. He had spent so hugely that the kingdom was almost bankrupt but, as Cromwell promised him, the wealth of six hundred monasteries would make him 'the richest prince in Christendom'.

In the space of four years, he closed them all and seized their lands, buildings and treasures. But he did not keep all to himself; gold and silver went into the Treasury, while many properties were sold to the highest bidders. In this way, a whole class of nobles, merchants and burgesses shared in the plunder and therefore remained strong supporters of Henry's policy.

There was however some resistance. In the North, where the monasteries were popular, and the old religion still widespread, a rising took place called the Pilgrimage of Grace, because the rebels carried banners proclaiming the Catholic faith. Henry met the situation with cunning, promising pardon if the rebels would disperse to their homes. Once they had done so, he pounced; the leaders were put to death and throughout the summer of 1537, he took his revenge, executing abbots and local gentry in Yorkshire, hanging thirty-six in Lincolnshire and seventy-four in Carlisle:

'You shall', he ordered, 'cause such dreadful execution to be upon a good number of the inhabitants of every town village and hamlet that have been offenders in the rebellion . . . by hanging them up to trees . . . and the setting of their heads and quarters in every town.'

By now, Anne Boleyn was dead. She had presented Henry with a daughter, christened Elizabeth, but two boys were born dead and the king was growing tired of her fiery, domineering ways. Moreover, he had taken a fancy to a young noblewoman called Jane Seymour, so he turned to his right-hand man to manage the business. Cromwell, who hated the Boleyns and had long spied on the Queen, came up with an accusation that she had made love to various gentlemen of the Court. Arrested and brought to trial, she contested the charges so hotly that even the King remarked,

'She hath a stout heart, but she shall pay for it.'

On the day of her execution, Cranmer produced a special licence enabling Henry to marry Jane and a month later she was proclaimed Queen.

Within a year, she, too, was dead, of fever, after giving birth to Edward, the longed-for heir to the throne. Henry, who seems genuinely to have loved Jane, was so grief-stricken that two years passed before he was once more looking for a wife. As ever, Cromwell was at his elbow, pointing out that, with France and Spain apparently on good terms, it would be as well to win the friendship of the German Protestant princes. By marrying a German princess named Anne of Cleves, he would gain some useful allies. Alas, when the lady arrived in England, she proved to be pock-marked and so plain and dull that Henry termed her 'the Flanders mare', and went through with the marriage with the greatest reluctance.

Once again, he had been made to look foolish and, the blame fell inevitably on Cromwell. Charged with 'treason' he could only write 'Your Majesty have been the most bountiful prince to me . . . Prostrate at your feet . . . I call for mercy, mercy, mercy.' But there was no mercy in the King's make-up and Cromwell was beheaded at Tyburn on the very day that Henry married Catherine Howard, niece of the Duke of Norfolk. His marriage to Anne of Cleves had been already 'cancelled' and the lady had cheerfully accepted a pension and retirement to a country house.

The King was greatly pleased with Catherine, a merry, empty-headed girl, the prettiest of all his wives, on whom he lavished jewels, furs and fine estates. In spite of his gross bulk and the pain from an ulcer on his leg, he himself was in great spirits, rising at dawn, attending Mass, riding out early to hunt before returning to an enormous breakfast and the affairs of the kingdom. Growing ever more tyrannical, he struck down anyone who aroused his suspicion, executing more northerners on charges of rebellion and 'clearing out' the Tower by sending all its prisoners to their death. He made a menacing tour of the North to receive its submission, along with gifts of money presented by the gentry, clergy and mayors of all the leading towns.

Mollified, he returned to London where Archbishop Cranmer slipped into his hand a note that struck the King speechless. Presently, he wept and roared out in grief and rage like a madman. It appeared that Catherine, no innocent maiden at her marriage, had been amusing herself with several gentlemen of the Court. Enemies of her family made sure that ample evidence was produced and, after her lovers had been executed and her nearest relatives thrown into prison, she herself went to her death on the scaffold.

Henry soon recovered from his grief, for there was plenty to occupy his energies, now that the Pope was encouraging Scotland and France to attack the defiant

kingdom. To counter the threat, the King sent an army north which routed the Scots at Solway Moss, whereupon James v died of shame, leaving, as heiress to the throne, his baby daughter, Mary, Queen of Scots. Henry could now turn his attention to France, though, first, he married his sixth and last Queen, Catherine Parr, an intelligent widow, who knew how to manage her husband and keep him in good humour.

Now in his early fifties, which he called his 'old age', Henry nevertheless donned a suit of armour, crossed the Channel and captured Boulogne in the autumn of 1544. The infuriated French prepared a counter-stroke and, in the following year, England faced the threat of invasion as the French fleet of a hundred and fifty ships put to sea and took control of the Channel. That the English were ready was due to the King, for it was he who had created the navy and, with Cromwell, had built forts and castles all along the coast. The nation rallied to him in the face of danger, with every able-bodied man standing ready to take up arms, while the forts were stocked with cannons and beacons were piled high to signal the invasion.

When the French fleet approached the coast off Portsmouth, it was fended off by the English navy, and the invasion troops who managed to get ashore were soon beaten back to their ships. With sickness aboard, and short of food and water, the French decided to withdraw, much to the disappointment of the English militiamen who had marched for days towards the coast and now had to be told to go back home.

With the danger past, Henry could turn to domestic matters. Money had to be raised somehow, for the Treasury was empty, so, to avoid more taxes, he compelled rich men to make gifts, called 'benevolences', and had coins struck containing less gold and silver. Peace was made with France but religion troubled him sorely. In overthrowing the Pope's authority, he had opened the flood-gates to Protestant ideas which he detested. A Catholic still at heart, he complained angrily to Parliament about the religions arguments that went on:

'Love and charity are not among you', he stormed, 'Ye presume to debate matters that are not for you to judge. Love, serve and dread God, as I, your supreme Head and sovereign Lord, do command you.'

Immensely stout and plagued by the pain in his ulcerated leg, Henry's temper was vile, but his brain was clear as ever and he could still ride to the hunt and journey about the kingdom. It was, however, prudent to make a will, leaving the crown to his son Edward, with succession, if the boy had no heirs, to Mary and then Elizabeth.

Suddenly, in the autumn of 1546, he become seriously ill. Knowing that he had little time, he acted swiftly, choosing a Council of Catholics and Protestants to rule until Edward came of age. Over the years, he had killed off practically everyone who might dispute the throne, but there were still Norfolk and his son Surrey. They belonged to the royal line and could well be troublesome, so, dying, he struck them down. Surrey was executed on a charge of treason and Norfolk, the cunning old aristocrat, who had survived a hundred dangers, was condemned to die on the morning of 28th January 1547. Once again, he escaped, because Henry died during that night.

The most ruthless tyrant who ever occupied the throne of England showed one touch of compassion as he neared his end. He sent for the Lady Mary, whose mother, Catherine of Aragon he had treated so cruelly, and whispered,

'Oh, daughter, fortune hath been hard against thee; and I grieve that I did not have thee married as I wished. Try to be a mother to thy little brother, for, look, he is very little.'

More about Henry VIII (1491–1547)

Henry was born in Greenwich Palace, the second son of Henry VII and Elizabeth of York, whose marriage had put an end to the feud between the houses of Lancaster and York and had founded the Tudor dynasty. Henry's older brother, Prince Arthur, died in 1502, leaving him as heir to the throne and he succeeded his father in 1509.

From his six marriages, only three of Henry's children survived: Edward VI, whose reign lasted for six years, Mary, who married Philip II of Spain and died childless in 1558, and Elizabeth I, who never married. At her death in 1603, the crown passed to James I, son of Mary, Queen of Scots.

Henry VIII was a tyrant, selfish, merciless and unprincipled, but he had great ability and his method of ruling was probably suited to the age in which he lived. He founded the Royal Navy and, strangely enough, encouraged the growth of Parliament's powers.

Rizzio, wild with terror, fell on his knees, holding the Queen's skirt and screaming to her to save him.

MARY, QUEEN OF SCOTS

When she was six days old, Mary Stuart became Queen of Scotland. She was six years old when the arrival of the English army caused her mother, Mary of Guise, to send her to France for safety.

The little Queen captivated Paris. With her four attendants, each named Mary, she bubbled with fun, and the French King, Henry II, was enchanted by the pretty child who was to marry his eldest son. Francis, the Dauphin, a pale little fellow of four and a half, bowed gravely to his future bride who took his hand in the friendliest manner. Even the French Queen, Catherine of Medici, who had no love for Mary's uncles and aunts, remarked:

'The Scots Queen has only to turn her head to make every Frenchman fall in love with her.'

It seemed as if a good fairy had given Mary every gift that a princess could desire. She was beautiful and gay; she danced and sang prettily, composed verses and played several musical instruments, but she also loved the out-of-doors and could ride as hard as any boy. By the time she was thirteen years old, she could speak half-a-dozen languages just as easily as the French she had learned from her mother.

As she grew older, Mary's beauty inspired the poets of the French Court. She was tall, like all the Guises, but her red-gold hair came from her Scots father and her eyes were so brilliant that no one could ever decide whether they were brown or yellow. No wonder it was said at Court, 'There is some enchantment in her by which men are bewitched.'

In 1558, Mary and Francis were married in a gorgeous pavilion erected outside the Cathedral of Notre Dame. But Mary's happiness was clouded by news from Scotland. The Queen-Mother wrote that John Knox was preaching furious sermons against the Roman Catholic religion, and, in some places, monasteries and churches had been destroyed. Many of the Scots nobles, calling themselves the Lords of the Congregation, supported Knox and the new Protestant religion: 'I hope you will restore them to God and their duty,' wrote Mary anxiously.

In the summer of 1559, the King of France held a great tournament in which he himself took part. He was an expert jouster but, as he rode in a contest against the

Count of Montgomery, a lance broke, knocking aside his vizor. A splinter pierced his skull and, in a few days, the King was dead.

Not yet seventeen, Mary Stuart became Queen of France but Francis, her delicate boy-husband, wrung his hands in helpless grief and left the affairs of state to his wife and uncles.

Ever since she came to France, Mary's life had sparkled with happiness and success, but, from now on, it was to be darkened by one tragedy after another.

Her mother died in Edinburgh Castle; then came news that, without consent of their absent Queen, the Scots lords had called a Parliament that abolished the Roman Catholic Church in Scotland. Mary angrily upbraided the noble who arrived with this information, 'I am your Queen,' she cried, 'or so you call me. But you do not use me so. Your Parliament is no Parliament without my consent and though you boast of the laws of your realm, you keep none of them.'

That same evening, Francis returned exhausted from the hunt. He always pursued his sports with furious energy, as if to prove he was as strong as other boys, but this time he seemed to have taken a chill. Despite all that the Court physicians could do, despite the prayers of his wife who would not leave his bedside, he became weaker and, in December 1560, he died.

Mary had been a widow for only a few days when Catherine of Medici asked her to return the Crown Jewels and she made it quite clear that there was no room at the French Court for one of the Guise family. Mary must go back to Scotland.

With the four Maries, her priests and attendants, Mary made her way slowly to Calais and went aboard ship with a heavy heart. All day, she stayed by the rail, watching the coast grow dim in the distance. It was a warm August night and a bed was made up for her on deck but, in the morning, France was still visible from the becalmed ship. Presently, a wind sprang up and the coastline faded from sight.

'Farewell, beloved France,' cried Mary. 'Farewell! I shall never see you again.'

It was a grey day when she came to Scotland. A wet mist blotted out everything except the dim shapes of a few spectators on the shore, and the procession to Holyrood had none of the splendour she had known in France. That night, some bonfires were lit and crowds came to sing under the Queen's windows. They sang doleful psalms and the music of the fiddles was poor thin stuff, but it was better than nothing and Mary graciously thanked the people for their welcome.

Clad in her widow's dress of white, with a little lace-trimmed cap from which her fair curls escaped, she was only nineteen when she first faced her Scottish subjects. There was no wise and trusty statesman to guide her, only a quarrelsome pack of greedy lords struggling for power. Almost at once, there was trouble.

On the first Sunday, when Mary went to Mass in her private chapel, a crowd led by by Knox forced its way into the Palace courtyard, demanding the death of her Catholic priests. The Earl of Moray, himself a Protestant, drew his sword and faced the mob, with his back to the chapel door, so Knox withdrew, growling mightily about 'the Papist woman'.

Yet, for four years, Mary did well. She held talks with Knox and showed herself willing to allow Protestants and Catholics to worship in their different ways; she did her best to soothe this turbulent kingdom and to make her jealous nobles live in peace. She recovered her high spirits and the Palace of Holyrood echoed with laughter and music, much to the disgust of the more solemn Protestants who were horrified by masked balls and wanton French dances.

People began to wonder when the most beautiful queen in Europe would marry again. There were plenty of suitors and advisers, but, in the end, Mary made her own choice. She fell in love with her cousin, Henry Stuart, Lord Darnley. 'My handsome long man,' as she called him, was young, with a carefree charm and all the courtier's skill in dancing and singing love sonnets. He was a delightful companion for a young girl who still sighed for the gaiety of France.

For a while, the marriage was perfect, but it could not last. Mary discovered that, beneath his charm, Darnley was a spoilt child. His head was turned by the thought that he was King of Scotland and he began to behave like an insolent ruffian, abusing the royal ministers and even shouting at his wife in public. Eventually, the Queen's love turned to contempt and she gave orders that he was to have no part whatever in State affairs.

Darnley went from bad to worse. He lost all sense of dignity and spent much of his time drinking and swaggering with the riff-raff of the Court, but he blamed his position, not upon himself, but upon David Rizzio, the Queen's secretary.

Rizzio was a clever young Italian who had made himself useful at Court. The Queen, with no one she could really trust, enjoyed his company, for he was not only a poet and musician, but he had a sharp brain for politics. He became the Queen's adviser and, as a result, he earned the hatred of Darnley and of a group of discontented nobles.

One evening, the Italian was at supper as usual with the Queen and a few of her closest friends. As they chatted, Darnley came in, apparently in good humour, for he joined the party and spoke to his wife with something of his old charm.

Suddenly, a crowd of armed men burst into the room headed by Lord Ruthven, in full armour. To the Queen's angry protest, Ruthven replied:

'We mean no harm to the Queen's Grace, but to yonder poltroon Davie. It is with him that I have to speak.'

The Queen demanded to know what he had done:

'Ask the King, your husband.'

'Ah,' cried Mary, turning to her husband, 'is this your work?'

Darnley, who had led the conspirators up by a private staircase, replied with a shrug:

'I? I know nothing of the matter.'

The armed men pressed closer and, as the Queen again ordered them out of her room, Rizzio backed away round the table. It was hurled aside with a crash and Rizzio, wild with terror, fell on his knees, holding the Queen's skirt and screaming to her to save him.

They dragged him away from her. Someone struck with a dagger and the Italian's last shrill scream was drowned in the trampling uproar as they roped him and bundled him outside. Later that night, Rizzio's body, with more than fifty stab wounds, was thrown out of a window into the courtyard below.

Next day, the conspirators forced Darnley to keep his wife a prisoner in the

Palace, allowing no one to go near her, not even her own servants. But Mary, whose love had turned to passionate hatred, was more than a match for her stupid husband. Smoothly, she worked on his vanity and cowardice, telling him that he now had less power than ever, for the rebellious lords were only using him for their own benefit. Eventually, she persuaded him to let her escape down a back staircase into a pantry, across a yard to a postern-gate where friends were waiting in the darkness.

They rode all night to Dunbar Castle and, in the morning, the lords in Edinburgh awoke to find their prisoner gone and their trump-card, Darnley, with her.

The conspirators fled and the Queen returned to her capital in triumph, but she had not forgiven Darnley for his part in the murder of her friend. Two months later, when her baby son was born, she told Darnley that his son looked so much like his father that she feared the worst.

At the end of the year, Darnley had gone sulkily to stay with his father at Glasgow where he fell ill with small-pox. By this time, the Earl of Bothwell had come into the Queen's life. He was a handsome man, brutal and reckless, but as brave as a lion and, though a Protestant, he had served Mary and her mother loyally. His devil-may-care manner and his great ringing laugh appealed to Mary who admired courage in a man, all the more because her own husband was a coward.

It is difficult to discover the truth in the events that brought Mary to ruin. Some people think that she was only too willing to get rid of her unpleasant husband; others believe that she was the innocent victim of a wicked plot. At all events, the Queen went to visit her sick husband and it seemed as if they were friends again, for Darnley promised to give up his evil ways and Mary appeared anxious to help him to get over his illness.

She arranged for Darnley to be carried in a litter to Edinburgh, where he stayed at a house at Kirk o'Field, just outside the town walls, amid the gardens of an old monastery where the air was sweeter for an invalid.

One evening, after the Queen had spent the day, as usual, with her husband, she remembered that she had promised to attend the wedding-ball of one of her pages. She would go back to the Palace, so she kissed her husband and promised to return in the morning.

That night, the citizens of Edinburgh were startled by a loud explosion and when daylight came, word went round that the house at Kirk o'Field had been blown sky-high and the body of the King, strangely unmarked by fire, had been found in the garden. There were rumours that men had been seen carrying sacks of gunpowder into the old house, that Bothwell had slipped away from the ball and that a band of men had hurried past some alarmed housewives just after the explosion took place.

No one knew what to believe. The only certain thing was that Darnley was dead and the Queen stayed in her room and would see no one.

Posters appeared in the capital accusing Bothwell of the crime and rumours grew so loud that he was brought to trial. But, when the town was filled with

Bothwell's troopers and the jury was packed with men who had been in the plot, the Earl was acquitted and he offered to fight anyone who disputed the verdict.

Soon afterwards, the Queen went to visit her little son at Stirling. On the way back, near Edinburgh, her company was met by a strong force of horsemen, with the Earl of Bothwell at their head. Seizing the Queen's bridle, he told her that she was in danger and that he was taking her to Dunbar for safety. One of the royal attendants drew his sword, but the Queen laid a hand on his arm.

'Nay,' she said gently, 'I would rather go with my Lord Bothwell than see one drop of Scots blood spilt.' As she rode away, someone whispered:

'Her Grace is a wonderfully willing prisoner.'

After a short stay at Dunbar, the dare-devil Earl took his willing captive back to Edinburgh, where, in the chapel of Holyrood, barely three months after Darnley's murder, they were married before a handful of nobles.

Blinded by love, Mary had not given a thought to the people she ruled. She had no idea that her conduct would fill them with disgust and anger. But, to them, she had betrayed her beauty and motherhood and they rose against a queen who could marry the man who had killed her husband.

An army took the field and almost captured Bothwell, but he escaped by a hair's breadth, and Mary, disguising herself as a boy, managed to join him at Dunbar Castle. They were too confident. Believing that their subjects would come to their aid, they rode towards Edinburgh with only a small force. An army barred the way and an envoy came forward to say that the lords had no quarrel with the Queen, it was Bothwell they would take.

The armies faced each other, but neither side would start an attack. Steadily, Bothwell's force dwindled, as some of his men stole away and there was no fight left in the others. Seeing that the position was hopeless, Mary offered to go with the lords if they would allow Bothwell to depart unharmed.

On an open hillside, they kissed goodbye and Bothwell galloped away and out of Mary's life forever. Weeping bitterly, she accompanied the lords to Edinburgh where the mob cursed her through the streets, as they paraded a banner showing her infant son by the body of his murdered father.

The Queen was taken to a castle standing in the middle of Loch Leven and here the lords forced her to give up her crown in favour of her son. When Mary's reign ended, she was only twenty-five.

Although she still had friends, it seemed impossible for her to escape from an island prison where the gates were locked every day at dusk and the keys delivered to the Governor himself. However, Mary won the hearts of the two little maids who were her attendants and of Willie Douglas, a fourteen-year-old page.

One evening, when the Governor was at supper, merry with drink, and the hall in an uproar, Willie Douglas dropped a napkin over the keys that were lying on the table. Presently, he picked up the napkin and the keys with it. No one noticed and soon the boy was able to slip away. A few minutes later, he and the Queen, followed by a trembling maid, tiptoed out of the castle and made their way towards a small boat. They rowed across the lake, the Queen eagerly taking an oar, to where friends were waiting on the shore with horses.

That night, the Queen reached Glasgow, where the Hamiltons had raised an army, but Regent Moray acted swiftly and marched to meet the Royalists at Langside.

From a little hill, Mary watched the battle and when she saw her troops routed by Moray's spearmen, she whipped up her horse and galloped away with a few attendants.

For three days, they rode south, sleeping rough and eating what they could find. It was impossible to get a ship to France, so Mary turned for help to her cousin Elizabeth. She reached England, almost penniless and without even a change of clothes, but she wrote proudly to her cousin as one Queen to another:

> *It is my earnest request that your Majesty will send for me as soon as possible, for my condition is pitiable, not to say for a Queen, but even for a simple gentlewoman.*

But Elizabeth did not send for her unhappy cousin. She ordered her to be kept in the north of England while Darnley's murder was investigated. Nothing came of the so-called trial, but Mary continued to be held a prisoner-guest in various castles. She was permitted to ride and hunt, to receive visitors and to write letters, but, wherever she went, there were guards and watching eyes.

Year after year, Mary pined for her freedom. She had the faithful Willie Douglas and her servants, her ladies-in-waiting and her dear friend, Mary Seton, one of the four Maries who had accompanied her to France as a child. She had her needlework and her pet spaniels. Above all, she had her letters and her hopes. She wrote incessantly to her friends in Scotland, in England, France and Spain. They sent gifts and prayers; the Duke of Norfolk and the Catholic Earls of Northumberland and Westmorland lost their lives trying to help her, but still she remained a prisoner.

For fifteen years, Mary was treated with dignity and respect, but, when the task of guarding her was given to a stern Puritan named Sir Amyas Paulet, her life became hard to bear. Walks and rides were forbidden, letters and visitors ceased and no word reached her from the outside world. By now, Mary was often ill, suffering from rheumatism and head pains caused by the damp conditions in which she lived, and her once-lovely hair was cropped short to make it easier to apply soothing fomentations to her aching head. She began to look old, but her courage was still high.

Hope never deserted her. Fresh plans were afoot and it became essential for Mary's Catholic supporters to get word to her. She was imprisoned now at Chartley Castle in Staffordshire where, every week, a barrel of beer was delivered for the Queen's servants. The drayman was bribed to conceal letters in the bung of the barrel. Thus, news came in to Mary and her replies went back with the empty barrel. In one of her letters, she thanked her friends for their support and gave her consent to a plot to kill Queen Elizabeth. She did not know that the drayman was also in the pay of her enemies and that every letter was copied and all her secrets known.

The letter may have been forged, but it was all that the English ministers, Cecil and Walsingham, needed. Mary was transferred to Fotheringay Castle in

Northamptonshire and put on trial for plotting against the Queen of England. When she saw the rows of lawyers and judges, she cried bitterly:

'Alas, how many lawyers here and not one for me!'

Nevertheless, she defended herself with spirit. Of course she had written to her friends, that was only natural after the way in which Elizabeth had treated her:

'I solicited them to assist me to escape from her miserable prisons,' cried Mary, 'in which she has kept me now nearly nineteen years, till my hopes and health have been cruelly destroyed, but I call on God to witness I never conspired the death of the Queen of England.'

It was in vain. She was sentenced to death and, on the 8th of February 1587, Mary, Queen of Scots entered the Great Hall at Fotheringay, supported by two of the Governor's servants, for her own attendants said they would die rather than lead their beloved mistress to the block. She said her prayers and then turned to the executioners who asked her forgiveness for what they had to do. 'I forgive you with all my heart,' she said, 'for now I hope you shall make an end of all my troubles.' Smiling, she knelt down on the cushion, murmured her last prayer, and laid her head upon the block.

More about Mary, Queen of Scots (1542–87)

Mary Stuart was the daughter of King James V who died of a broken heart after the defeat of his army by the English at Solway Moss; her claim to the throne of England arose from the fact that her grandmother was Margaret Tudor, sister of Henry VIII. Roman Catholics believed that she was the rightful Queen of England because, in their opinion, Elizabeth's mother was not legally married to Henry VIII. This explains why Elizabeth, never a cruel person, would not set her free.

Mary's life was a tragedy. Even if she had always acted wisely, the influence of Knox would have made the position of a Roman Catholic queen very difficult, but the murder of Darnley and the marriage to Bothwell brought her to ruin. Evidence that she helped to plan Darnley's murder depends upon the famous Casket Letters, which she was supposed to have written to Bothwell and which were found in a silver casket after he fled. If the letters were genuine, Mary was guilty, but many people believe that they were forgeries. The argument has never been settled.

Bothwell escaped to Norway and led a wild, adventurous life until he was imprisoned by the King of Denmark: he went mad in prison and died before Mary. Regent Moray who defeated the Queen's troops at Langside was her own half-brother. Mary's little son, James VI of Scotland, was brought up as a Protestant and, in 1603, he became James I of England.

Philip lost all control and snatched the nobleman's sleeve while he jabbed him with an accusing finger, 'Not the Estates,' he hissed. 'But you, you, you!'

WILLIAM THE SILENT

The name of Holland's national hero suggests a brooding, iron-jawed leader, but William the Silent was really a gay and charming prince who was not even a Dutchman. His story is as curious as his nickname.

William was born in Germany at the castle of Dillenburg whose old-fashioned turrets overtopped the roofs of a pleasant village near to the River Rhine. His father, the Count of Nassau, had married a beautiful widow named Juliana, and William, born in 1533, the same year as Elizabeth Tudor, was the eldest son of a large family.

The castle was a lively home, full of children, governesses, tutors, grooms and riding-masters, for Juliana not only presided over her family with loving devotion, but she formed a school at the castle, inviting children from noble families in the district to ride in for lessons. The Count was not rich, but he busied himself on his estates, taking more interest in farming and in the welfare of his people than in the quarrels of the German princelings.

The Dillenburg children were brought up to plain fare and to the enjoyment of family games and country festivities. William and his brothers, especially John and Louis who were nearest to him in age, learned to ride and hunt with their neighbours but, above all, their mother taught them to behave with kindness and dignity, to love justice and to respect the opinions of others.

At this time, the religious teaching of Luther and Calvin was sweeping across Germany into France, the Netherlands and England, much to the alarm of Roman Catholic rulers who saw in the Protestant religion a threat to their own power. The Emperor Charles v began to punish heretics with death, but at Dillenburg, although the Count and his wife became Protestants, life went along quietly enough until William reached the age of eleven.

An astonishing piece of news reached the castle. A rich cousin had been killed in France and all his wealth was left to William. By a fluke, the boy became one of the richest nobles in Europe, far higher in rank than his own father. His new-found fortune included hundreds of estates, great stretches of land in France, Italy and the Netherlands, with the title Prince of Orange from the name of a small principality in the south of France which William never visited in his whole life.

The young Prince could no longer stay at Dillenburg. Custom demanded that he should be brought up at the Emperor's Court at Brussels, so William said good-bye to his brothers and sisters and to his mother who prayed, amid her tears, that he would not forget the lessons she had taught him. The boy rode with his father to the Netherlands and there was handed into the care of the tutors, priests and gentlemen-in-waiting who had been specially chosen by the Emperor himself.

The magnificence of the Court was a startling change from Dillenburg, but if William was homesick, he did not show it. The merry, handsome boy accepted his new life with such eager charm that he soon became a favourite with everyone. Charles V so delighted in his company that he would keep him by his side, even when the greatest courtiers had to withdraw from the royal presence. When the Emperor was away, his sister, the Regent of the Netherlands, looked after the boy with tender affection and took him with her to the cities and villages of the Low Countries.

At this time, the Netherlands consisted of modern Belgium and Holland, seventeen provinces that made up the richest country in Europe. There were more than two hundred towns, most of them walled and semi-independent, and the people, under their proud nobles, were boisterous and hard-working. Their wealth came from the skill of the weavers and tapestry-makers, from trade with Germany and the Baltic, from farming and fishing, from money-lending and banking.

These lively people were ruled by the Emperor, and the wealth of their cities was absolutely essential to him, for, despite his possessions in Austria, Italy and Spain, despite the gold from the New World, he was always short of money for his wars.

William, Prince of Orange, grew up into a gay leader of fashion. He built himself several palaces where the dazzling extravagance of his parties became famous. The Emperor chose an heiress to be his bride, made him governor, or Stadtholder, of three provinces and Commander-in-Chief of an army.

At the age of twenty, William was campaigning in the war against France, taking part in sieges and night-attacks, enduring the life of camp and fortress. He also learned about the sufferings of common soldiers and did all he could to ease their hardships. But he hated the looting of captured towns and he was constantly asking the Emperor to send pay for the soldiers who otherwise had to steal. Most of all, he was sickened by the horrors of public executions and the burning alive of humble citizens who had, he knew, committed no crime except that of worshipping as Protestants.

In William, the fashionable world saw a gifted prince, blessed by fortune and good looks, a man whose courtesy was as remarkable as his kindness to servants and even to criminals. He lived like a prince, but underneath all his extravagance and easy charm, there was still the open-hearted boy of Dillenburg whose mother had taught him to love justice.

Charles V suddenly decided to give up all his titles to retire to a monastery. Leaning on the arm of his beloved William, the weary Emperor handed over his power to his son, Philip II of Spain, who came to Brussels for the ceremony. Philip was thin and ugly; he seldom spoke or looked anyone in the face and he was a fanatic. The one object of his life was to crush the Protestant religion and to stamp out its beliefs by torture and the sword.

Philip immediately sensed that his father's favourite was at heart an opponent, but for the moment he showed favour to William. When the war with France was ended, he sent him to Paris to arrange the terms of the peace treaty and here, as usual, William enjoyed the luxury of a brilliant Court.

One day, he was out hunting with the royal party and by chance found himself alone in the woods with King Henry II of France. The King began to speak of a secret that lay on his mind. In horrified amazement, William heard him describe Philip's plan for the two monarchs to use Spanish soldiers to massacre the Protestants in their countries, beginning with the stubborn Netherlanders. But though deeply shocked, William gave no sign, beyond a murmur of polite interest, so Henry never suspected that under that courteous manner, William was burning with indignation.

Later, he said he felt overcome 'with pity and compassion for all these good people doomed to destruction.' This moment was the turning-point of his life. Yet, for the time being, he said nothing—as his enemies always declared, no one knew his thoughts; he was sly, he was William 'the Silent'.

Soon afterwards, Philip decided to go back to Spain, but first he must have a huge sum of money from the Netherlanders whose Parliament, called the Estates, granted it, providing he would take his soldiers with him. Furious, he had to agree but, as he was about to sail, he turned to Orange who was bidding him a courteous farewell, and bitterly complained about the impudent Netherlanders. 'It was the decision of the Estates, my Lord,' replied Orange gently.

Philip lost all control and snatched the nobleman's sleeve while he jabbed him with an accusing finger, 'Not the Estates,' he hissed. 'But you, you, you!'

In the absence of the King, the Netherlands were governed by his sister, the Regent, and a Council of State, but the real ruler was Cardinal Granvelle. This priest was so greedy and cunning that the Dutch nobles, led by Count Egmont, began to mock his extravagance, calling themselves 'the Beggars' in derision.

At last, Philip was obliged to recall Granvelle but he made up his mind to crush these uppish Netherlanders. Men were forbidden to be Protestants or even to discuss the Scriptures and anyone suspected of heresy was tortured and put to death.

So far, the Prince of Orange had kept quiet. The Spaniards distrusted him, because he was so widely loved by the people, but he had never sided openly with the Beggars and he was still a Roman Catholic, though he believed that men should worship as they chose. The situation grew worse and William resigned his governorships and retired to Dillenburg.

It was just as well. The Duke of Alva arrived with an army of Spanish soldiers; Egmont was executed, William's estates were seized and his eldest son was kidnapped and taken away to Spain. The Netherlands suffered a ghastly wave of terror as Alva rooted out the Protestants, with cruel relish: 'I have tamed men of iron,' he boasted, 'shall I not now be able to tame men of butter?'

More than 18,000 died for their religion and thousands more fled to Germany and England.

At Dillenburg, where Juliana still exercised her gentle rule, the family rejoiced to have William home after so many years. He could do little at first, except appeal for help to Elizabeth Tudor and the German princes, but he knew that cruelty was not stamping out the Protestant faith in the Netherlands. It burned all the more fiercely, and he himself turned to that religion.

After four years of exile, he raised an army of refugees and hired soldiers, selling his jewels and plate to help find the money. Then he set off with his brothers, Louis, Adolphus and Henry, to make war against the Spanish tyrant.

But the Protestant force was small and many of the mercenaries were faint-hearted. The Prince lost battle after battle; his brother Adolphus was killed and Alva laid waste the countryside.

Presently William was forced to wander about, too weak to make a major attack, but always hoping to hear news of help from the French Protestants (the Huguenots) who had powerful leaders and great hopes. But on St Bartholomew's Eve 1572, a terrible massacre in Paris destroyed the Huguenot cause, and William, with only 70 men left, was forced to retreat into the northern provinces of Zealand and Holland, where, amid canals and islands, it was difficult for the Spaniards to follow. Alva was triumphant everywhere and towns like Haarlem that defied him were put to the sword.

William did not despair even when his position was hopeless. Once, he was asked if there was any chance of an alliance with a foreign power. 'I have entered into a close alliance with God,' he replied. 'And I am firmly convinced that all who put their trust in Him shall be saved by His almighty hand.'

He was saved, not by an army, but by a fleet composed of fishing-boats manned by the seafaring folk of the northern provinces. Calling themselves the Sea-Beggars, they began to work along the coast, attacking Spanish ships and destroying Philip's reinforcements. By a bold stroke, they captured the port of Brill which gave them a valuable base from which to carry out their raids, and they often slipped into Dover to sell the booty, for Elizabeth turned a blind eye to their exploits and was secretly sending arms and men to William.

As the tide turned and towns held out against the Spaniards, Alva lost heart and resigned his command. William advanced and captured an important fortress, while his brothers Louis and Henry were leading a small army from Germany. He waited for their arrival, but there was no news. Days passed and then came the awful tidings that both brothers had been killed in a desperate charge against the enemy.

This disaster allowed the Spaniards to besiege Leyden, a prosperous town, some six miles from the sea and vital to the defence of the north. The town was completely surrounded and though the townsfolk held out behind their battered walls, their valiant Burgomaster knew they could barely last a month. William had no soldiers left and he could only send in messages by carrier pigeon until he fell so ill from fever that men despaired of his life.

Leyden held on, for a month, for two months and the people began to die of hunger. At last, Orange asked the Estates to cut the dykes and let the sea flow across their precious fields, so that the Sea-Beggars could sail in to the rescue. 'Better a drowned land than a lost land,' they cried, and the dykes were cut.

The sea crept in and the dismayed Spaniards fled from the rising waters as the ships manoeuvred between the trees and farm roofs.

Now William went to live in Delft with his wife and children, no longer rich but loved by everyone, and he worked with all his soul to unite the provinces. It was a slow task, for the Dutch loved independence and the south was still Catholic. But when 8,000 Spanish troops made an attack on Antwerp so savage that it was known ever afterwards as 'the Spanish Fury', the Estates agreed to form a Union of all the provinces.

This was the greatest triumph of William's career. The Spaniards retreated and he entered Brussels after ten years' absence through streets lined with the cheering populace.

To hold the Netherlands together, a monarch was needed. William refused the crown because he wished to serve rather than to rule, but he hoped that Elizabeth of England might accept. When she refused, he persuaded the Estates to invite a French prince, the Duke of Anjou, an absurd little fellow, as ugly as a bull-frog and quite untrustworthy.

Anjou arrived, full of promises and fair speeches, but within a year, he was gone, driven out for his miserable treachery. Meanwhile, as the Spaniards recovered, the South wavered and fell away. The northern provinces formed a separate Union and William went back to live in Delft. In this town of canals and quiet streets, 'Father' William was often to be seen, walking along deep in thought, his handsome head now grey and his once-gorgeous clothes as shabby as those of any poor townsman.

There was much to worry about; he had not been well since a would-be assassin shot him in the face at Antwerp, but he had to work ceaselessly to persuade the cities and provinces to stay united. He persuaded; he would never force or bully. But the Spaniards, under a brilliant general, the Duke of Parma, were steadily winning back the South and drawing nearer to the United Provinces.

Still, there was much to be thankful for. The people trusted Orange and loved him, though they made him sad when they repaid cruelty with cruelty. He wanted freedom for all men and he hoped, for he was only fifty, that he had many years left in which to serve his adopted country. He did not reckon with the dark mind of a fanatic.

The Spaniards regularly employed spies and assassins, but even they would not pay money to Balthazar Gerard, a crack-witted apprentice who had vowed to kill the Prince of Orange. Somehow, Gerard reached Delft where, pretending to be the son of a murdered Protestant, he got to know a friend of the Prince, was employed by him as a messenger, and, once, he actually entered William's house, only to find that he had no weapon.

Gerard hung about the courtyard, chatting to the guards and telling them that he would enlist in the Protestant forces if only he could afford a pair of stout shoes.

This was reported to Orange who, with his usual generosity, sent down a sum of money to the poor messenger.

Next day, Gerard bought a pair of pistols and returned to the courtyard. After dinner, as the Prince was leaving his room by an outside staircase, the assassin stepped from an archway and fired twice into his body. William staggered and gasped, 'My God, have pity on my soul; my God, have pity upon my poor people.' He was dead by the time they had carried him indoors.

Gerard was caught and put to a horrible death, smiling and praying to the end, but William the Silent was buried in the great bare church of Delft, where he still lies under the canopy of a marble tomb, with an angel sounding a trumpet above his head. He has been called 'the wisest, gentlest and bravest man who ever led a nation' and when he died, the little children cried in the streets.

More about William the Silent (1533–84)

When William, son of the Count of Nassau, went as a boy of eleven to the Court at Brussels, the Emperor Charles V was the greatest monarch in Europe. As Holy Roman Emperor, he had great possessions in Germany and power over many of the princes; he ruled Austria and the Netherlands, he was King of Spain with all its colonies and the kingdoms of Sicily and Naples. These huge territories caused him endless trouble for he was opposed by France, by the Turks and by the Protestants in Germany and the Netherlands. At last, worn out, he retired to a Spanish monastery and died there in 1558.

Although William did not live to complete his task of freeing the Dutch people from Spanish rule, his sons, Maurice and Frederick Henry, carried on his work. For a time, it seemed as if the Duke of Parma must defeat them, despite the help sent by Elizabeth from England. However, Parma had to prepare an army to invade England and, after the Armada, Philip II ordered him to France.

Meanwhile, William's son, known as Maurice of Nassau, proved himself the best soldier in Europe and the Dutch fleet grew ever stronger. By 1609, Spain had to agree to a twelve years' truce and in 1648, the Netherlands (known as the Dutch United Provinces) finally won their freedom.

ELIZABETH OF ENGLAND

On a November day in 1558, Elizabeth rode into London. The gorgeous procession, headed by the Lord Mayor and the Garter King-at-Arms wound slowly through streets hung with tapestries and silks. The narrow way was jammed with citizens who shouted with joy for their new Queen and also with relief that her sister was dead.

Cannon boomed down the river as Elizabeth came to the Tower of London. Turning to those about her, she said,

'I am raised from being a prisoner in this place to being a Prince of this land.'

From babyhood, her life had been in danger. She had known four stepmothers, a brother surrounded by scheming nobles, a sister hated for her religion and her Spanish husband. In a world of plots and treachery, she had been imprisoned, questioned and spied upon, so that she knew more about lies than truth, more about the value of keeping silent than about love and kindness.

But the lonely, frightened child had grown into a striking woman who looked every inch a queen.

In the minds of the cheering Londoners, there was no doubt that this was Henry VIII's daughter. They could see that in the reddish tint of her curly hair, in the firm set of her mouth, in the shrewd blue eyes that looked everywhere and missed nothing. Her manner reminded them of the great Henry. Now and then, she paused majestically to let the people see her in her jewels and purple velvet; she picked out someone in the crowd to praise, another to pity. She replied wittily to a compliment and then hurled back a coarse jest to some brawny carter waving to her from a barrel-top. The crowd roared with laughter:

'God save your Grace!' they bellowed.

'God bless you all, good people!' answered the Queen.

But Elizabeth had heard cheers before. She remembered how her sister Mary had been cheered only five years ago, and now she was dead, a tragic failure.

The kingdom had sunk low in those five years and now was only 'a bone between two dogs'—France and Spain. The people were divided by religious hatred, the Treasury was empty, the warships were rotten and the French had captured Calais. But Spain was equally interested in controlling England, for

Queen Mary had married Philip II of Spain, so, if French troops landed, Spanish armies would surely follow.

Thus, in 1558, it seemed certain that Elizabeth's reign would be short and bloody. She was only twenty-five and she had no powerful friends to help her; half the people were still Roman Catholics at heart, believing that the rightful queen was Mary, Queen of Scots, now in France. Nevertheless, Elizabeth faced the situation bravely.

First, she found advisers who could be trusted. She kept some of the nobles who had served Mary, but she also chose men from the middle-class, solid, faithful men like William Cecil, her greatest minister, Nicholas Bacon, Thomas Gresham and Walsingham, the master of her secret service.

The nobles and courtiers who made the Court so gay and colourful, men such as Leicester, Raleigh, Sidney and Essex, were given fine-sounding appointments. Yet, although she delighted in the company of handsome young men and kept them always close to the throne, Elizabeth never told them the innermost secrets nor gave them the trust that she gave to quiet Cecil.

England's new Queen had to settle the religious struggle by somehow satisfying the Protestants without driving the Roman Catholics into rebellion. She herself could not understand why men should torture and kill each other for religion— once she wrote to Philip:

'What does it matter to your Majesty if they go to the Devil in their own way?'

So, as long as people went regularly to Church of England services and did not openly worship as Roman Catholics, Elizabeth did not enquire closely into their beliefs. She wanted religious peace, and for eleven years, no one in the realm was executed for religion or treason.

Money was the next pressing problem. Kings were expected to keep up a handsome Court and to pay for most of the country's expenses out of their own pockets, for Parliament met only from time to time to make special 'grants' for such expenses as wars. Prices were going up and the Queen's income, mostly from the rents of farms on her estates, stood still.

So, for the whole of her reign, Elizabeth had to pinch and scrape to make ends meet. She earned a name for being mean and it was even said that she kept her sailors short of powder and shot. The truth was that she was careful about money because she would not grind her people with heavy taxes and she hated waste. She sold much of her own land and died poorer than at her Coronation.

In Thomas Gresham, the Queen found a man who was a genius with money and she gave the people a new coinage in place of the clipped coins that hampered trade because no one trusted their value. Above all, she avoided war. Kings, nobles and even common citizens loved the glory and excitement of war, but she, a woman, knew better. It was risky and expensive.

By every possible means, Elizabeth kept out of wars. She made no threats or defiant speeches to her enemies. When she had to act, she acted craftily, sending 'underhand' help to the Dutch Protestants and French Huguenots, but always unofficially, so that she could say she knew nothing when an angry king accused her of aiding his rebellious subjects. She encouraged her sea-dogs to rob and her merchant-adventurers to trade, often providing ships and some of the cost of an expedition so that she could take her share of the profits. But if her captains ran into trouble with the Spaniards or the Portuguese, that was their affair.

When it suited her, Elizabeth was all innocence about the behaviour of her subjects in the English Channel or on the Spanish Main. She would promise to find out, she would punish; but she did nothing. The Spanish ambassador fumed and wrote to his master,

'This woman is possessed of a hundred thousand devils.'

Craftiness and silence were two of Elizabeth's qualities that infuriated her friends and enemies alike. Poor Cecil was always begging her to make up her mind; so were the Scots, the Dutch, the French, King Philip and all the princes who wanted to marry her. But she would not answer. She would put off a decision until the morrow in case something better turned up. Then she would take a different course, change the subject and laugh at her grave statesmen as she turned to flirt with the courtiers who hovered about her like so many gorgeous butterflies. Few of them realised that this maddening, enchanting Queen was playing her own game.

Elizabeth played for time. By trickery and lies, with courage and love, she was steering her country out of its troubles, but time was everything.

At first, there was more danger from France than from Spain. King Philip certainly offered to marry Elizabeth and she pretended to consider the matter, though she had no intention of repeating her sister's mistake. For years, she kept on good and even affectionate terms with Philip, because neither wanted a war and both were frightened of France.

The French King had captured Calais; his son had married the beautiful young Mary Queen of Scots and his troops were looking after Scotland in her absence. It seemed only a matter of time before he would place her on the thrones of both Scotland and England.

But a storm drowned another French army that was on its way to Scotland and the Scottish Protestants, with cautious help from Elizabeth, were able to drive out the French Regent and her soldiers. Then came news that the French King had been killed in an accident, and therefore Mary was Queen of France, Queen of Scotland and, she claimed, Queen of England too.

Elizabeth's luck held. Mary was soon a widow and she had to return to Scotland where she made a disastrous marriage with Lord Darnley, her worthless cousin. Darnley was murdered and when Mary married the man who probably killed him, a worse ruffian named Bothwell, the Scots were so angry that they drove the pair out of the kingdom.

Penniless and without so much as a change of clothes, Mary escaped to England and appealed to her cousin Elizabeth for help.

Elizabeth sent a paltry gift of clothing but no promises, for, although she disliked rebellion, she was not eager to help a rival who had claimed her own throne. So she did nothing, apart from keeping Mary a prisoner in various castles for eighteen years.

It was a dangerous policy, for, as long as Mary was alive, Catholics at home and abroad plotted to rescue her. There was a rebellion in the North and the rebels were punished with horrible severity. For once, Elizabeth showed a glimpse of her father's savage temper, but she was badly frightened—not for herself, she was never scared of assassins—but for the kingdom. If the revolt had been successful, there would have been civil war, and England would have been a battleground for foreign troops.

The Queen's ministers begged her to execute Mary. Time after time, they produced proof of plots to overthrow the government, to kill the Queen and to restore the Roman Catholic religion, but Elizabeth hesitated. Mary was her cousin; she was a queen and, in a sense, a guest. Perhaps the plots were exaggerated, perhaps her cousin knew nothing about them. But the proofs piled up and, at last, Elizabeth signed the death-warrant. Afterwards, she wept bitterly and laid the blame upon her Council.

For Philip, the execution of Mary Queen of Scots was the last straw. Elizabeth had deceived him for thirty years, pretending she was about to change her religion, pretending she was going to marry this prince or that one, pretending she was his true friend, and all the time she had been secretly helping the Protestant Netherlanders and encouraging her pirates to rob his ships. Now she had killed the cousin whom for so long he had meant to place on England's throne. He must put everything else aside in order to destroy this deceitful woman and to bring her kingdom back to the true faith.

He assembled the greatest fleet that had ever put to sea. Drake delayed its sailing by a whole year but in July 1588, the Armada entered the English Channel.

Elizabeth's people were ready to defend their island. The Queen had found the money to build some warships and the sea-towns supplied the rest of the fleet that harried the Armada like a swarm of hornets, and finally, with the aid of a storm, broke its majestic power to send the fragments flying northwards to escape the weather and the English guns.

The Queen herself went down to Tilbury on the north bank of the Thames, where Leicester commanded the army that stood ready to oppose the Spanish soldiers if they got ashore. As ever, she rose to the occasion, put on a steel breastplate, mounted a white horse and, with a page carrying her plumed helmet before her, rode into the ranks of her army:

'I am come amongst you, as you see,' she cried, 'to lay down for my God and for my kingdom and for my people, my honour and my blood, even in the dust. I know I have the body of a weak and feeble woman but I have the heart and stomach of a king, and of a king of England too, and think foul scorn that Parma or Spain or any prince of Europe should dare to invade the borders of my realm!'

Parma's soldiers never arrived and Elizabeth did not have to lead her countrymen in defence of their land, but it was the pinnacle of her reign. All Europe was dumbfounded by this extraordinary woman, Queen of only half an island, who had defied and defeated the greatest King on earth.

Danger was not ended, for Philip never gave up his dream of conquering England and there was war for many years—at sea, in Ireland and in the Netherlands. But England had grown up.

Under such a queen, the people found confidence in themselves. They had beaten the Spaniards, they could do anything. Their sailors, explorers and merchants went farther afield and brought home greater riches; their poets, writers and scientists suddenly found amazing energy and skill. New ideas, new buildings, better crops, more trade, more beauty, more splendour were to be seen on every side. It was as though, after a long winter, a tree had burst into blossom.

The Queen grew old and her moods more uncertain than ever, though she still delighted in the company of her young men whom she kept so jealously at Court. They wrote poems in her honour and praised her with lavish compliments. It seemed ridiculous that an ageing woman with bad teeth and a red wig should be courted as if she were a beautiful princess, but Elizabeth had the power to inspire the young men who would serve her at sea and on the battlefield to their last breath.

They called her 'Gloriana' and 'the Faery Queen'. 'She is our God on earth,' said one of her ministers and when Drake returned to Plymouth after his three-year voyage round the world, his first question to a passing skiff was, 'Is the Queen alive and in good health?'

What was the secret of her fascination and how did she raise a bankrupt little island to the ranks of the Great Powers?

Elizabeth was an actress in an age that loved a show. She looked a queen and dressed like a queen. On her Progresses, those summertime journeys about the country, she travelled like an empress, with 300 wagons and 2,000 horses, kindling her people's love by her heartiness and acts of royal generosity. The country people flocked to see her pass, as she rode by on horseback or was carried in a litter in the midst of her splendid Court. She was better-known and better-loved than any previous English monarch.

She was vain, but she could do all the things that people admired. She danced and rode superbly; she could kill a running deer with a shot from her bow and she hunted until she was nearly seventy. As a musician, she was almost as good as her father; as a scholar, she could converse with the university dons and, as she said herself, she could speak six languages better than her own.

Like her father, Elizabeth was royal to her fingertips. When she was angry, the Court trembled, and when she smiled, the sun shone, but she was neither cruel nor greedy. In one of her tempers, she would swear like a sea-captain, box the ears of her courtiers and, once, she took off a shoe and hurled it at Walsingham. Then suddenly, she would sparkle with fun, calling her ministers and suitors by the nicknames she invented—'my faithful Moor', 'my monkey', 'my Frog prince' and 'my little black husband'.

At a solemn ceremony, she could not help tickling the neck of the kneeling Earl of Leicester, and when an ambassador from Poland delivered a threatening message, she rose with a flood of furious insults and turned away in outraged dignity to remark in a loud whisper that it was a pity her favourite Essex was not present to hear how good her Latin still was.

No wonder she never married. All the world, except Elizabeth, thought it impossible for a woman to rule alone, but she kept her princely suitors dangling for thirty years and never intended to share her throne with any of them.

She loved England. She said she had taken England for her husband and wanted no other:

'Nothing, no worldly thing under the sun, is so dear to me as the love and goodwill of my subjects,' were her words to her first Parliament and, when she was not far from death, her last speech was almost the same:

'Though God has raised me high, yet this I count the glory of my crown, that I have reigned with your loves.'

There was one thing she could not do. To name her successor, to think of someone else in her place, was unbearable.

Towards the end, after days and nights in a great chair or lying on piled cushions, her ladies got her finally to bed but she refused food and medicine. Semi-conscious, her mind went over the old perils and she seized a rusty sword that was always kept on her bed and laid about her, slashing and stabbing at the curtains. Then, when she could no longer speak, the Secretary of State dared to breathe the name of James Stuart, and Elizabeth raised her hand to her head to show that the crown should go to the son of the cousin whom she had executed.

In the early hours of the next morning, in her seventieth year, the Great Queen died in her sleep and James VI of Scotland became King of England.

More about Elizabeth I (1533–1603)

Elizabeth was the daughter of Anne Boleyn, King Henry VIII's second wife, who was executed before the child was three years old. During her childhood, the Princess was often lonely and neglected but she found a kind stepmother in Catherine Parr, the King's sixth and last wife.

When Henry died in 1547, he was succeeded by his nine-year-old son, Edward VI. During the reign, Admiral Seymour was executed for treason on the grounds that he planned to marry Elizabeth and seize power, and, although the girl was innocent, she was kept in semi-captivity.

Edward died in 1553 and Mary Tudor became Queen of England. Like her mother (Catherine of Aragon), Mary was a Roman Catholic; she married Philip II of Spain and hoped to bring England back to the authority of the Pope. Mary and Elizabeth were fond of each other but, since the hopes of the Protestants centred on Elizabeth, she was imprisoned in the Tower for a time. Afterwards, she was closely guarded in various country houses until her half-sister's death in 1558.

Mary, Queen of Scots, was only six days old when she became Queen of Scotland but she was brought up in France where, at fifteen, she married Francis, son of the French King. She was nine years younger than Elizabeth and far more beautiful but, although she was charming and tragically unlucky, she lacked her cousin's cool commonsense. She was executed in 1587 and, in dying, she left her claims to the English throne not to her son James, a Protestant, but to a daughter of Philip II who therefore prepared the Armada in order to take the English crown.

*The most elegant Court in France was startled by a woman who appeared in a tight-fitting
military jacket, a crimson scarf and a vast hat with black feathers.*

QUEEN CHRISTINA

The only child of Gustavus Adolphus, 'the Lion of the North', was born in 1626 when Sweden was the leading Protestant power in Europe. Gustavus Adolphus was a wise statesman and a great leader but his marriage to Maria Eleanora of Brandenburg was far from happy.

The Queen was a jealous, tempestuous woman who despised her husband's country and was angry with herself for not giving him the son he longed for. At last, the astrologers announced that from their study of the stars they could forecast the birth of a son and heir to the royal House of Vasa.

A lull in the war with Poland allowed Gustavus to hurry back to Stockholm where the people waited eagerly for the arrival of the infant prince. On December 7th, the bells pealed out the joyful news to a snow-clad countryside. But the baby was not a son. The midwives had not dared to tell the truth and it was left to the King's sister to inform Gustavus that his child was a daughter. He looked down at the tiny dark-haired baby in his arms:

'It is God's will, sister,' he said quietly. 'My daughter shall be called Christina after my mother. She is a Vasa and will rule Sweden as well as any man.'

From that moment, Gustavus was devoted to the child, but the Queen, whose mind seemed to have been unhinged by the birth, disliked her daughter and could not bear to see her.

'Why am I so luckless in this accursed country?' she cried. 'Instead of a son, I am given a daughter, dark and ugly, with a great nose and black eyes. Take her from me, I will not have such a monster.'

It was even whispered that in her madness the Queen tried to kill the child. Once, a beam fell mysteriously upon the cradle and on another occasion a nursemaid was blamed for dropping the baby on to a stone floor, injuring a shoulder that ever afterwards remained a little crooked. But Christina grew rapidly into a strong, lively child. She was by no means the ugly duckling of her mother's imagination, for her bright eyes and sparkling laughter made her attractive to everyone in the Palace.

Whenever he was at home, Gustavus took the little girl with him when he visited fortresses and inspected his troops. Seated on the pommel of his saddle, she laughed gleefully as the soldiers marched past and clapped her hands as the cannons thundered out in salute. Perched on her father's shoulder or seated quiet as a mouse by his side during the deliberations of the Swedish Parliament, Christina was absolutely happy as long as she was near to this wonderful man who loved her so deeply.

The war took Gustavus away from Sweden but before he left he placed his daughter in the care of his sister and of the Chancellor, Axel Oxenstierna, his most trusted friend. The Queen was to be allowed no say in the child's upbringing, but to the State Council, he gave these orders:

'Her Highness shall be reared as a Prince of Sweden. In horsemanship, shooting and sword-play, she shall excel boys of her age and besides the studies that are proper to a Prince, she shall be taught the arts of government and of war.'

In the summer of 1632, Gustavus was commanding no fewer than eight armies in Germany. His victories over the armies of the Catholic Union had forced the Emperor to retreat and Gustavus advanced across a devastated countryside to attack his opponent at the town of Lützen where a savage battle took place in a thick mist. The Swedes were driven back in one place and the King became separated from his own troops. Making a detour to regain his lines, Gustavus was shot down by a squadron of enemy cuirassiers. His horse, with its empty saddle and royal trappings, galloped along the line and was recognised by the Swedes who charged in maddened rage to avenge their King and recover his corpse. They won a complete victory, but the body of Gustavus was embalmed and carried back to Sweden to be buried amid the mourning of his people.

A lonely little girl of six became Queen Christina, though the proclamation named her 'King of Sweden'. Until she came of age, a Regency of nobles was to rule the kingdom, for Queen Maria Eleanora was now almost out of her mind.

Christina was brilliantly clever and, by the age of ten, she could speak German, Latin and French and was learning Spanish, Italian and Greek. Her lessons started at six o'clock each morning and, in addition, there were riding exercises and physical training as laid down by her father. But, although Axel Oxenstierna strove gravely to teach the child the duties that lay before her, no one remembered that she was a little girl who needed kindness and love, as well as playmates of her own age. Brought up among court officials, Army officers and ministers of State, Christina lived in a man's world where fun was only to be found among the stable-lads and private soldiers who adored the royal tomboy with her coarse untidy hair and reckless skill on horseback.

Her aunt died and the only companion to whom she could ever open her heart was her cousin, Charles Gustavus, a stocky little boy who could not match her at lessons or games. As Christina reached her teens, however, and began to show remarkable ability to understand the affairs of State, her nurse was replaced by a companion of her own age named Edda Sparre. Christina was fascinated by her dainty companion and for many years the two became close friends, although Edda was really a vain, empty-headed little creature who was quite incapable of understanding Christina's restless mind.

Another friend entered Christina's life when the handsome young Count

Magnus de la Gardie came to Court. He was charming, with perfect manners and a mountain of debts which Christina was forever trying to settle by gifts of gold and land. In time, she learned that Magnus was no more than a greedy spendthrift, as treacherous as he was idle.

Meanwhile, the Thirty Years' War dragged on, with all the horrors that made it the most cruel war in history. When, on her eighteenth birthday, Christina formally took over her duties as 'King' of Sweden, Swedish soldiers were still fighting in Denmark and Saxony. Soon afterwards, however, there was talk of peace which Christina did everything to hasten. In this, she quarrelled with Oxenstierna, for the cautious old statesman felt that Sweden would gain more from the peace treaty if he could proceed slowly. As it was, he was hustled along by an impatient young woman who reminded him sharply that she was now Queen and intended to have her own way.

Although Sweden was almost bankrupt after the long struggle, Christina was full of ideas. Her wide reading and her discussions on art and philosophy with men who had travelled abroad had convinced her that she could turn Stockholm into the Athens of the North. She sent agents far and wide to buy pictures, classical statues and whole libraries of rare books which were stacked higgledy-piggledy in the corridors of the Palace.

In her enthusiasm, she rose at dawn to examine and sort the treasures that arrived by the ship-load. Then, realising that she knew all too little, she sent for the cleverest man in Europe, the French philosopher, Descartes. Flattered by a Queen's invitation, the bent, little man made the long journey and was installed as guest of honour in the Palace.

Christina was delighted. Here at last was a man with a better brain than her own. She swamped him with questions and arguments, continuing their conversations far into the night and resuming them at five o'clock in the morning. The bitter Swedish winter and the exhausting discussions in an icy library proved too much for the old Frenchman. He caught a chill but Christina, as healthy as a sleigh-dog herself, did not notice. One morning, three months after his arrival, Descartes was found dead in his room.

Christina was heartbroken. She was alone once more, for Magnus was abroad and Edda was now married. There were marriage offers for herself from all over Europe, and the Senate pressed her to marry her cousin Charles Gustavus, but she brushed the subject aside. She wanted friendship and love, but she was determined to remain free, so, to quell arguments that she might die without a successor, she forced the Senate to recognise Charles Gustavus as heir to the throne.

The next thing to do to keep boredom at arm's length was to plan her own Coronation. Without consulting Parliament, Christina made arrangements for a magnificent ceremony. It began with a triumphal procession of all the Swedish nobility, the crack regiments, the Senate and foreign ambassadors, with the Queen herself seated in a sumptuous coach smiling happily at the continuous thunder of cannon which she had specially ordered. After a State Banquet, the Coronation itself took place in the Great Church of Stockholm and was followed by several days of festivities that exhausted everyone except the Queen.

After the costly excitement of the Coronation, Christina turned to science, to medicine, to laboratory experiments, to music, folklore and even, it was rumoured, to witchcraft. Nothing satisfied her long. She squandered money on quack doctors, foreign adventurers and anybody who could capture her interest. Even her behaviour in public became scandalous. At one moment, she was the haughty Queen; at another, she was cackling with laughter or cursing like a guardsman.

The Swedes took their Lutheran religion seriously, but Christina seemed to go out of her way to offend them by chattering and playing with her pet dogs in the royal pew. Perhaps religion had been dinned into her too severely during her childhood. At all events, she began to be attracted to the religion which her father and the Swedish nation regarded as their most bitter foe. She made secret enquiries about the Roman Catholic faith.

A Jesuit priest attending the Portuguese Ambassador carried this astounding news to Rome and, some time later, two cloaked figures were admitted to the Palace. The visitors were learned professors from Italy who had been specially sent by the Pope.

For days, the Italians visited the Palace in the guise of art experts. But, in their long discussions behind closed doors, they were not advising the Queen about her collection of treasures, they were instructing her in the Catholic religion. They were astonished by her knowledge of the subject, by her endless questions, sudden changes of mind and bursts of impatience and laughter. Eventually, the strange woman turned away from them and whispered, almost to herself:

'There is no help for it. I must give up the throne.' For once, she did not act quickly. It was months before she sent for Charles Gustavus and said abruptly:

'You might as well know that I have decided to abdicate. You can begin to prepare yourself for your duties.'

Next, she summoned Count Oxenstierna and told him to call the Swedish Parliament at the ancient city of Uppsala. Christina strode into the Great Hall, between rows of representatives who stood respectfully until she had flung herself into the Chair of State. Presently she stood up and made a short speech in her deep, vibrating voice:

'I think you know the reason for my coming here. I have made up my mind to abdicate and nothing can change my resolution. I thank you for your loyalty and trust that you will remember that I have done what has to be done out of love for our country.'

To the sorrowful speeches and pleadings of the representatives, she turned a deaf ear and listened aloofly to the discussion on the subject of her income. She had asked for a fantastic sum but although the Diet reduced this figure, it was still far more than the country could afford.

The final act took place at the Ceremony of Abdication when, sensing the reluctance of the aged Count, Christina removed the crown from her own head. Then she took off the cloak of royal purple and stepped down from the throne. That evening Charles Gustavus was crowned King of Sweden and the reign of Christina came to an end.

At twenty-eight, Christina had abdicated without being quite certain why she had done so. She told herself that it was in order to become a Roman Catholic but she knew in her heart that she had given up the task entrusted to her by her father because she was bored and lonely. Most of all, perhaps, she wanted to startle the world.

To show that she was different from everyone else, she cut her hair short, put on a man's suit, stuck a couple of pistols in her belt and rode away from Uppsala accompanied by only five attendants. From Stockholm, disdaining the fleet of warships offered by the King, she crossed to Denmark in a small ship and started out on a flamboyant tour to Europe.

Dressed like a cavalier, and accompanied by an increasing retinue of hangers-on and money-lenders, she travelled from city to city, embarrassing the authorities by her demand to be treated like a reigning monarch.

From Germany, she went to Antwerp and then by canal to Brussels, where she arrived in a gilded barge pulled by twelve horses. By this time, her conversion to Roman Catholicism was known all over Europe and inquisitive crowds thronged the streets to see the Queen who had forsaken her homeland and her native religion.

She had not forsaken pleasure, however. Balls, revels, firework displays, tournaments and hunting-parties followed one another in unending succession but, by this time, the people of Sweden, horrified by her change of religion, were holding up payments essential to keep up this glittering way of life. Careless of her mounting debts, Christina continued her leisurely progress towards Rome, calling on the way upon Charles II, the exiled King of England. In December 1655, she rode on a white horse into the great square of St Peter's at Rome, where priests conducted her to the Pope's chapel.

The conversion of a Protestant Queen so soon after the great wars of religion was a triumph that deserved every reward, so the Farnese Palace, one of the most magnificent buildings in Europe, was placed at her disposal. Surrounded by priceless paintings and treasures, Christina held Court as if she were Queen of a new kingdom. To stifle her inner loneliness, her days and nights were filled by entertainments of the most lavish kind. Yet, to draw further attention to herself, Christina adopted manners that were suitable only for the stable, guffawing like a peasant, mocking the ladies and treating the men as if she were their equal in every repect.

Polite society was shocked. The best families in Rome began to stay away and the Court of the Swedish Queen went steadily downhill. In place of the aristocrats, a gathering of rogues made themselves welcome in the lovely palace. One of the worst scoundrels was Count Cantinelli, another was the Marquis Monaldeschi, who quietly removed the treasures from the palace and sold them for his own benefit.

Christina seemed not to care. Robbed right and left, flattered by rascals who posed as her friends, she blinded herself to what was going on. In any case, she no longer had the money to pay her servants' wages.

Eventually, the Pope made her a huge gift and arranged for his embarrassing

guest to go on a visit to France. At first, all was well. Louis XIV owed vast sums to Sweden for the recent wars and all the way to Paris the towns of France decked themselves in Christina's honour as she rode through like a man, accompanied by some of the greatest nobles in the kingdom.

The most elegant Court in France was startled by a woman who appeared in a petticoat laced with gold and silver, a tight-fitting military jacket, a crimson scarf and a vast hat with black feathers. The aristocrats were as surprised by her language and ribald laughter as by her perfect French and knowledge of their country, and although Louis XIV found her interesting for a short time, her behaviour became so shocking that he was glad to see her depart and she returned to Italy penniless, and as lonely as ever.

From this time onwards, Christina's life was a succession of scenes, scandals and disappointments. Her dream of becoming Queen of Naples ended in ridiculous failure, as did a later plan to take the throne of Poland. She returned to France where, discovering the treachery of Monaldeschi, she had him murdered in the presence of a priest, while she herself stood in the next room with the door ajar. This was too much, even for the French Court, and Christina was obliged to quit the kingdom.

In Rome, where another residence was provided to take the place of the gutted Farnese Palace, the Queen made plans to visit her own country, for Charles Gustavus was dead and she felt that the people might welcome her back. As always, the visit was a failure, for Christina persisted in offending everybody by celebrating Mass in a room of the palace. This was brave but tactless and the Swedes reacted by sending a party to pull the room down, whereupon their ex-

Queen was seen punching and kicking the workmen who were trying to carry out their orders. Amid much ill-will, she left the country and went back to her hard-up, tempestuous existence in Rome.

Years went by and the Queen, growing middle-aged and stout, began to realise that all her great plans had come to nothing. She had made her mark in the world only as an oddity, a bizarre figure who could shock but could not win the love and affection for which she craved, nor even the fame that her talents could have earned.

She lived on a pension given her by the Pope. There were quarrels, bouts of temper and scenes in plenty to keep people's tongues wagging but, by this time, the Swedish Amazon was part of the landscape. With a certain amount of pride, people pointed to the plump little woman going by in her shabby old coach—she was a rarity, that one, and whatever was said about her, she had plenty of spirit.

She defied the Pope, defended her rascally servants from the police, half-throttled one who disobeyed her and brandished a pistol in the face of the authorities who came to protest. Yet she was deeply fond of her maid Georgina and her generosity to her friends was as open-handed as ever.

Cheerful and fiery to the end, she died at Rome in 1689, in the presence of Georgina and an old friend, Cardinal Azzolini, the only persons in the world who really cared for her.

More about Queen Christina (1626–89)

The strange career of Queen Christina occurred during Sweden's brief period as a Great Power.

Her ancestor, Gustavus Vasa, threw off the Danish yoke and was proclaimed King of Sweden in 1523. Gustavus was a strong ruler who controlled the nobles and greatly increased Sweden's trade. In his reign, the country adopted the Lutheran religion. Two sons tried to restore Roman Catholicism and his grandson, Sigismund, who was also King of Poland, was deposed in favour of his uncle Charles IX, in 1600.

Charles IX restored order but was constantly at war with Denmark, Poland and Russia. He left a vigorous kingdom and his aim of forming a Protestant League to his son, the great Gustavus Adolphus (1594–1632), who was killed in battle during the Thirty Years' War. In Christina's reign, Sweden controlled large areas of northern Germany and most of the trade of the Baltic Sea, which was called 'the Swedish Lake'.

Christina's cousin, Charles Gustavus (Charles X) added more territory to Sweden's empire. He died in 1660, leaving a baby son (Charles XI) who proved to be yet another warrior-king.

It was under Charles XII (1682–1718), 'the wonder of Europe', that Sweden's fortunes began to decline. This brilliant general won many victories over his enemies but the effort exhausted a country whose real wealth and population were small. By the middle of the 18th century, Sweden could no longer rival Russia and Prussia, the rising giants of the North.

The two fugitives climbed into a huge oak-tree, in which they were hidden by dense foliage.

CHARLES II, THE KING'S ESCAPE

At about six o'clock in the evening, Cromwell's Ironsides had forced their way into Worcester where, in cobbled yards and streets slippery with blood, they tore the Royalist army to pieces.

Charles II was twenty-one. He had fought well and was still trying to rally his men when the fleeing cavalry swept him out through St Martin's Gate. A mile away, he pulled up on a heath with fifty of his officers and lords and angrily surveyed the remnants of his army pounding by in headlong flight.

'My Lord Wilmot,' he cried, 'Can we not make a stand?'

'Men who desert when their ranks are whole, are worthless in defeat,' answered the stout cavalryman. 'Let us quit their company, Sire, while we can.'

Leaving the line of fugitives, the Cavaliers galloped across country, guided by a Catholic gentleman and his servant, Francis Yates, who was later hanged for his part in the adventure. They passed through the sleeping town of Stourbridge, walking their horses to avoid attention, and came at dawn to the ruined convent of Whiteladies.

Here they were met by the Penderels, a loyal family of five brothers, small farmers and foresters, who did their best to supply the tired horsemen with beer and bread. Lord Derby told them that they must preserve the King.

'We are honoured, my lord,' replied Richard Penderal, 'if it cost our lives.'

Within an hour, the King was dressed in a coarse shirt, green threadbare breeches, and old leather doublet and darned stockings. A pair of patched shoes were too small until they were slit down the back and the King grinned ruefully as he tried a few steps in them. A greasy steeplechat did not hide his black curly locks, so Wilmot began to hack them off with a knife, until Richard Penderel completed the job with a pair of shears. Laughing at his lords' dismay, Charles put his hands into the chimney-place to complete his make-up by blackening his face and neck with soot.

Since a troop of followers would be fatal to the King's chance of escape, his lords left him but, first, they begged him not to tell them his plans, lest they gave him away under torture. Only Wilmot knew that Charles hoped to reach London and he promised to meet him there at a certain inn.

By this time, it was growing light and Richard Penderel took Charles to hide in a little wood. All day, he crouched in a spinney, alone with his thoughts. He remembered how, as boys, he and his brother had watched the first battle of the Civil War when his cousin Rupert had charged so gallantly. He remembered how his father had lost the war and, afterwards, his life. There had been years in France with his mother and then, only a year ago, he had landed in Scotland full of high hopes of marching to England to win his throne. He had got as far as Worcester where Cromwell had crushed his hopes as if they were eggshells and now, hungry and drenched with rain, he had sunk as low as the poorest fugitive in the kingdom.

A twig cracked and Charles sprang up, clutching his hedger's bill-hook, but it was Richard's sister, Elizabeth Penderel, who had come with a bowl of milk and some boiled eggs. Presently, Richard himself arrived. The roads, he said, were choked with troops and Roundheads were everywhere. It would be madness to try to reach London but, in Wales, there were many who would befriend their King. The best hope, therefore, lay in crossing the Severn that night.

It was nine miles to the ferry where they hoped to cross the Severn and Charles was soon exhausted. He had had no rest for days; it was pitch dark and he stumbled repeatedly as he followed Richard across rough country. Every step was an agony in those ill-fitting shoes, so he threw them away and walked in his stockinged feet which were soon raw and bleeding.

At one place, the King and his guide passed through the yard of a small mill disturbing the miller, who came out with a lantern: 'Who's there?' he called.

'Neighbours, going home,' answered Richard.

'If ye be neighbours, show yourselves!' roared the miller but, taking him for a Roundhead, the two fled blindly up a muddy lane and through a thicket until the shouts had died away. Charles flung himself down, declaring he could not go another step. Anxiously, Richard helped him up and persuaded him to make one more effort to reach the house of an old Royalist named Woolf.

It was midnight when Richard tapped at Woolf's door and asked him to help an escaped Cavalier across the Severn. The old fellow shook his head: 'With the village full of soldiers, I would not venture my neck for any man, unless it were the King himself.'

Penderel blurted out that it *was* the King and Woolf at once offered to help him. His own house had already been searched, so the travellers must hide in the barn until he had seen what could be done.

Next evening, Woolf and his daughter came to the hayloft with food, clean stockings and shoes, but they also brought word that the ferry was heavily guarded and there was no hope of crossing the river. There was nothing for it but to go back.

Another night of hard trudging brought them to Boscobel House, the home of William Penderel, where the King was delighted to find Colonel Carless who had fought at Worcester and who had news that Lord Wilmot was hiding not far away at Moseley Hall.

By the time William's wife had washed the King's feet and lanced the blisters, it was daylight and unsafe to remain in the house. The barns and ricks were such obvious hiding-places that the two fugitives climbed into a huge oak-tree, in which they were hidden by dense foliage. Almost at once, a party of soldiers arrived to patrol the woods.

Presently, the tired King fell asleep on the colonel's shoulder. Carless dared not move and his arm became numb and extremely painful. He was about to wake his companion when he realised that Cromwellian troopers were immediately below the branches. Charles stirred in his sleep and Carless feared that he would fall, since his own useless arm could no longer support him; very gently, he pinched the King until he awoke sufficiently to realise their peril. At last, the soldiers went away and the pair descended, cramped and stiff, from their hiding-place.

Next day, being Sunday, when the Puritans were at their prayers, the fugitives were able to rest in an attic. Humphrey Penderel came in to tell them that a proclamation threatened death to anyone who should conceal 'Charles Stuart, a long dark man above two yards high', and there was a reward of £1,000 for his discovery.

'Such a sum is a sore temptation to poor people,' remarked Charles.

'Were it a thousand times as great, it were to no purpose,' replied the faithful Penderel.

It was agreed that Charles should join Lord Wilmot, who was reported to be as bold and cheerful as ever. He scorned disguise, declaring, 'Cromwell's rogues be too thick-headed to recognise a gentleman.'

That night, having said farewell to Colonel Carless, Charles made the eight-mile journey to Moseley with the Penderels and Yates. Near the house, three of the brothers turned back with the old horse that had carried the lame King. A little way on, Charles realised what he had done. Limping back after the three, he whispered: 'I do beseech your pardon for forgetting, in my troubles, to thank my friends.' In the dark wood, the brothers knelt and kissed their sovereign's hand.

At Moseley, Mr Whitgreave, owner of the house, and Father Huddlestone, a priest, conducted the bedraggled King to an upstairs room where Wilmot was waiting. Charles was still cheerful and declared that the priest-hole was the most capital place he had ever been in. With a clean shirt on and a glass of wine in his hand, he cried to Wilmot, 'If God provide me with an army, I am more than ready and willing to drive all the rogues out of my kingdom.'

Not long afterwards, Colonel Lane rode over from Bentley, near Wolverhampton, with a plan to take Charles to Bristol, disguised as 'Will Jackson', a servant of Jane, the colonel's young sister, who had a pass to visit her cousin. Another cousin, Henry Lassels, would accompany the pair, while Wilmot made his own way.

Jane's mother, who was not in the secret, was puzzled that 'Jackson' seemed so clumsy for a servant and, somewhat doubtfully, she waved goodbye to her pretty daughter, riding pillion behind the tall young man in a brown suit.

The travellers made good progress and reached Stratford-on-Avon that evening, where they had to ride past a troop of horses in the main street. Jackson raised his tall hat civilly and they returned the salute, noting with approval, the cropped hair of the serving-man.

Having ridden fifty miles, the three stopped for the night at Long Marston at the house of a relative of the Lanes. Charles took supper in the kitchen, where the cook told him to turn the roasting-jack. He was so awkward that the other servants guffawed and the cook angrily asked what sort of a countryman was he who could not even wind a jack.

'I am a poor tenant's son from Staffordshire,' said Charles dolefully. 'We seldom get roast-meat and when we do, we never use a jack.'

Next day, they rode through the Cotswolds, staying a night at an inn in Cirencester, and then came to Bristol and, by late afternoon, to Abbotsleigh, the home of Jane's cousin, Mrs Norton.

As they approached the big house, Charles whispered to Jane that among the spectators of a game of bowls on the lawn, he could see a certain Doctor George, who had once been his chaplain. The man would surely recognise him and give him away, if only through surprise. Jane was equal to the occasion. She told Pope the butler that her servant was sick and must have a room to himself. However, the Doctor, learning that there was a sick man upstairs, insisted on going to feel his pulse. Fortunately, the room was dark and Charles, already in bed, answered in a mumbling kind of way and kept his face in the shadows, pretending to be sleepy.

The Doctor departed next morning and Charles went cheerfully to breakfast in the kitchen where the servants were discussing the recent battle. One gave such a detailed account that Charles asked him how he knew so much.

'Because I fought in the King's regiment.'

'What, in the regiment of Colonel King of Cromwell's army?'

'Not I. In Major Broughton's company of the guards of His Majesty the King!'

'And did you see him?'

'As plain as I see you. Dark, he is, of countenance, long hair and tall—taller than you, my good fellow, by three inches!'

This narrow squeak startled Charles who, realising that Pope the butler was staring at him in a curious way, went into the garden. Presently, Lassels came out in great alarm to say that Pope had recognised him. Charles went upstairs, asking that the butler be sent to see him. Pope closed the door and fell on his knees, declaring that, far from betraying the King, he was more than willing to risk his life to save him.

The butler was as good as his word. He met Wilmot and hid him, lest any of the guests recognised him; then he went into Bristol, only to find that no ship was sailing to France for a month, so he made arrangements for a safer hiding-place in Colonel Wyndham's house at Trent, on the borders of Somerset and Dorset.

Wilmot slipped away unseen and Charles, Jane and Lassels were about to set off when Mrs Norton gave birth to a still-born child and was gravely ill. How could her cousins depart at such a time? Charles had a quiet word with Pope who, at supper, handed a letter to Mistress Jane. Acting her part, Jane tearfully told the company that her father was so ill that he was likely to die. Jackson must take her home at once.

They started out as if to the Midlands but presently turned south and came eventually to Trent where Colonel Wyndham, having got his servants out of the way, hustled the travellers indoors. Jane and Lassels said good-bye and Charles lay hidden upstairs for several days, unknown to any of the household apart from the Colonel's family and two loyal maids who cooked the King's food and conveyed it to him by a rope and pulley in the chimney.

The villagers were Cromwellians and, one day, on enquiring why the bells were ringing, Charles was amused to learn that a returned trooper was boasting that he had killed the King and was wearing his buff coat. In celebration, his neighbours had lit a bonfire and were pealing the church bells.

Meanwhile, Colonel Wyndham had been visiting his Royalist friends. He brought back money and the names of two gentlemen in Lyme Regis who might know of a boat. One of these, Captain Ellesdon, found a skipper named Limbry who was willing to carry two Cavaliers to France.

At this splendid news, Peters, the colonel's trusted servant, went to the coastal village of Charmouth to book two rooms at the inn. To disarm suspicion, he told the landlady a tale about a nobleman who was running away with an orphan girl because her guardian opposed their marriage.

On 22nd September, Charles left Trent in the guise of groom to Juliana Coningsby, cousin to Colonel Wyndham. Wilmot and Peters followed. At the inn, Juliana and Wilmot played the part of the runaway lovers and Charles served at table, while Wyndham and Peters went to the beach to await the arrival of Limbry's boat.

Hour after hour they waited until, by dawn, it was clear that Limbry had failed them. They did not know that the skipper's wife, discovering the reason for his voyage, had locked her husband in a bedroom until he promised to give up so risky a venture. It was essential to get Charles away from the inn, where the visitors had caused far too much excitement, so he, Wyndham and Juliana set out for Bridport, leaving Wilmot and Peters to follow.

Wilmot's horse had cast a shoe and was taken by the ostler to the local smith who noticed that the other shoes were of Midland make which tallied ill with the story that the lovers had come from Exeter. The ostler, already suspicious, returned the horse and hurried off to see the parson. However, the clergyman was at his prayers, so the ostler went back to the inn in time to see the jovial Wilmot ride off with Peters. He gazed after them and scratched his head. Suppose Charles Stuart was one of the the mysterious visitors, there was a fine reward going a-begging. He went with his tale to his local Justice of the Peace who merely hummed and hawed. The ostler reported next to Captain Massey, commander of a troop of Roundhead Militia, who immediately called out his men and galloped away to Bridport.

Unaware of their danger, the royal party had reached an inn at Bridport where Wyndham and Juliana went in to a meal, while Charles took the horses past a knot of soldiers into the yard. An ostler came across with some oats and, looking hard at the King, said: 'Sure and I know your face?'

Charles, keeping cool, replied: 'Well now, where could it be we met? Was it here?'

'Not here,' said the ostler, 'I have it! In Exeter, where I worked at the inn next to

Mr Potter's, the merchant.'

Without turning a hair, Charles answered: 'Friend, you certainly saw me there, for I served Mr Potter above a year.'

'Ah, that's it then. I remember you a boy there. We must drink a pot of beer together.'

Charles excused himself, saying that he must attend to his master's dinner. As quickly as possible, the three left by the London road and met Wilmot and Peters outside the town. A quarter of an hour later, Massey's troopers arrived at the inn and, discovering the route taken by the fugitives, came on after them.

Luckily, the travellers had found the main road too busy and had turned inland. By dusk, they were lost in the Dorset uplands but, on enquiring the way at a lonely inn, Wyndham recognised the landlord as an old family servant and was able to obtain rooms for the night. No sooner were they in bed, than a company of soldiers arrived and demanded lodging. Fortunately the troopers were so noisy and quarrelsome that they did not bother to penetrate to the attics where Charles and his companions lay listening to the uproar.

At daybreak, the soldiers resumed their march to the coast and the King was able to make his way back to Trent with his friends.

He stayed there for another eleven days, while the Royalists did their utmost to find a ship. Fresh plans were made and a new hiding-place was agreed upon at Heale House, near Salisbury, the home of Mrs Hyde, whose family had served Charles I. When the King arrived, riding as groom to Juliana, Mrs Hyde immediately recognised him but managed to conceal her excitement until, at supper, she could not help serving him first from a dish of larks. She raised her glass and Charles, seeing that he was known, returned the toast with a silent smile.

For several days, unknown to the servants, Mrs Hyde and her sister waited on the King in a tiny room, while Wilmot got into touch with a Sussex gentleman named George Gounter who had already been heavily fined for his Royalist activities. When he heard what was afoot, the gallant Gounter declared: 'The rogues have had my estates, they can have my life into the bargain if we can but get the King safe into France.'

With the help of Mr Mansell of Chichester, Gounter made an agreement with Nicholas Tattersall, master of a coal-brig, to carry two Cavaliers across the Channel for the sum of sixty pounds. All that remained was to get them down to the fishing village of Brighthelmstone or Brighton.

Gounter had a sister, Mrs Symons, living at Broadhalfpenny Down, Hambledown, and he called on her to tell her that he would bring some friends to stay the night after a day's coursing. On October 13th, the party arrived and was welcomed into the parlour by Mrs Symons. Presently, Mr Symons came home, merry with drink and determined to make his guests equally happy.

Filling the tankards with a generous hand, he peered at the King's solemn face and cropped hair. 'H'm, what's this?' he cried, 'A Roundhead in my house. I never knew you to keep Roundhead company, brother-in-law.'

Gounter assured him that the man was a friend and harmless, but Symons

insisted on calling him 'Brother Roundhead' throughout the evening until, at ten o'clock, pretending to dislike drink and strong language, Charles departed to bed, leaving the others with their host.

Early next morning, Wilmot, Gounter, his cousin and a servant set out with Charles on the long ride to the coast. They had some narrow shaves on the way, passing close to the Governor of Arundel Castle and being forced off the road by a cavalry troop which galloped past without a glance but, at length, they reached the 'George Inn' at Brighton where they sat down to supper with Mr Mansell and the skipper, Tattersall. The King was in high spirits, drinking their healths and joking with 'Mr Barlow', which was his name for Wilmot.

After the meal, Tattersall took Mansell aside, 'You have not dealt fairly with me, sir,' he muttered. 'That gentleman Mr Jackson is the King and I know him to be so.'

Mansell denied it but Tattersall was certain. He remembered the King from the time when Charles had commanded his father's fleet in the Channel. He had actually been captured but Charles had let him go.

'So be easy in your mind,' went on the skipper, 'I know my duty and with God's help will set His Majesty safe on shore in France.'

The fugitives sighed with relief, but Charles sensibly insisted on keeping Tattersall with them in case he changed his mind.

There was one more incident. The landlord, an old guardsman, approached the King and suddenly seized his hand and kissed it, saying, 'God bless you, Sire, wheresoever you go. I do not doubt, before I die, to be a lord and my wife a lady!'

The King laughed and said he would not forget a soldier's loyalty.

At two o'clock in the morning, Gounter called Charles and Wilmot and led them down to the beach. Bidding farewell to their friend, they went aboard Tattersall's brig, 'The Surprise', to wait for the tide.

At seven, the vessel was under way, sailing along the coast as if for Poole, with Charles, who loved the sea, walking the deck, happily cracking jokes with the crew, while the faithful Gounter rode along the shore anxiously watching the receding sails. In the evening, Charles set about persuading the crew to alter course, telling them that he and Wilmot were distressed merchants, afraid of being arrested for debt, but if only they could get to France, there was money owing them in Rouen.

When their likable passenger produced twenty shillings for drink, the crew declared that they would do it if he would talk the master round. Tattersall pretended to be unwilling but he eventually yielded to the arguments of his own crew.

On Thursday, 16th October 1651, two ill-kempt men stepped ashore near Fécamp. One was the King of England and the other was Lord Wilmot. It was exactly six weeks since the battle of Worcester.

More about Charles II (1630–85)

Nine years passed before Charles returned to England to be welcomed joyfully by a nation tired of Puritan rule. He rewarded those who had helped him to escape, but he was not able to restore the fortunes of many ruined Cavaliers.

His reign was marked by the Plague, the Great Fire, the Dutch Wars and many secret intrigues with France. Charles longed to rule without his argumentative parliaments, but he was careful to avoid endangering his throne, for he was determined, he said, never 'to go again to my travels'.

Years of exile and poverty had made him easy-going and fond of pleasure. He appeared to be lazy, preferring a witty jest to serious business and his Court was notorious for its scandalous gaiety and for the number of the King's lady-loves.

'The Merry Monarch', as he was called, was really an intelligent, talented man. He was fascinated by scientific experiments, astronomy, and everything to do with ships. Maps, clocks, mathematics, architecture, yachts, race-horses, flowers, music and the theatre all filled him with enthusiasm and, in his reign, there were many important advances in Britain in science and in the arts.

That Charles was able to wander about the country for six weeks after Worcester was not entirely due to luck. Cromwell's spies and agents were everywhere but, as we have seen, there were still many Royalists ready to die for the cause they believed in. Moreover, Charles was only sixteen when he had been forced to leave England after his father's defeat, so very few of his enemies knew what he looked like, only that he was 'a tall black man, six feet two inches high'.

Opposite *Portrait of Queen Elizabeth around the time of the Armada*

LOUIS, THE SUN-KING

At the age of five, Louis XIV became King of France. He was a grave, quiet little boy, whose only playmates were the children of palace servants. 'He laughs rarely in his childish games,' remarked a foreign ambassador, 'and stands for long periods without moving. He knows he is the King and wishes everyone else to know it too.'

Knowing that he was King did not help Louis very much because, although his Spanish mother, the Queen Regent, adored him, she was entirely under the influence of Cardinal Mazarin who was determined to be the real ruler of France. So the boy was kept in the background, surrounded by the Cardinal's spies.

Louis' mother gave him religious instruction every day but he had little other training or education. The Royal Tutor reported that he was so lazy that he could teach him nothing: 'I see no point in reading books' retorted the young King.

But the lonely boy who hated lessons was naturally charming and polite. An Englishman in Paris saw him riding in a procession, 'like a young Apollo, in a suit so covered with embroidery that one could perceive nothing of the stuff under it; he went almost the whole way with his hat in his hand, saluting the ladies. He seemed a prince of a grave yet sweet countenance'.

While Louis was a boy, there was civil war between the followers of the Queen Regent and some of the great nobles, and the young King suffered the humiliation of being hustled into a coach to escape from Paris, of being peered at and pawed by the mob. When the Royal Family returned, the Parisians insisted on seeing the King to make sure he had not been murdered, and Louis lay in his bed, trembling with rage, while some of the mob burst into his room and stared at him.

He kept silent but he never forgot. All his life he hated Paris, and distrusted the great nobles:

'When I am master,' he said to himself, 'I shall not live in Paris and I shall not allow the nobles to behave like princes with their private armies and fortified towns. There will be no royal uncle and no Mazarin to tell me when I may come and when I must go. I shall be King!'

He had to wait until Mazarin died in 1661. On the next day, Louis announced that he would be his own Prime Minister. He was 22 years old and his reign had really begun.

Opposite *King Louis XIV at the age of ten*

France was delighted. The people were sick of Mazarin's rule, and all classes gave a joyous welcome to their young King. He was handsome and wonderfully dignified; his marriage to Marie-Thérèse of Spain brought peace between the two countries and everyone felt that a glorious reign was beginning.

At first, all went well, Colbert, the Minister of Finance, was a brilliant man with many ideas for improving the kingdom; industry was encouraged, trade grew prosperous and colonies were founded overseas; roads and canals were improved, the Army was reorganised and the strength of the Navy was increased from 20 to 200 ships.

Though the King still disliked his capital, Paris was cleaned, paved and given a police force.

In all these reforms, Louis showed enthusiasm and ability. He had an excellent memory for detail, and he had entirely thrown off his boyish laziness. Every morning he worked with his ministers and in the afternoon, he met his Council. He also spent an hour or two at Latin or another language, because, he said, 'I find it shameful to be ignorant.' In all his activities—working, building, hunting, dancing, even eating—Louis exhausted his ministers and companions by his tremendous energy.

The evening entertainment at Court began punctually at six o'clock and went on until ten, when the King supped in state and afterwards attended a ball, a musical concert, the ballet or some magnificent form of amusement until two or three in the morning. Often, he would slip away from the festivities to continue his work, and he kept up this programme year in and year out, for his sense of duty and an iron constitution never allowed him to be tired.

He trusted no one and meant to keep all power in his own hands: 'Never leave to another anything which you can do yourself,' was one of his sayings, but there were problems that even the Grand Monarch could not solve.

The curse of France was unfair taxation. The nobles and the rich churchmen paid almost no taxes at all; the middle-class paid as little as possible, and the cost of all Louis' schemes, of the Court, the Army and the Navy fell heaviest upon the poorest citizens in the land. Worse, the taxes were collected so dishonestly that barely half the money squeezed from the groaning peasants ever reached the Treasury.

Although Louis XIV is often regarded as a hard-hearted tyrant, he was naturally a generous man who was moved by suffering when it came to his notice.

At a time of famine, he had foreign corn given away to the poor: 'I never spent money to better purpose,' he said, and he was constantly making gifts to courtiers who were in difficulties, and to his servants, even remembering to send £100 as a wedding-present to the granddaughter of his old nurse.

He punished officers who cheated the soldiers and executed an overseer who defrauded the workmen at Versailles but, despite his generosity, Louis did not understand money. He squandered fantastic sums on wars and palaces, without a thought for where the money came from and, although he compelled the nobles to obey him like puppets, he did not use his power to make them improve their estates and care for the downtrodden peasants.

The first years of the King's 'personal rule' were brilliantly successful. He had a number of able ministers besides Colbert, all men of the middle-class who owed everything to his favour and were therefore absolutely loyal. As for the nobles, Louis cut away their power by insisting that they should live permanently at Court under his eye. He never forgot a face and knew every nobleman by sight. If one was absent from the evening ceremony, he would say sharply, 'I do not see him here', and afterwards, the culprit was out of favour, out of the sun. The worst fate of all was to be banished from Court to a distant estate.

To occupy these perfumed courtiers, Louis invented numerous posts that were as useless as they were decorative. At the top, there were the Grand Master of the Household, the Grand Chamberlain, the First Gentleman of the Bedchamber, the Grand Falconer and so on. Hundreds of lesser noblemen held less important positions and their wives and daughters held similar titles in the Queen's Household. As the Royal Family increased, there were more posts of honour in the Dauphin's Household and in the service of the younger princes and princesses.

Thus, the King had endless opportunities to reward those who were obedient, and the nobles of France passed their time in a ceaseless scramble for favour, fluttering about the King and living for the moment when they might be noticed, might catch his eye or actually be spoken to.

In the centre of this glittering Court which included the leading painters, architects, writers and poets of the day, Louis shone like the sun that was his emblem. He wanted glory and where should he find it except in war?

He soon found an excuse to invade the Spanish Netherlands where he captured several frontier towns.

The Powers of Europe were alarmed but Louis soothed their fears by making peace. They did not know that he planned to conquer Holland. Playing the game he loved, the Grand Monarch bought off Charles II of England by a secret treaty, and bribed Sweden and the German princes to keep aloof; then his armies, under a brilliant general named Turenne, attacked Holland and overran its defences. Just in time, the Dutch flooded their countryside to save Amsterdam and the French army was forced to retreat for the time being.

When peace was made in 1678, Louis had gained many towns and duchies, parts of the Rhineland and a new province. True, the cost had been staggering and Turenne was dead, but France—that was to say, Louis XIV—was supreme in Europe.

Naturally, the flatterers gave all the victories to the King, not to his generals. He loved military life, for he revelled in hard exercise and was quite indifferent to discomfort and cold. He would spend ten hours at a time in the saddle, reviewing troops and inspecting positions, and he liked to see to the welfare of his soldiers, to visit their bivouacs and to taste their soup to make sure it was good. But the King was no general. He busied himself so much with petty details that he could not realise the plan of a battle or of a campaign. What he really enjoyed was a siege and there were occasions when his generals would arrange a siege for his benefit instead of getting on with the war.

In later years, Louis tried to command his armies from his desk at Versailles but,

by then, his good generals had died and the younger ones were men of lower ability whose chief concern was to please their master at all costs.

However, for the moment, Louis was supreme and it was time to dazzle the world with a monument to his own glory.

From boyhood, the Monarch had loved hunting in the woods round Versailles, where his father had built a hunting-lodge. Here, in a Royal Park of 15,000 acres, in a setting of lawns, ornamental lakes, and woodlands, rose the Palace of Versailles whose extravagance astonished the world. Big enough, with the town that grew up outside the park, to house five thousand courtiers, with servants, tradesmen and hangers-on, the Palace was built to provide a sumptuous background for the Sun-King whose golden emblem blazed on every door.

Never, since the days of the Roman Emperors, had one man been surrounded by such pomp. Beneath painted ceilings, in rooms hung with tapestries and masterpieces, where the priceless furniture was changed according to the season of the year, where silent lackeys in uniforms of blue and silver lit 10,000 candles for an evening's pleasure and where hundreds of the most beautiful women and the most elegant gentlemen in the world loitered and gossiped, the Grand Monarch presided over a perpetual ballet.

The first performance took place every morning. The King's rising, or levée, was a solemn ceremony attended by only the most highly privileged. First, the Royal Family, the loftiest nobles and officials entered the Bedchamber and, as the King rose, his dressing-gown was held ready by the Grand Chamberlain. The Master of the Wardrobe pulled off the King's night-shirt by the right sleeve, the First Valet of the Bedchamber by the left sleeve. The King's brother presented the royal shirt, while the Master of the Wardrobe stood ready to pull on the royal breeches. Meanwhile, double-doors were opened and other courtiers were admitted according to rank, until four separate waves of spectators had been privileged to witness the completion of the King's toilet.

Presently, with equal solemnity, Louis proceeded to Mass in the Chapel where he gazed at the altar and the courtiers gazed at him. The whole day was parcelled out into exact periods of work for the Monarch and of idleness for the courtiers until the evening. Then, with the King's punctual appearance, came the games, the dancing and supper in state to the music of massed violins. The day ended with the ceremony of the King's retirement to bed when the most envied privilege was the right to hold the royal candlestick!

This daily routine would have been ridiculous without the King's matchless dignity. Dressed in a plain brown suit, he moved like a god among the glittering men and women, bowing here, speaking a gracious word there and lifting his hat in a manner that was grandeur itself. It was said that the brims of his hats were always encrusted with grease from his habit of raising his hat at mealtimes when he spoke to a lady. Even kings still used their fingers when eating and, for all its magnificence, the Palace was so cold in winter that soup brought from distant kitchens became congealed grease and wine froze in the glasses. But the King was never cold and no one dared to shiver.

Immensely polite himself, Louis gave new standards of behaviour to European society, for he allowed no brawling or raised voices, and he loved elegance, music and the arts. Yet he was selfish. He had no thought for anyone, only for his pleasures and his dignity, and beneath its brilliant surface, the Court was bored and spiteful. It must be said, however, that the King never shirked any of his duties and, despite his heartless treatment of the Queen, he genuinely loved children. In his old age, his greatest pleasure was to visit Saint Cyr nearby, the school for young ladies founded by Madame de Maintenon, his second wife, who was formerly governess to his children.

If the pomp of Versailles showed the world that Louis was rich and all-powerful, it so alarmed the rest of Europe that a league was formed to oppose his ambitions. When William of Orange, the bitterest enemy of France, became William III of England in 1688, the tide began to turn against the Grand Monarch.

Although the French armies won many land victories, they could not break the resistance of England and Holland and, after nine years, France was so exhausted by the struggle that Louis had to ask for peace.

Only three years later, the half-witted King of Spain died leaving all his possessions to Philip of Anjou, grandson of Louis, who immediately announced that he would support the young man and allow him to accept the Spanish crown. This situation provoked another war between France and the rest of Europe, a war in which English and Dutch sea-power and the military genius of the Duke of Marlborough were too much for France.

The battle of Blenheim destroyed a French army; the battles of Ramillies and Oudenarde wrecked the prestige of Louis and brought his country close to surrender. By 1709, a terrible year of frost and famine, France was bankrupt, its armies beaten and its King forced to sell his gold dinner-service and the silver tables from Versailles.

The allies offered peace if Louis would turn his grandson off the Spanish throne, but, in disaster, the old King showed that he still possessed his dignity: 'If I must fight,' he said, 'I prefer to fight my enemies rather than my grandchildren.'

He made one last appeal to his ragged soldiers and they responded magnificently in defence of the soil of France. News came that Marlborough had lost the favour of Queen Anne and was removed from his command:

'This will do for us all that we desire,' remarked Louis for he sensed that, with Marlborough gone, the war would peter out.

Throughout the disasters, the French King had never lost his majestic calm, but Versailles was sadly changed. The stately routine went on as punctually as ever. The courtiers still promenaded among the statues and fountains, still put on full Court dress for dinner, and schemed to catch the Sun-King's attention. But the sparkle had gone, and the Grand Monarch was an old man who had lost his glory.

His last two years were spent in sorrow for the sufferings of France and for the loss of his son, his grandson and an elder great-grandson who died one after another, leaving an ailing child as heir to the throne.

In the evenings, the King would retire to a private room to join Madame de Maintenon, and there they would sit in their armchairs like any other old couple. He was still difficult to manage, but she had turned his mind to religion and he felt more comfortable in her company than with any other human being he had ever known.

In February 1715, the Sun-King held a pageant to show a foreign ambassador that he and France were not finished. He ordered the Court to be as magnificent as in the old days and he himself appeared in gold and black, blazing with jewellery worth £50,000. He held himself as upright as ever but he looked ill and was heard, for the first time in his life, to mention the cold. Yet in July, at the age of seventy-six, he actually hunted again and took a long walk across his favourite estate. Obstinately, he carried out all his usual duties but his leg was hurting him and he began to grow weak.

When he was too ill to leave his room, he ordered his orchestra to play outside the doors during dinner, as though nothing were amiss. Then he said good-bye to his family and his servants, apologising with his usual courtesy for the trouble he was causing. On September 1st 1715, he died at Versailles, having been King of France for seventy-two years and three months, the longest reign in European history.

The Sun-King, who had dazzled Europe for more than half a century, gave France the kind of glory that the 18th century admired, but it was glory founded upon the people's poverty. Seventy-four years after his death, a hungry mob marched to Versailles and put an end to the monarchy and its splendour.

More about Louis XIV (1638–1715)

During Louis XIV's immensely long reign (1643–1715), France was the foremost country in Europe, but there was little competition from the other nations. Certainly, Holland became a prosperous sea-faring Power and Sweden was important for a short while, but Spain was declining, Austria and Germany were terribly weakened by religious wars, Prussia had not yet trained a remorseless army, Russia was only beginning to stir and England was suffering a great many ups and downs.

In the course of Louis' reign, England knew six monarchs and a dictator (Charles I, Cromwell, Charles II, James II, William III, Anne and George I), a Civil War and the bloodless Revolution of 1688. There were wars with Spain, Holland and France, battles in Ireland and Scotland, Jacobite plots and religious unrest. Yet, at the end of the reign, England was stronger and France was weaker than at the beginning.

There were four main reasons why Louis failed to take advantage of his position and abilities: his extravagance, his neglect of trade and sea-power, his persecution of the Huguenots and his ambition. This caused most of Europe to unite against him and the alliance produced, in Marlborough, one of the greatest generals in history.

Louis was succeeded by his great-grandson, Louis XV (1715–74), who tried to rule in the same manner, but he was lazy, immoral and weak. Wars and misrule increased the misery of the peasants and it was upon Louis XVI that their vengeance fell. The French Revolution broke out in 1789 and, in 1792, Louis XVI and his wife, Marie Antoinette, were guillotined.

The Tsar dealt out punishment with horrible zest.

PETER THE GREAT

The Kremlin is a vast fortress-palace in the heart of Moscow. Behind its red-brown walls are churches, towers and onion-shaped cupolas, green and gold in the winter sunlight. The gloomy palaces are honeycombed with rooms, passages, and chapels where the Dukes of Muscovy once lived and prayed.

One night, in 1683, the dim corridors rang with screams and the clatter of armed men as the fur-hatted guardsmen of the Streltzy, the Royal Guard, burst into room after room stabbing the occupants and hacking down any who stood in their way. A boy of eleven and his mother fled in terror through the passages and out by a secret doorway into the streets of Moscow to the house of a merchant in the Foreign Quarter. From there, they escaped to a lonely township where they lived in a wooden hut near a lake.

The boy was Peter and his mother, Natalie, was the second wife of the dead Tsar Alexis. After his death, there had been a ferocious struggle between the families of his two wives until Sophia, a daughter of the Tsar, urged the Streltzy Guard to cut the throats of Peter's family so that she could rule as Regent for her idiot brother, Ivan.

Peter never forgot that fearful night, nor the time when he had to fly from his hut and hide all night in the woods clad only in a night-shirt, while Sophia's men searched everywhere to kill him.

The boy grew up wild and savage-tempered. He could not read or write until his mother found a Dutch tutor to give him some lessons, but he preferred working with hammer and chisel. Best of all, he liked the games he invented for a gang of playmates, sons of cooks, grooms and seamen. Along the shore of the lake and aboard a rotting, stranded ship, the boys played battles and sieges in which Peter fought and kicked like a madman, beating his companions with whip or club and hurling them into the shallow water. Then suddenly his mood would change, and the boy, as strong as a young bear, would be all laughter and generosity, rewarding his ragged friends with gifts and with the firework-shows that fascinated him all his life.

At 17, his mother's supporters came and took him back to Moscow where he was set up as joint-Tsar with his idiot half-brother. But Peter was not yet interested in

143

ruling Russia. He left that to others while he spent his days and nights with his boon companions in the Foreign quarter, still playing crazy games and hooligan jokes. His closest friends were Patrick Gordon, a wild Scot, and Lefort, a Swiss exile with plenty of money. For several years, this trio went everywhere together, fighting, drinking and sailing boats.

When he was twenty-four, Peter decided to stop playing the fool. He would rule as Tsar of All The Russias and make his country great. He was now a giant of a man, six feet six inches tall, with enormous limbs and coarse powerful hands; his face, when not angry, was handsome, with big intelligent eyes and an eager expression. Yet he had the habits of a savage.

His country was as savage as his own character. Hardly anyone in Europe had heard of Russia in the seventeenth century, for the vast country, still known as Muscovy, admitted only a handful of foreigners to trade in furs and tallow. Ruled by the Tsar and the boyars, or nobles, the people lived in misery and fear.

There were no schools, factories, law-courts or Parliament; no navy or worthwhile army, no ports or handsome towns. The nobles were uneducated brutes who treated their wives and children as cruelly as the serfs who toiled on their vast estates. The whole country was sunk in ignorance and superstition.

This was the nation that Peter vowed to make as strong as the countries of the West that his foreign friends described. He had heard enough to know that the secret of power lay in armies and navies. Very well, he would have them both. But Russia had no seaports, except Archangel in the frozen North, for the Turks barred the way to the Black Sea and Sweden ruled all the coasts of the Baltic.

'War is the occupation of kings,' said Peter, and he made a surprise attack on Turkey and managed to capture Azov on the Black Sea. Then, realising that there was much he did not know about ships, he resolved to go to Europe to find out for himself.

The boyars and the priests were horrified. No Russian ever travelled abroad for it was death to leave the country, except as a pilgrim or diplomat. Peter therefore announced that he would permit a party of nobles to go abroad to find allies for a crusade against Turkey.

In 1697, the Grand Embassy set out, with Lefort as Ambassador-in-Chief, eleven diplomats and numerous pages, valets, musicians and four dwarfs. Also in the party was a sergeant of the guards called Peter Mikhailov, in reality the Tsar himself, who hopped in and out of this disguise whenever it suited him.

Travelling through northern Europe, the Embassy came to Holland where Peter worked for five months as a ship's carpenter in the dockyards at Amsterdam. Though he enjoyed himself, living in a little hut near the shipyard, he was disappointed to find that the Dutch built their ships out of age-old skill and knowledge of the sea. He wanted to learn about shipbuilding in a more scientific way, so he decided to go to England whose King, 'Dutch Billy', William III, was ready to welcome him as a possible ally.

To the Tsar's delight, William gave him a splendid new yacht, the *Royal Transport*, and offered him the use of Sayes Court, a beautiful house that belonged to John Evelyn, friend of Sam Pepys. Sayes Court had a famous garden but, from

Peter's point of view, its best feature was a private gate into the Royal Dockyard of Deptford. Here he could roam as he pleased, examine vessels and work—an old shipwright said afterwards, 'The Tsar of Muscovy worked with his own hands as hard as any man in the yard.'

He also went about London, visiting the Tower and Windsor Castle, calling upon William III at Kensington Palace where he went in one of the backdoors like a coachman. He went down to Portsmouth and was as excited as a schoolboy to be present at a mock sea-battle. 'I would rather be an admiral in England,' he declared, than Tsar of all the Russias.'

The Bishop of Salisbury was sent to tell him about religion and government in England. 'He is,' said the Bishop, 'a man of very hot temper and very brutal in his passion . . . has a larger measure of knowledge than might be expected . . . and seems to be designed by nature rather to be a ship-carpenter than a great prince.'

Peter liked the Bishop but he was less interested in religion than in workshops and factories. He was fascinated by the Royal Observatory, the Woolwich Arsenal where guns were made, and by the Mint. He had coin-making machinery sent back to Russia and also a coffin which was far superior to the Russian way of hollowing an entire oak tree. He loved watches and clocks and found out how to repair them; the streak of cruelty in his nature rejoiced at watching surgeons at work or at acting as dentist to his unfortunate companions.

All the time, the Tsar was enlisting seamen, shipwrights, builders and engineers to go to Russia to work for high wages, and he was also enjoying himself. With his friends, he would go roistering in the taverns or sailing on the Thames. There were mad games at Sayes Court where a fine holly hedge was ruined by wheelbarrow races in which the object was to force the Tsar and his drunken companions through the prickly wall and out the other side!

Indoors, the Muscovites behaved like barbarians. An old servant wrote to Evelyn that the house was full of people who were 'right nasty', but his master had no idea what they were at until after they had gone. The floors were covered with burns, grease and ink; the panelling and tiled stoves were smashed; door-locks and window-catches ripped out, pictures slashed, curtains and bed-linen torn to ribbons; 300 window-panes broken and all the chairs, over fifty in number, gone, probably for firewood. As for the green lawns, the trim gravel walks and flowerbeds, they were ruined beyond repair.

The Grand Embassy left England for Vienna where the Court was horrified by the Tsar's clownish pranks. Then news of a revolt by the Streltzy Guard caused Peter to hurry back to Moscow. Although Patrick Gordon, now a General, had easily put down the mutiny of a few troops, the Tsar dealt out punishment with horrible zest.

He took his revenge for the night when his family was murdered. After torture had wrung every secret from the wretched Guards, hundreds were beheaded in the Red Square, many of them by Peter himself who gloried in the slaughter. Two hundred men were hanged outside Sophia's convent and the rest were sent to die in Siberia. The power of the Streltzy was destroyed and Peter could rule as he pleased with the aid of spies and secret agents.

In this atmosphere of terror, he dealt with the boyars, ordering them to discard their old-fashioned robes, to dress as Europeans and to shave off their shaggy beards, many of which he himself hacked off with brutal relish. The nobles were forced to serve him, to pay taxes and to send their sons to be trained to work for the government. The lazy priests and monks were stripped of their riches and the peasants were dragooned into the army or into battalions for building and draining.

Russia trembled but all were helpless. 'To be near the Tsar is to be near to death', ran a popular saying, for Peter went about with a heavy stick and would thrash anyone, courtier or workman, whose stupidity roused his anger. But those who could stand his savage rage were usually well rewarded for their service.

In 1700, war was declared on Sweden, and after several defeats from the great Charles XII, the Russian generals lured the Swedes into Russia, destroying everything as they went, so that the enemy starved and died of disease. By 1709, Sweden was defeated and Russia had gained a strip of the Baltic sea-coast.

On a piece of marshy ground, Peter built the port of St Petersburg (now Leningrad), one of the marvels of the world.

He dug the first turf himself and lived in a log hut while around him thousands of serfs, prisoners and convicts built a city where there had been nothing but a desolate swamp. Architects were sent to Holland to study the methods of building on marshy land, the use of stone anywhere else in Russia was forbidden, the nobles were forced to build palaces, and 200,000 men died from exhaustion and fever. It was 'a city built on bones', but in less than ten years, Peter had one of the finest cities and best ports in Europe.

Wars went on throughout most of the reign and, as the years went by, Peter grew ever more tyrannical as he began to fear that the sullen boyars would undo his work when he was gone. For this reason, he killed his own son Alexis, and forced everyone into grovelling obedience.

The only person who could control him at all was his second wife, Catherine, formerly a servant-girl and camp-follower of the army. She was fat, dirty and dishonest; she loved drink and the barbaric jewellery with which she decked herself from head to foot. But Peter loved her for her cheerful unshockable character. He made her Empress, allowed her to cook his food and wash his clothes and, after his death, she ruled Russia for a time almost as brutally as he.

Was Peter the Great mad? His experiences as a boy left him with terrors and a love of cruelty that could never be put to rest. The Courts of Vienna and Paris certainly regarded him as an insane gorilla and he undoubtedly suffered from fits; his face constantly twitched and his great body often seemed uncontrollable. There were days when he stayed sunk in hopeless gloom, filthy and unkempt, then, suddenly, he would emerge magnificently dressed, filled with energy and gaiety. He cared nothing for human life, murdering countless people by his orders and with his own hands. He was a monster and all Russia sighed with relief when he died at the age of fifty-two. Yet he is called Peter the Great.

By superhuman will, he made Russia into a modern Power. He built an army and his beloved navy, factories and industries to supply them, a government system to support them.

He reformed the Church, the coinage, the alphabet, the calendar. He built a capital in a swamp, gave Russia a coastline, founded schools, hospitals, museums and even a newspaper.

He could not give his people justice, goodness or dignity, for he understood none of those things. But what might he have done for Russia and the world if he had been brought up with kindness and educated with goodwill?

More about Peter the Great (1672–1725)

Peter the Great (Tsar Peter I) succeeded in making Russia into a European Power. His reforms were brutal and rapid, but most of them lasted, although the nobles hated progress and the peasants became worse, rather than better off.

Peter left a line of rulers, most of them women, who were generally healthier than the male members of the Romanov family in which there was such a marked streak of insanity. Peter's second wife became the Empress Catherine I for a short while and she was followed by his grandson, the weakling, Peter II, who reigned from 1727 to 1730. Next came Peter the Great's niece, the Empress Anne and then his daughter, the Empress Elizabeth (1741–62). She chose a German princess to be the wife of her nephew Peter III, who was soon assassinated by the friends of his wife. She became the Empress Catherine the Great. Thus, it was a German woman and not one of his own descendants who was destined to carry on the work of Peter the Great.

He was forced back to the window to behold the body of his friend and the patch of blood-stained sand in the castle yard.

FREDERICK THE GREAT

'The boy is a fop, a miserable, whining nincompoop,' roared King Frederick William.

'But he is only six,' protested the trembling Queen. 'You forget that he has never been strong.'

'Forget! I do not forget that my son is Crown Prince of Prussia,' replied the furious King, banging a table with his cane. 'I'll make a man of him the same way as I make a soldier out of a ploughboy. Drill, drill, drill. I'll drill your Frenchified ideas out of the ninny!'

The little prince had fled to Madame de Roucolle, his French governess, but he was fetched back and made to stand before his father. Between blows, he learnt that two Army officers would take charge of his education from six o'clock in the morning until bedtime.

Family life at the Prussian Court was severe. At a time when every other monarch in Europe did his best to copy the elegance of Louis XIV's Versailles, the King of Prussia lived like a sergeant-major in barracks. His palace was furnished with bare boards and plain wooden furniture, the royal meals were so scanty and bad that his children were always hungry and foreign envoys could hardly swallow the food. Not a farthing was wasted and everyone in the palace, from the Queen to the cooks in the kitchen, lived in dread of the King.

Frederick William was hardly sane. He bullied his wife and his fourteen children, whom he often struck in full view of the horrified Court and he ruled his kingdom like a savage old squire on a country estate. When he went out into the streets, it was said that people fled from him as though from an escaped tiger. He would rain blows on a workman who had rested for a moment on his shovel, would aim a kick at a passing housewife and tell her to get home to her brats and he would stalk into houses to peer at the dinner on the table to make sure that there was no extravagance.

Frederick William's passion in life was the Army. He turned Prussia, a poor little country with sandy soil and barely two million inhabitants, into a military camp. He drilled his soldiers until they were the best in Europe, and the pride of his heart was the regiment of Potsdam Guards. Every man was a giant. The King who lived on bread and cabbage soup employed agents to scour Europe for tall recruits and he would order one of his ill-paid ambassadors to offer a thousand pounds to a seven-foot Irishman for joining the King's regiment.

This strange, brutal monarch made up his mind that his little son Frederick should grow up exactly like himself. He laid down rules for every minute of the boy's day, but somehow Frederick persuaded his tutors to let him dance and listen to music. He loved his French books and wanted to learn Latin and Greek which the King had forbidden. Two nervous conspirators encouraged him. His mother, Queen Sophia Dorothea, and his older sister, Wilhelmina, longed for the elegance of polite society and they rejoiced that Frederick had inherited his mother's taste for music and books. The Queen secretly hired a tutor named Quantz to teach her son to play the flute and she hoped that one day he and his sister would marry their royal cousins in England.

Meanwhile, the King had chosen one hundred and ten boys for his son to drill every day in the palace yard.

'I'll make a man of him yet,' he said with satisfaction, as he looked down from a window at the small figure marching at the head of the cadets.

But, one day, the King heard the sound of a flute from an upper room and he learned that his son was practising in secret. His anger was terrible. The boy was brought down and questioned. His father beat him with his fists, knocked him down and dragged him by the hair to a window where, but for the Queen, he would have throttled him with the cord of a curtain. After this, the King's hatred for his son became a mania.

'You think you can deceive me with your disobedience,' he bellowed, 'but I'll show you who is master of Prussia.'

The Queen did what she could to shield her son, but she had a large family and many anxieties, so it was to pretty Wilhelmina that Frederick turned for comfort. She was gay and daring, for she invented games in which they mimicked their terrible father whom she called 'The Ogre of Potsdam' and she would hide Frederick's flute in her dress, so that the King could not break it.

At fourteen, Frederick entered the regiment of guards and two years later, he was promoted to the rank of major. At last, he began to have friends and a little freedom. When his father was away inspecting the provinces, he would turn eagerly to his books and to the poems he wrote in French. His closest friend was a young officer named Lieutenant Katte who often accompanied him when he played the flute.

One evening, the friends were enjoying some music with the tutor Quantz, when Lieutenant Katte happened to glance out of the window.

'Quick!' he cried. 'The King has returned.'

Frederick tore off the silk dressing-down he was wearing and struggled into his tight uniform jacket while his friends began to gather up the piles of books and music that littered the room. A heavy tread on the stairs sent them flying into a large cupboard just before the King entered the room. He peered suspiciously at his son who was reading a military drill book. The Prince sprang to attention but the King caught sight of the edge of the red silk dressing-gown under the sofa.

Opposite *The Pope looks on as Napoleon raises the imperial crown, while Josephine kneels before him*

'What's this, you scoundrel?' he roared, pulling it out, 'What else, hey, what else have you concealed, you puppy?'

Snatching up a bundle of French books, he hurled them out of the window and bellowed to the servants to clear the room of every book and every sheet of music. As he stamped about the room, flinging Frederick's treasures to the floor, he paused now and then to rain blows on the white-lipped Prince.

At last, the Ogre departed and the terrified friends came out of their hiding-place to comfort Frederick.

'It is the end,' he cried, 'I will bear this no longer.'

That evening, he decided to escape. With Katte and another friend, Lieutenant Keith, he meant to leave Prussia and make his way to England.

In August 1730, the attempt was made. The young men planned to ride away from the royal camp at dawn and Frederick was about to place his foot in the stirrup when a hand fell upon his shoulder.

'Good morning, Your Highness,' said Colonel von Rochow. 'It is early for a ride.'

Rochow, guardian of the Crown Prince, had heard a rumour on the previous evening and had arisen in time to see two cloaked figures waiting in the mist for their horses. He reported to the King and was ordered to keep the culprits under close arrest and to kill them if they attempted to escape.

Frederick managed to get word to Lieutenant Keith, who fled to England, but he and Katte were imprisoned in the fortress of Kustrin, where they were to be tried as deserters from the army.

Frederick remained noticeably cheerful.

'I ask no favours for myself,' he said haughtily to the officers who were sent to question him. 'But Lieutenant Katte is guiltless. The plan was mine and he acted only as I commanded him.'

But there was no mercy. The Crown Prince was treated worse than a criminal. His cell door was opened only to admit food three times a day and he was not allowed visitors, books, papers, nor even a light. He received no word from the outside world, apart from a message that his mother was never to hear his name again and his sister was locked up in Berlin.

In November, two officers entered his cell at five o'clock in the morning.

'What news do you bring me?' enquired Frederick.

'His Majesty the King commands that Your Highness shall witness the execution of Lieutenant Katte.'

Frederick was horrified. For two hours, he stormed, wept and pleaded with the officers to carry a message to the King. He offered to give up his right to the Crown, his liberty, his own life, if Katte could be spared.

At seven o'clock, held against the bars of the window by two soldiers, the Prince saw Lieutenant Katte marched into the courtyard below.

'Pardon! Pardon me!' shrieked Frederick.

The condemned man paused and looked up smiling. 'Do not ask for pardon, Sire,' he called, 'I am happy to die in the service of my beloved prince.'

When the axe descended, Frederick fainted, but he was brought round and

Opposite *George VI and Queen Elizabeth in the royal lodge, Windsor, with Princess Elizabeth and Princess Margaret*

forced back to the window to behold the body of his friend and the patch of blood-stained sand in the castle yard.

Next day, when the prison chaplain came to urge him to repent, Frederick was delirious. He fainted many times, raved like a man in a fever and often dragged himself to the window to peer at the spot where his friend had died. Nine days later, his brain cleared and the chaplain reported to the King that the Prince was a changed man.

He was very quiet and submissive, declaring in a low voice that he repented his wicked disobedience and asked only for his father's pardon. Some weeks later, the King ordered him to be sent to work as a clerk in one of the State offices, where he was to be guarded, to speak to no one and to be allowed no liberty whatsoever.

A year after the execution of his friend, Frederick was summoned to Berlin for the wedding of Wilhelmina who had agreed to marry a man whom she did not love if her beloved brother could come to the wedding. Frederick hardly dared speak to her or to show sympathy in the matter of her marriage.

'My son begins to know his duty,' muttered the King with approval and he promised to restore him to his army rank.

Frederick breathed a sigh of relief. He had forced himself to act the part of a sorrowful son, to hide his feelings and to deceive everyone. He hated his father but he knew that he was the master. His own heart had died when his one true friend had been executed; nothing could hurt him anymore and he lived only for the day when he would be King of Prussia.

He learned that his father considered it was time for him to marry. His bride was to be Princess Elizabeth of Brunswick, a sweet, timid girl of sixteen, who had never seen her future husband. Frederick received the news with cool contempt.

'Then there will be one more unhappy princess in the world,' he remarked, 'I shall put her away as soon as I am master, but at least she has won me my liberty.'

When the young couple were married, the King gave them an estate at Rheinsberg where, for the only time in his life, Frederick was happy. He ignored his poor little bride, but he rejoiced in freedom and built a charming chateau called "Sans Souci", which means 'Without Care'. It was decorated and furnished in the French style and laid out with lawns, gardens, pavilions and a lake.

At Sans Souci, Frederick studied hard and surrounded himself with a gathering of scientists, writers and musicians. Concerts and plays were held in which the Prince himself took part and every evening, there was a dinner-party at which the conversation, always in French, became famous for its wit and new ideas. The Prince wrote many essays and poems and he began to exchange letters with Voltaire, the most brilliant writer in France.

'It was at Sans Souci,' he said, 'that I began to live.'

This pleasant life was interrupted when Frederick had to take his regiment to serve with the Austrian army under the command of the aged hero, Prince Eugene. Frederick did not see much action but he noted the way a great commander bore himself and he also noted that the famous Austrian troops were not a patch on his own Prussian soldiers.

The taste of war was enough to make him ask the King for permission to return in the following year, but Frederick William refused. He did not want to risk his precious guardsmen and he was beginning to fail. He suffered from dropsy and his temper was as vile as ever but he had come to approve of his son.

'I've done it,' he growled, 'I've made a man out of the weakling. He's a soldier now, my son, and he'll be a King of Prussia after all.'

Towards the end of his life, the old ogre believed that he had been tricked by Austria and by some of his own ministers: pointing to Frederick with his cane, he roared, 'There stands one who will avenge me. When I am dead, you will say, "Well that's the end of the old bully"—but believe me, he who is to succeed me, will tell you all to go to hell!'

In 1740, the King died and Frederick became King of Prussia. His friends at Sans Souci rejoiced at the thought of a poet-king and they saw themselves raised to fame and wealth. They were sadly disappointed. Looking round at his friends with their violins and books, Frederick snapped: 'No more of these fooleries. I have other work to do.'

More than anything else, he wanted fame as a general and the opportunity came almost at once. The Emperor of Austria died and was succeeded by his daughter, Maria Theresa, a beautiful, noble-hearted young woman, who received messages of friendship from many of Europe's princes, including the King of Prussia.

Yet, as he wrote so kindly, Frederick had already ordered his army to readiness. He wanted Silesia, one of Maria Theresa's richest provinces that lay next to Prussia.

'The question of right is your affair,' he said to a minister. 'Work it out secretly, for my orders to the troops have been given.'

The Prussian army seized Silesia without warning and then Frederick sent letters to the rulers of Europe explaining his 'right' to the province. He knew it was untrue, for he admitted to his old tutor, 'I did it for glory, to make people talk about me and to see my name in history.'

Once Frederick had turned thief, there were others to follow his example and Maria Theresa found herself surrounded by greedy foes. With brave indignation, she appealed to her people and fought back with all her strength: she never forgave Frederick and always spoke of him bitterly as 'the Monster'.

The Austrian army met the Prussians at Mollwitz, and, at first, the Austrian cavalry swept all before them. Frederick, confused in his first great battle, was persuaded by his generals to escape before he was captured and he galloped away at such speed that he outdistanced all his attendants, save one. Meanwhile, the Prussian infantry fought so stubbornly that they turned defeat into victory and the news was carried to Frederick, thirty miles away. He was so shocked by his own conduct that he could never speak about it, but for the rest of his career, he put himself into danger with a recklessness that filled his men with dismay and admiration.

Next year, Maria Theresa made peace, allowing Prussia to keep Silesia, though she intended to win it back as soon as possible. Knowing this, Frederick worked

untiringly to strengthen his army and when, in 1744, he learned that Maria Theresa, having defeated her other foes, was about to turn on Prussia, he again attacked without warning.

Two more seasons of war brought victory and Frederick returned to Berlin in triumph. He still had Silesia but it had been a hard struggle. His treasury was empty and he had even had to melt down the family silver to pay for his soldiers' rations. Clearly, he must give his country a breathing-space to build up a class of prosperous farmers and peasants who could pay the taxes to support a huge army.

For ten years, Frederick worked harder than anyone in the kingdom and it was astonishing how like his father he became. He had the same love of order, the same passion for soldiers, the same tight-fistedness with money and something of the same delight in giving pain to others. Every day, he rose at four or five o'clock and went to his desk to read the despatches that came in at night; he then saw his ministers, directed replies to foreign governments and gave orders for every detail in the kingdom, from military pay to the method of draining marshes. When dealing with business, he often walked about from room to room playing his flute. 'It composes my mind,' he would say. He drilled his troops and regularly inspected the countryside, for he knew that farming was the source of the kingdom's wealth, but he also encouraged trade and manufactures.

Hungry for military fame, Frederick was just as eager to be known as a man of letters. He still wrote poems and volumes of history; the concerts and the learned dinner-parties still went on far into the night at Sans Souci. For nearly three years,

Voltaire himself was the star of the Court but the brilliant Frenchman, with his sharp tongue and thirst for money, outstayed his welcome and was almost chased back to France. Yet, Frederick forgave his treacherous idol and went on sending his poems to be corrected.

'The King sends me his dirty linen to wash,' remarked Voltaire when he received a batch of poems. 'He sends me more verses than he has battalions. . . . He is an exceptional man—very attractive at a distance.'

All this time, Maria Theresa remembered Silesia. She formed a league to overthrow Frederick, winning to her side the rulers of Sweden and Saxony, Louis xv of France and the Empress Elizabeth of Russia. Frederick's only ally was England but, as usual, he struck the first blow by suddenly invading Saxony.

The Seven Years' War was a long bitter struggle in which Frederick won a world-wide reputation as a general. At first, he gained a number of brilliant victories but gradually the superior numbers of his enemies wore him down. Time after time, he seemed to be doomed but always he managed to escape from the tightest corner; he was a master of manoeuvre and retreat and, just when his foes thought he was at his last gasp, he would somehow scrape together a fresh army and savagely attack the enemy. Often defeated but never routed, his Prussian soldiers served him with dauntless obedience because they knew that in 'Old Fritz', as they called their granite-hearted King, lay Prussia's only hope.

Gradually, the net tightened, as the Austrians, Russians, French and Swedes closed in upon Frederick's sorely-stricken army. Prussia was surrounded and everyone expected it to be wiped from the map. Even Frederick could see no hope.

'Next month will decide the fate of my poor country,' he wrote a friend. 'I intend to save it or to perish with it. . . . I will be buried beneath the ruins or I will put an end to my sufferings.'

At this moment, when Frederick was ready to take his own life rather than surrender, a miracle occurred. Elizabeth of Russia died as she was leaving church and her successor, the mad Tsar Peter III, a warm admirer of Frederick, immediately ordered the Russian army to withdraw. The Swedes followed and, in the next year, Frederick managed to make peace with his tired enemies.

Somehow, Prussia had survived and her King, a haggard little man, in an old uniform soiled with grease and snuff, was acclaimed the foremost general in the world. Praise made no difference to Frederick's cold nature; his mother, his sister Wilhelmina, a brother and all his friends were dead, so he avoided the festivities in his honour and went quietly home to Sans Souci.

'I have fought and struggled for twenty-three years,' he said, 'I intend to devote the rest of my days to my country's recovery.'

Prussia needed Frederick. Whole districts had been laid waste by the enemy; people, animals and buildings had disappeared and the fields lay empty for want of workers. The army's store of corn was distributed for seed, artillery horses were harnessed to ploughs, taxes were lifted in the worst-hit provinces and grants were made from the King's private fortune to build cottages and barns.

Gradually, Frederick brought his country back to life. He lived and worked like a peasant, dressed always in the same faded uniform coat, old breeches and campaign boots and, throughout his life, he never possessed more than one suit for State occasions. His people were expected to work as hard as their King but he did not mind when they grumbled; 'I let them *say* what they please,' he remarked, 'but I *do* what I please.'

Nine years after the long war, Frederick took the chance to grab another slice of territory for Prussia, when he and Catherine of Russia agreed to divide Poland. They offered a share to Austria whose ministers persuaded Maria Theresa to accept.

'The Empress wept but she took her share,' sneered her old enemy.

It was Frederick's last theft. He was growing old and attacks of gout had put an end to his flute-playing. He wrote little now but lived almost alone at Sans Souci, with only a few servants and his greyhounds for company. A few guests came occasionally to visit the bent and shabby King and, for a time, the conversation would go round with something of its old sparkle. Once, a veteran of the wars fell asleep at supper and the other guests were about to remind him of his manners when the King said, 'Let him sleep. He kept watch often enough for us.'

One day, in August 1786, Frederick began work, as usual, at five o'clock in the morning. He dictated replies to despatches, made arrangements to inspect the Guards at Potsdam and carried out the business of the day in an agony of pain. By evening, he went to sleep in his chair until eleven, when he awoke, enquired the time and said that he would rise at four next morning: there was much to be done. Then he asked for his favourite dog and told his servant to cover it with a quilt as the night was cold. He closed his eyes and never woke again.

More about Frederick the Great (1712–86)

Frederick the Great of Prussia inherited a kingdom that had been part of the Duchy of Brandenburg, one of the many small states that made up the Holy Roman Empire. His grandfather was a Duke or Elector until he coaxed the Emperor to give him the title of King Frederick I in 1701. Thus, the brutal Frederick William (who reigned from 1713 to 1740) was only the second king of Prussia.

Frederick II, 'the Great', is often regarded as the founder of modern Germany but, in fact, he had little or no interest in any of the German states except Prussia. By the end of his life, the lonely, bitter king was very unpopular, but he had shown his people that hard work and military skill could raise a poor country to the level of the Great Powers. He wished to be buried on the terrace of Sans Souci with his greyhounds, but his coffin was taken to Potsdam from which it was removed during the Second World War when the Russians were approaching Berlin, and hidden in a castle at Marburg.

Frederick was undoubtedly a wonderful general; as for his character, this is what his ally King George II of England, said about him:

'The King of Prussia is a mischievous rascal, a bad friend, a bad ally, a bad relation and a bad neighbour, in fact, the most dangerous and ill-disposed prince in Europe.'

MARIE ANTOINETTE

'She has a most graceful figure, her character, her heart are excellent. She is more intelligent than has been generally supposed. Unfortunately, up to the age of twelve, she has not been trained to concentrate in any way. Since she is rather lazy and extremely frivolous, she is hard to teach.'

This report was written by the Abbé Vermond after he had come to Vienna to act as tutor to the thirteen-year-old Archduchess Marie Antoinette. He soon discovered that the pretty little princess preferred romping with her brothers and sisters to learning her lessons with a grave Frenchman.

But the good Abbé did his best to change this merry child into an accomplished young lady. Her mother, Maria Theresa of Austria, had made an alliance with France, and Marie Antoinette was to marry the Dauphin, grandson of Louis xv. So the Empress anxiously urged her daughter to concentrate on her lessons, to acquire a perfect French accent and to try to behave in a ladylike manner.

'Do read your books, 'Toinette,' she said, 'you need reading more than almost anyone, since it is about all you are capable of, for you know little of music or drawing or dancing or painting.'

At length, Marie Antoinette said goodbye to her mother and stepped in the sumptuous carriage that was to carry her to France. Escorted by a brilliantly uniformed bodyguard, she was greeted all along the route by music and petal-strewn streets until she came at last to the park where Louis xv and his Court waited to receive her.

The elderly monarch was so enchanted by the fair-haired princess who skipped from her glass chariot and curtsied daintily that he almost forgot to introduce his grandson, Louis. The Dauphin, a tall, awkward youth, peered short-sightedly at his bride and mumbled a few words of greeting. The whole affair bored him, especially as he had had to forgo hunting for a whole day.

After their marriage, the young couple were given an apartment at Versailles. The famous palace had lost something of its glory since the days of Louis xiv, for, although it seemed as elegant and luxurious as ever, the King minded nothing but his own pleasures and the Court had become a hothouse filled with flatterers and place-seekers.

In this atmosphere, Marie Antoinette was the centre of attraction. Critical eyes watched every movement as she walked lightly through the Hall of Mirrors, accepting curtsies and bows with the grace of a born princess. It was noticed, however, that on other occasions she would skip rather than walk, would run along corridors with skirts flying and would rather romp with the Dauphin's lively brothers than pass the time with her dull husband.

At sixteen, Marie Antoinette detested the rules that governed every moment of the day at Versailles and she saw no reason for carrying on with lessons when there were so many new and delightful things to do. There were banquets, balls, concerts and riding-parties and there were gay people who were far more amusing than the sour-faced old aristocrats.

On a cloudless June day, the Dauphin and Dauphiness made their State Visit to Paris, driving through cheering crowds to the Palace of the Tuileries where, from a balcony, Marie Antoinette looked in wonderment at a sea of citizens, all of them waving and cheering with frenzied enthusiasm.

'Heavens!' she exclaimed, 'How many of them there are!'

The governor of Paris gallantly replied, 'Madam, you have before you two hundred thousand persons who have fallen in love with you.'

From that moment, Marie Antoinette was in love with Paris. She went there whenever she could steal away from her husband and the stuffy Court. When Versailles was asleep, she and her friends would visit the Opera, the theatres, the masked balls and the gaming houses. Then, at dawn, as the workers were beginning their day, the carriages bowled back to Versailles. The tired Princess believed in her innocence that not one suspected that the masked lady who danced so gloriously was really the Dauphiness. Everyone knew, of course, and since many of her so-called friends were worthless idlers, her reputation began to suffer.

But when, in 1774, Louis xv died, the people greeted the news with joy. Their young king was pious, thrifty and simple in his tastes, his wife was charming and they felt that a new age had arrived. Yet the state of France was too desperate for Louis xvi to cure.

Millions of heavily-taxed peasants toiled like beasts to support the aristocrats who did no work and paid next to nothing in taxes. The middle-class of business folk had no share in the government and they hated the privileges of the nobility. Trade, farming, the law, the army, and even the supply of food to the capital were in confusion and decay because the government was the King and for sixty years the King had neglected his duty. The new King was quite incapable of ruling.

Poor Louis xvi ought to have been a country gentleman or a blacksmith. He wished no harm to anyone in the world and merely wanted to enjoy his hunting and to follow his hobby of making locks in an upstairs workshop. Strong as a peasant, he was curiously lifeless, for nothing ever seemed to rouse him. He simply ate and slept and did what he had to do like some amiable dray-horse. His only trouble was that he was born to be King of France.

So, while one minister after another tried to set the kingdom right, Louis tinkered away at his locksmith's bench and Marie Antoinette continued to enjoy

herself. Dresses, jewels, cards and horse-racing were far more interesting than affairs of State, unless she wished to reward a relative of one of her friends. The Queen was not greedy or wicked, merely thoughtless, and when her easy-going husband mentioned some particular extravagance that a worried official had brought to his notice, she pouted sweetly and said:

'I cannot think what all the bother is about. I only want to enjoy myself.'

To please her, Louis gave the Queen a delightful summer-palace called the Little Trianon that stood in a corner of the park at Versailles. Here, Marie Antoinette created a toy realm of her own, decorating the house in delicate blues and pinks and laying out the gardens with a child's eagerness. There were little woods and winding paths that led to fairy grottoes, and the waters of a babbling stream that fed the tiny lake were brought across country to the park in specially laid pipes.

One fancy led to another. To satisfy a craze for the 'simple life', eight model farms were built in the grounds, with thatched barns, dove-cots and pretty cow-sheds. Real shepherds and milkmaids looked after real sheep and calves and the Queen and her friends, dressed enchantingly for the part, were to be seen leading woolly lambs by silken cords or milking carefully scrubbed cows into porcelain buckets.

All this time, the Queen's friends were becoming more unpopular. Marie Antoinette became fascinated by the Countess de Polignac whose relatives fastened on the friendship like vultures. Money, titles and pensions poured into their greedy palms, for the Queen could refuse nothing and the King merely shrugged his shoulders.

Suddenly, the nation learned that France was bankrupt. Venomous blame was laid on the Queen. Had she not lavished money on the Polignac set? Had she not sent millions to her brother, Joseph? Had she not spent even more on the Trianon, on jewels, dresses and gambling-parties? A flood of pamphlets, filled with lies and vile accusations, made Marie Antoinette the most hated woman in France.

Hurt, but with the pride of a Hapsburg, Marie Antoinette withdrew from the public gaze and tried to reduce her expenditure, while her husband did his best to solve the country's difficulties. Alas, he could never make up his mind to do anything definite but kept hoping that all these troubles would soon die down.

The situation grew worse and bad harvests brought hungry people crowding into Paris where, inflamed by agitators, the mob began to riot. In May 1789, the King summoned the States-General or Assembly to its first meeting for 175 years.

In an atmosphere of enthusiasm, the three 'estates'—nobility, clergy and commons—met at Versailles where the Commons, calling themselves the National Assembly, swore an oath never to go home until they had given France a new system of government.

Weeks went by and while the lawyers at Versailles made one fine speech after another, mob-leaders were at work in the back-alleys of Paris, urging the unemployed and criminals to fresh deeds of violence. On July 14th, 1789, a mob broke into a storehouse where arms were kept. Someone yelled, 'To the Bastille!' and twenty thousand excited citizens surged towards the ancient fortress. It fell with ridiculous ease and the Governor, who had seen his own troops making friends with the attackers, was murdered with horrible brutality.

The news reached Versailles after the King had gone to bed, but a Duke was sent to waken him:

'Sire, the Bastille has been taken by storm. The Governor is dead and the streets are filled with armed men.'

'You are telling me of a riot?' enquired the sleepy King.

'No, Sire, it is a revolution.'

The King could not believe it. Surely there were loyal troops in the city and was not the National Assembly forming a government to please everyone? He would go to Paris himself, but instead of punishing the Governor's murderers, he listened courteously to the complaints of the people and pinned on his hat the red-white-and-blue rosette of the Revolution. The crowd was delighted but the royalists despised a king who would not lead them.

As stories came in of landowners murdered and mansions looted, many of the aristocrats, including the King's brothers, fled from France. Carriage after carriage rumbled away from Versailles where Marie Antoinette penned a note to her friend, the Countess of Polignac: 'Goodbye, dearest friend. What a dreadful word, "goodbye" ... Here is the order for your horses. ... I am fairly well, although shaken by this succession of blows. You may be sure, however, that adversity has not lessened my strength and courage. These I shall never lose.'

By October, food was desperately short in Paris and a rumour went round that there was plenty at Versailles. Agitators egged on the women in the empty markets until, led by a brawny young woman with a drum, a procession seven thousand strong set out to ask the King for bread.

Cold and hungry, drenched to the skin by a downpour, the women reached Versailles and sent in their leaders to see the King. He received them politely and promised a supply of food if they would go home on the morrow. That night, as the tired women dried their sodden clothes in the Hall of the Assembly, agitators prowled from group to group.

'Have we tramped all this way to be fobbed off with empty promises?' they whined. 'There's food enough here for our empty bellies. If we're not careful, the King will join the runaways. Let's take him back to Paris to keep an eye on him.'

In the early hours, a crowd gathered in the courtyard of the Palace. A shot was fired. Pikes and muskets appeared as if by magic. A shout went up:

'To the Queen's apartments!'

The mob broke in and flooded up a marble staircase where the Royal Bodyguards were swept back and clubbed to the ground. As a bearded rag-picker hacked off their heads, the rabble tore upstairs. While crowbars smashed into the gilded door of her room, Marie Antoinette slipped a petticoat over her nightdress and ran along the corridor to the King's apartment, where she comforted her children and the terrified maids.

By daylight, the rebels had left the building, but a crowd outside, now ten thousand strong, kept up an incessant chant, 'The King to Paris! The King to Paris!' Eventually, Louis said that he would yield to the people's wish and when this was known, his appearance on the balcony was greeted by tumultuous cheers. But it was not enough. The hated Austrian must be humiliated.

'The Queen, the Queen on the balcony!' they yelled.

Perfectly calm, Marie Antoinette appeared with her son and daughter. 'No children!' shrieked the mob. She stepped forward alone, a pale, beautiful woman facing a crowd who loathed her. The mob stared up at the motionless figure and suddenly someone shouted, 'Long live the Queen!' Everyone took up the cry and cheered themselves hoarse as the commander of the National Guard bowed and kissed the Queen's hand.

At noon, the Royal Family left Versailles for ever. Waving the heads of the murdered guards on pikes, the mob sang songs of triumph all the way. Behind them rumbled wagons loaded with flour. 'Here we come!' they yelled as they entered Paris. 'We have brought the Baker, the Baker's wife and the Baker's son! They will give you bread!'

The captives were taken to the Tuileries, a rambling Palace with broken windows and grass-grown courtyards, but servants, furniture and carpets were soon brought from Versailles, for people pretended that the King had merely changed his residence.

Louis seemed to be paralysed. He made no move to join his brothers, to raise an army or to win popularity by appearing in public. The Queen was far more resolute. She wrote letters to her brother, the Emperor of Austria, and to many foreign rulers appealing for help, though it was difficult to see what anyone could do while her husband meekly accepted captivity. In the capital, evil, violent men took over the reins of power and even Louis came to see that his position was hopeless.

One evening, in June 1791, Marie Antoinette told her daughter's governess to dress the Princess, while she woke the Dauphin:

'Come, darling,' she whispered, 'we are going on a journey to a place where there will be lots of soldiers.'

'Then I must wear my uniform and my sword, Mamma,' replied the little boy, though he was disgusted to find that he had to put on a girl's frock and a bonnet.

When the children had been got away by friends, the Queen pretended to go to bed but, once in her room, she changed into a plain grey gown and a black hat with a veil. By a side-door, she slipped away from the Tuileries and was presently joined by the King, wearing a wig and dressed as a servant. A hackney cab brought them to the outskirts of the city where a coach stood waiting.

Alas, even when escaping, royalty had to be royal. The coach was brilliantly new, with yellow panels and white velvet upholstery. There were piles of luggage, postillions, two ladies-in-waiting and, from time to time along the route, troops of dragoons to accompany the party. The dullest country bumpkin could see that these were no ordinary travellers.

Nevertheless, the coach made good progress all night and by the following evening, when Paris was in an uproar over the escape, the fugitives were nearing the frontier. At almost the last stop to change horses, a young man named Jean Drouet noticed the magnificence of the coach.

'Hm, aristocrats escaping,' he said to himself, 'I must report this to the authorities.'

By the time Drouet had obtained a horse, the coach had rumbled on but, by taking a short cut, he got ahead and at Varennes, he told the Mayor of his suspicions. Half an hour later, when the coach arrived, an excited crowd barred the way. A lantern was thrust into the King's face and the Mayor informed the travellers that they must spend the night in a little room above his grocer's shop while enquiries were made. The travellers protested but had to agree and the King was soon helping himself to generous slices of cheese, comfortable in the knowledge that his cavalry would soon appear to rescue their sovereign.

But Drouet had roused the local populace who filled the streets and surrounded the grocer's shop. By morning, the town was packed with National Guards summoned from the surrounding villages and presently two members of the Assembly arrived. The King was recognised. The escape had failed.

A journey of bitter humiliation brought the Royal Family back to the Tuileries where their guards were doubled. From now on they were regarded as enemies of the people who had tried to join the foreign armies across the frontier. With the rallying cry, 'Our country is in danger!' the Assembly declared war on Austria and Prussia.

At first, the war went badly for the revolutionists. Some French fortresses were captured, the army was defeated and royalists took up arms in distant provinces. When the commander of the enemy forces issued a proclamation that he would destroy Paris if the King and Queen were harmed, the people of the capital rose in wrath. A vast crowd invaded the Tuileries and massacred the Swiss Guards while the Royal Family was hustled for safety into a stifling little room next to the Hall of the Assembly.

When the riot had spent itself, the King was informed that he would be moved to a gloomy fortress known as the Temple. All his personal servants were dismissed and although he and the Queen were allotted four rooms each, with reasonable food and a daily walk in the castle garden, they had to suffer gibes and insults from their undisciplined guards.

More devoted than they had ever been, the royal couple bore their lot with dignity. They took turns in giving lessons to the two children; the King read and prayed devoutly with his sister, Madame Elisabeth, and the Queen busied herself with embroidery and with mending their slender stock of clothes. No news reached them, for newspapers were forbidden and even their bread was cut up into cubes lest messages should be concealed in the loaves. Perhaps it was fortunate that they did not know that Paris was in the grip of the Terror and that every day dozens of persons suspected of royalist sympathies were beheaded by the guillotine.

The monarchy was abolished and Louis XVI was given the name of 'Citizen Capet', but far from gaining their liberty, the unfortunate family was treated more harshly than ever. Louis was no longer allowed to see his wife and children and they only knew that he was alive through listening for his heavy tread on the floor below. In January 1793, after the Queen had been permitted to bid him farewell, Louis went to the guillotine as calmly as he had faced every other disaster.

The only hope for Marie Antoinette now lay with her brother the Emperor, but that cold-hearted man and the kings of Europe had no thought for a woman in prison unless they could make some gain for themselves.

'Everyone has forsaken me,' she cried in despair.

Not everyone. There were men in Paris ready to risk their lives to rescue the Queen. By bribing officials and guards, they almost succeeded, but a plan to smuggle out the Dauphin and his sister with a lamplighter went wrong and Marie Antoinette refused to leave without them.

'However great my happiness at getting away from here,' she wrote, 'my son's interest is my sole guide. I cannot possibly consent to part with him.'

But the Committee of Public Safety ordered the tearful little boy to be taken away from his mother and placed in the charge of Simon, a shoe-mender, who soon taught him to sing revolutionary songs and to accuse his mother of horrible crimes. Marie Antoinette was heart-broken. She would stand for hours peering through a window-slit in hope of catching a glimpse of her bright-eyed son at play in the courtyard, but she never spoke to him again.

The summer wore on and no news or comfort came to the two women and the Princess in their prison. Although she was only thirty-eight, Marie Antoinette's hair had turned white; she was unwell, but she made no complaint to her captors. They were merciless. One night, she was ordered to dress, for she was leaving immediately for another prison; she could take nothing with her but a handkerchief and a little bottle of smelling salts. Quietly she said goodbye to her daughter and her sister-in-law and turned to follow the jailers. As she did so, she struck her head against a low arch: an official asked if she was injured.

'No,' she replied, 'nothing can hurt me now.'

The last seventy days of the Queen's life were passed in a cell furnished with an iron bedstead, a basin and a jug. She had no drawer for her last few garments, no candle at night and no privacy from the guard who watched her every movement. She was searched daily and even her rings and her watch were taken from her, but she was comforted by the devotion of Rosalie, a little serving-maid. Rosalie brought her food and performed small services such as warming her nightdress in her own room and hurrying back to the damp cell to place it in her bed. She also managed to bring a cardboard box for her linen and a cheap little mirror which the Queen received as if they were treasures.

In October 1793, Marie Antoinette was brought before the Tribunal to face a long list of charges, many of which were ridiculous and disgusting but the serious ones accused her of plotting with the enemies of France. To every charge and to every insult from the Public Prosecutor, she gave a firm denial, but when she was accused of undermining her son's health and teaching him evil ways, she refused to answer.

The President pressed her to speak. Raising her head in utter disdain, she said clearly:

'If I have made no reply, it is because nature refused to answer such a charge brought against a mother. I appeal in this matter to all the mothers present in court.'

The fish-wives who had come to gloat over the Widow Capet ceased their knitting and sat absolutely silent.

That evening, Marie Antoinette wrote her last letter to Madame Elisabeth:

'I have just been sentenced—not to a shameful death, for execution is shameful only to criminals, whereas I am going to join your brother. Being innocent like him, I hope to show the firmness which he showed in his last moment. I am calm, though deeply grieved at having to leave my dear children. . . . I hope my son will never forget his father's last words, "Let him never try to avenge our deaths".'

At seven o'clock next morning, Rosalie persuaded the Queen to taste a few spoonfuls of soup and offered to help her to dress. The Tribunal refused to allow her to wear mourning, so she had to change into a white dress and, since the guard would not leave, the serving-maid stood between her and the wall to allow the Queen to change her clothes with as much modesty as possible. Then she arranged her hair carefully and put on a little linen cap. She refused the services of a priest of the Republic and when they came to her cell a second time to ask if she wanted to confess, she replied in a low voice:

'To a priest of Paris? There isn't such a thing.' The official confessor still came forward and asked:

'Would you like me to accompany you, Madame?'

'As you please, Monsieur,' she answered but she did not speak again to the man.

Citizen Sanson, the executioner, arrived and took his stand in the cell, looking the Queen up and down.

'You have come very early, Monsieur,' she said, 'could you not have waited?'

'No, Madame, my orders were to come now,' replied Sanson gruffly. He noticed that beneath her linen cap she had cut off her hair leaving her neck bare, so there was nothing for him to do except to wait, fingering a piece of rope.

Just before eleven, the executioner indicated with a jerk of his head that it was time to leave the cell. Marie Antoinette rose and followed him into the yard where a flicker of indignation passed across her face to see that she was to ride in the tumbril, the executioner's open cart. Her husband had at least been permitted a carriage. No one gave her a hand as she clambered into the cart and seated herself on the wooden board with the unwanted priest and Citizen Sanson standing behind. When the executioner had tied her hands behind her back with his piece of rope, the cart moved into the street where an escort of mounted and dismounted civil police took up their stations on either side.

Cannons had been placed at the cross-roads and in the squares of the city and armed patrols were everywhere to guard against the possibility of a last-minute rescue. But Marie Antoinette saw nothing of that. The vast crowds, silent for the most part except for an occasional jibe shrieked by some guttersnipe, made no impression upon the daughter of Maria Theresa. She sat erect, gazing with unseeing eyes above the heads of those who had come to see a Queen die.

In the great Square of the Revolution, she mounted the steps of the guillotine unassisted and knelt down without a quiver. There was a moment of utter silence. Then the blade fell and a tremendous roar went up:

'Long live the Republic!'

The last entry in the pathetic history of Queen Marie Antoinette was the undertaker's bill to the revolutionary government:

'Widow Capet: for the coffin, 6 francs; for the grave and grave-diggers, 15 francs.'

More about Marie Antoinette (1755–93)

Marie Antoinette the fourth daughter of Maria Theresa, Empress of Austria, was married at fifteen to the Dauphin, who became King Louis XVI in 1774. Her unpopularity arose from her extravagance, from dislike of the Austrian alliance and from her opposition to the popular party. People believed that she would not allow the King to make reforms and they made her the scapegoat for centuries of misrule and aristocratic privilege.

Her son, the Dauphin, known as Louis XVII, was treated with revolting cruelty after his mother's death and he almost certainly died in a prison cell at the age of ten, though in afteryears, various pretenders came forward. His sister, 'Madame Royale', as Marie Thérèse Charlotte was called, was exchanged in 1795 for certain Republican prisoners taken by the Austrians. They included Jean Drouet who had the royal coach stopped at Varennes. The Princess was fifteen at the time of the family's imprisonment and in later years she could not bear to speak of their sufferings. Madame Elisabeth, the King's sister, was guillotined in May 1794; she never received Marie Antoinette's last letter, which only came to light twenty years later. The brothers of Louis XVI who did so little to help him, regained the throne after the fall of Napoleon; one was Louis XVIII, who reigned until 1824, and the other was Charles X, who lost his crown in 1830.

NAPOLEON BONAPARTE

On August 15th 1769, in the Corsican town of Ajaccio, a second son was born to Marie, wife of Charles Bonaparte, a lawyer of Italian descent whose family had lived in Corsica for more than 200 years.

The boy was christened Napoleon and, when he was nine years old, his father sent him away to France to a military school at Brienne. At 16, young Bonaparte entered the French army as a sub-lieutenant in the artillery. He was poor and unhappy, but he worked hard at his profession and studied during the evenings when most young officers were enjoying themselves.

At school, the young Corsican had been unpopular. He was very small, only five feet two inches tall, and his olive-skin and strong accent marked his Italian origin, so that he felt a foreigner among the sons of French gentlemen. But in his work, they had to admit that the sullen Corsican was outstanding, and there was a kind of brooding ferocity about him that prevented them from tormenting him.

When the French Revolution broke out in 1789, Bonaparte remained in the Army for he sympathised with those who believed in liberty and justice, but he soon came to hate the rule of the mob and their utterly unscrupulous leaders.

The violent events in France and the execution of the King and Queen brought about war with several European countries, including England and Austria. The year 1793 found Captain Bonaparte in the Revolutionary force outside Toulon, which was held by French Royalists with the aid of British warships. Bonaparte placed his guns with such skill that the town was captured and the British ships had to withdraw.

He had made his mark and was rewarded with promotion to the rank of brigadier.

Young Bonaparte went to Paris where he found the government in confusion while a cut-throat struggle for power was being waged by the politicians. In this dangerous atmosphere, Bonaparte himself was struck off the list of officers and put into prison for a short time, but luckily he had won the notice of Carnot, the War Minister, and of Barras, a rascally politician.

The Parisians were preparing to overturn the corrupt government when Barras remembered the pale young officer who had captured Toulon.

'I have the very man we need,' he told the frightened Members of the Assembly, though they were hardly impressed when they saw a puny youngster in a threadbare uniform.

Once again, Bonaparte seized his opportunity. He placed field-guns where they could command the bridges and rake the streets leading to the Tuileries Palace where the Assembly was sitting and, at the decisive moment, he gave the order to fire into the advancing crowds. Having saved the government, he looked for his reward, and Carnot obtained for him command of the French army in Italy. At the age of twenty-six, he was a general.

Settling his affairs in Paris, among them his marriage to Josephine, a beautiful widow, Bonaparte hurried to take up his command. He found his army dispirited, ill-armed and hungry. Their officers resented the arrival of the youthful commander who had been placed above them, though Masséna, afterwards one of his most famous marshals, remarked, 'The moment he put on his general's hat he seemed to grow two feet taller'.

Bonaparte addressed the soldiers, telling them that he would lead them to victory and wealth if they showed courage. Then, with lightning speed, he dealt blow after blow upon the Austrian armies that had been holding Northern Italy. He drove the enemy out, forced his own treaty upon them, took up residence in a palace near Milan and conducted affairs without a word to the government in Paris: 'Do you think I triumph in Italy, in order to glorify that pack of lawyers?' he said.

Wagon-loads of treasure were sent back to France and Bonaparte's soldiers were now well-fed and splendidly equipped. They adored him and hailed him as their 'Little Corporal', an affectionate nickname which stuck to him all his life.

The conquering hero returned to Paris where the government was only too anxious to find fresh employment for this terrifying young general. His victories had caused all the enemies of France to retire, except Britain, so it was suggested that he should invade England. Bonaparte had other ideas: 'Europe is too small a field,' he said. 'Fame can only be won in the East.'

To win an Empire and to bar the British route to India, he sailed his army to Egypt, captured Malta on the way and speedily defeated the Mameluke tribesmen at the Battle of the Pyramids. Ten days later, Bonaparte learned that his fleet at Alexandria had been totally destroyed by Admiral Nelson and therefore his army was cut off from France:

'This is the hour when men of superior ability show themselves,' he remarked and began to prepare for a campaign against Turkey.

He won victories but the stubborn defence of Acre denied him a road to the East so he skilfully withdrew to Egypt where serious news awaited him.

The government in France was tottering and all his Italian conquests had been lost to the Austrians. Leaving his army, Bonaparte went aboard a frigate which managed to evade the British warships and to put him ashore on the coast of France.

As the one man who could restore order and deal with the foes who were closing in, Bonaparte swept aside the government and, by the people's vote, he became

First Consul, with two other Consuls of no importance to assist him. He was ruler of France.

With superb energy, Bonaparte crossed the Alps and routed the Austrians at Marengo, while General Moreau, in the north, won a victory at Hohenlinden. For the time being, the Allies had had enough, and in 1802 the Peace of Amiens was signed.

Now, at last, Bonaparte could show that he was more than a successful general.

He put France upon her feet and gave her many of the benefits for which the Revolutionaries had fought. Law and order were established, with an efficient system of government that has remained, little changed, until the present day. Trade, agriculture, education and scientific studies were encouraged; religious freedom was permitted, and careers were opened to men of ability whether they were rich or poor.

'I wish to do something both great and useful for Paris,' declared the Consul, and orders were given to pull down slums, to lay out parks and wide streets and to construct handsome buildings and riverside quays.

In addition, the country was given new roads and canals, but the greatest gift to France was the Code Napoléon, a system of laws that established justice and provided the foundation for the laws of many other countries in the world.

In 1802, Bonaparte was only thirty-three. He had no rival, and had just been made Consul for life. With a stable government in France, trade and prosperity were on the mend everywhere. If only he could have devoted the rest of his life to serving his country peacefully, he might have been the greatest figure in history. Clear-sighted, imaginative, fired with enthusiasm and knowledge of his own great ability, he had all the qualities of a born commander; unfortunately, he chose to use them almost entirely for war.

In 1804, the little Corporal became Emperor of the French. Other emperors might go to Rome but he had the Pope brought to France, and at the coronation ceremony, he took the crown from the hands of His Holiness and crowned himself. Then he turned and placed a crown on the head of Josephine. The Court was soon as magnificent as in the days of the Bourbons. Generals became dukes and princes, former republicans became courtiers and barons, their ladies' dresses changed the fashions of Europe and everyone, even his mother, had to address the Emperor as 'Sire'.

Meanwhile, war had broken out again and the 'Army of England' was assembled on the cliffs at Boulogne, but the French fleets could not win command of the Channel for a few vital days. In disgust, Napoleon broke up his camp and was already marching against Prime Minister Pitt's allies, when Nelson's victory at Trafalgar made England safe from invasion.

The master of war was now at his best. He had a superb army and a corps of generals who had made their names under his leadership. At Ulm, the Austrian commander surrendered with 70,000 men and at Austerlitz, in 1805, perhaps the greatest of Napoleon's victories, the joint armies of Russia and Austria were smashed.

This was the victory that killed Pitt, for men said his face never lost 'the Austerlitz look'.

Next, the King of Prussia's army was destroyed in a single day at Jena. The French Emperor entered Berlin as he had entered Vienna. He went on to defeat the Russians and to make peace with the Tsar who was utterly captivated by the charm that Napoleon could turn on as easily as the ferocious brutality with which he subdued anyone who opposed him.

Now, at last, he was astride Europe. He made and unmade kings as he pleased. He oppressed and robbed countries whose simple people had believed that the French came to bring liberty; whereas he declared, 'the states of Europe must be melted in one nation and Paris must be its capital'.

When it came to sharing out crowns, he did not forget his family, as long as they showed proper respect. One brother, Louis, was made King of Holland; another, Jerome, became King of Westphalia; Joseph was placed on the throne of Naples and Sicily and when he was 'promoted' to be King of Spain, Naples was given to a sister who had married Murat, one of his generals. Another of his officers, Count Bernadotte, ruled in Sweden, and Napoleon himself took the title of King of Italy. Only England, 'perfidious Albion', remained beyond the conqueror's reach.

Plans were made to bring England to her knees by destroying her trade and all Europe was forbidden to do any business at all with the nation of shopkeepers. Since Portugal was a door through which English goods might enter the continent, a French army was sent to crush that small country and Joseph was given the Spanish crown. But the Spaniards and the Portuguese were obstinate people whose countryside was ideal for guerilla warfare, even if they could not face the French in battle. With the help of the Duke of Wellington and his British redcoats, they defied the best generals whom Napoleon could send and tied up a quarter of a million of his veterans. The 'Spanish ulcer' drained the strength of the Grand Army.

Once more, Austria raised an army but again Napoleon triumphed at Wagram, a victory that was followed by his divorce from the Empress Josephine who alone loved and understood him. She had not given him a son, so she was put aside for Marie-Louise, daughter of the Austrian Emperor, who bore him a son known as the King of Rome.

Still, Napoleon could not rest, for Tsar Alexander was defying his orders about trading with Britain and in 1812, the greatest army ever assembled in Europe perished in the snow on the way back from Moscow.

This disaster gave fresh heart to the oppressed peoples of Europe and the armies of Russia, Austria, Prussia, of the German states and even of Sweden were assembled against the Corsican tyrant.

Faced with overwhelming numbers, commanding troops that were mostly young and untrained for war, Napoleon was never more brilliant. He defeated the Allies twice and was only beaten at Leipzig because his guns ran out of ammunition. 'If I had had 30,000 rounds, I should today be master of the world,' he wrote afterwards. Retreating into France, he won one action after another, but

Blücher and the Allies plodded on and, from Spain, Wellington was driving towards the French border.

France's terrible losses were too much to bear and on April 11th 1814, Napoleon abdicated, said a sorrowful farewell to the Guard, and left France for the Isle of Elba, amid the curses of the people who had once adored him.

Ten months later, a short figure in a grey overcoat and a cocked hat stepped ashore in the South of France, and the eleven hundred veterans who were with him wept as they formed in ranks once more behind their Emperor. They had no horses yet, so they set out to march to Paris with Napoleon at their head, stick in hand.

The news of his escape flew ahead and all along the route, he was greeted with cries of 'Long live the Emperor!' His old soldiers fell into step with their comrades, for the Bourbon king, Louis XVIII, was already unpopular and France wanted its glory back. Troops were sent to arrest him, but at the sight of their former commander, they rushed to greet him and he entered Paris in triumph.

The glory was short-lived, for the dismayed Allies could not trust the man who had towered over Europe. In June 1815, his hopes were broken on the ridge of Waterloo when the Old Guard made its final charge and was driven back by Wellington's infantry and cut to pieces by Blücher's Prussians.

The Emperor reached Paris but found no more support. He tried in vain to reach America and, in the end, he surrendered to the nation which had fought him for twenty years, for he went aboard H.M.S. *Bellerophon* which sailed to Plymouth.

Though he asked for the hospitality of the British people, the fallen Emperor was taken to the lonely island of St Helena in the South Atlantic, from which there was no escape. After six years spent in writing his memoirs and quarrelling with the Governor, Napoleon died and was buried on the island. Twenty years later, his body was brought back with great pomp and placed in a magnificent tomb in Paris.

Napoleon was probably the greatest general who ever lived. Unlike Alexander and Caesar, he started with no advantages of birth and made his way by sheer brilliance and the force of his personality. Yet all his conquests brought only disaster to France and at the end, he left his country weaker and smaller than when he mounted the guns at Toulon.

His real gift to France was his system of civil government and laws. As he said himself,

'Waterloo will wipe out the memory of my forty victories, but that which nothing can efface, which will live for ever, is my Civil Code.'

More about Napoleon Bonaparte (1769–1821)

What happened in Europe after Waterloo? Napoleon, as we know, died in 1821 on St Helena, but the effects of his extraordinary career did not die.

The rulers of Europe, particularly of Austria, Russia and Prussia, wanted to put things back much as they were before the terrible Corsican overturned so many thrones. Above all, they were determined to stamp out everything that might lead to revolution.

But, in many countries, Napoleon's tyranny had awoken a spirit of patriotism in ordinary men and a desire for liberty. So, for years, there were uprisings and revolutions. Greece and Belgium gained independence, the Germans tried hard to become a united country, the Poles, Italians and Hungarians rebelled against their foreign rulers.

In France, the Allies had put Louis XVIII on the throne, and he was followed, in 1824, by his brother Charles X, who behaved as if the Revolution had never happened. In 1830, Charles was deposed in favour of Louis-Philippe, 'the Citizen King', who gave France 18 years of peace.

But kindly old Louis-Philippe brought no glamour to the throne and France was bored. The terrific excitement that arose when Napoleon's body was brought home in 1840 showed that the French had not lost their thirst for 'glory'. There was a revolution in Paris in 1848; Louis-Philippe abdicated and Louis Bonaparte, a penniless nephew of Napleon, became President of a new Republic. Three years later, he seized complete power and soon afterwards was hailed as Napoleon III, Emperor of the French.

She worked hard at her lessons to please her governess, 'dear Lehzen, the best and truest of friends'.

THE PRINCESS VICTORIA

On the 24th of May 1819, a baby girl was born in one of the many rooms of a shabby royal residence called Kensington Palace. She was the daughter of the Duke and Duchess of Kent and grandchild of His Majesty King George III, but her arrival caused no excitement and hardly a mention in the newspapers.

At the baby's christening, her father wished her name to be Elizabeth, but the Prince Regent insisted upon Alexandrina, in honour of her godfather, the Tsar of Russia. Her mother's name, Victoria, was added as an afterthought.

The birth of a princess aroused no rejoicing because at this time, the Royal Family was very unpopular. George III, very old, blind and quite mad, was pitied, but his seven sons were universally hated.

'Prinny', the eldest son, still fancied himself as 'the first gentleman in Europe', but his elegance had long since faded and he was now disgustingly fat and disagreeable. His only daughter, the charming Princess Charlotte, had died soon after marrying a German prince called Leopold and, since none of his brothers had produced a single heir, it had seemed likely that the House of Hanover would come to an end.

To prevent such a calamity, two of the royal Dukes looked round for wives and they found them, as usual, among the numerous princesses of Germany.

The lady chosen by the Duke of Kent was a sister of the Prince Leopold already mentioned. She was a widow with two children, a boy Charles and a pretty twelve-year-old daughter named Feodora.

The Duke of Kent was a stiff military man, with dyed hair and enormous debts which he hoped Parliament would pay when he had done his duty by marrying. Parliament, however, was not very generous, so the Duke grumbled and stayed on in Germany until it was known that his wife was expecting a baby.

An heir for the House of Hanover had to be born in England, so the royal couple hurried back as cheaply as possible and were given a suite of rooms in Kensington Palace where little Alexandrina Victoria was born. Soon afterwards, the family travelled down to Sidmouth in Devonshire where it was thought the sea air would be better for the baby's health than the sooty atmosphere of London.

At Sidmouth, the peppery Duke went for a walk one day, got his feet wet, took a chill and died. Six days later, poor old George III died at Windsor and fat Prinny became King George IV. The little princess at Sidmouth was now an important baby, for the King had no children nor had his next brothers, the Duke of York and William, Duke of Clarence.

The Duchess of Kent was fully aware of her daughter's importance, but for the moment, she was in a difficult situation. She had little money and few friends. She could hardly speak a word of English and she was faced with the mountain of her husband's debts and the dislike of the Royal Family. King George made it quite clear that he expected her to take herself and her baby back to Germany.

The Duchess refused to go. She was determined to bring up her daughter as an English princess and if the Royal Family would not help, there was the child's Uncle Leopold, living in Surrey on a large income, who would come to the rescue.

So the Duchess and her small household came back to the rooms at Kensington Palace. She was a stout cheerful person, fond of chatter and of bright silk dresses, but she was also fussy and tactless and she had a marvellous way of making people dislike her.

The household consisted of the Duchess herself, Feodora and her German governess, Fräulein Lehzen, and Sir John Conroy, who was agent and adviser. There were some female attendants and servants, all of them drilled by the Duchess to form a protective ring about the baby, in order to screen her from the outside world and the influence of the Court and her scandalous old uncles.

Princess 'Drina, as she was called at this time, was spoilt. The chubby, flaxen-haired child who reminded everyone of her grandfather, captivated the household with her blue eyes and pretty ways. Feodora and her nurses adored her and she did as she pleased, demanding her own way and screaming with temper when anything was not to her liking. Yet she was warm-hearted and she was always sorry for her naughtiness when the tantrums were over.

In later years, Feodora spoke of this period as 'those years of imprisonment', but, for the moment, little 'Drina was happy enough. She had a donkey, a present from Uncle York, to ride in the lovely grounds about the Palace; there were elderly aunts and uncles living in the various apartments who petted their tiny niece and took her for walks among the flowers and there were a few, though very few, little girls who came to play and look at her dolls.

When she was five, the self-willed princess came under the guidance of Fräulein Lehzen who declared 'there never was such a passionate and naughty child'. With her beady eyes, sharp nose and shining black head, the German governess resembled a watchful bird, but, for all her odd habits and plain appearance, Fräulein Lehzen was a remarkable woman.

By instinct, this German clergyman's daughter seemed to know exactly what was needed for bringing up an English princess. She stood no nonsense from the wilful child but, while she was teaching her to be self-controlled, she somehow won Victoria's heart. Mamma was strict and always in a hurry; the child loved her Mamma of course, but Lehzen was the person she talked to, the person who understood her. She became obedient and worked hard at her lessons to please her governess, 'dear Lehzen, the best and truest of friends'.

Under Lehzen's watchful eye, a team of tutors took over Victoria's education. The Dean of Chester was in charge, with another clergyman to teach Latin, a Frenchman to give French lessons and various artists to teach drawing which was one of the Princess's best subjects. She also liked music and singing, and when she was given an examination at the age of eleven by two bishops, they reported that her knowledge of Scripture and History was 'remarkable in so young a person'.

Life was not very exciting at Kensington. Feodora went to live in Germany, the time-table and the rules were very strict, the food was plain and lessons lasted a long time. There was no fun and even books had to be serious, for Victoria was not allowed to read stories or a novel until she was almost grown-up.

The Duchess guarded the child so closely that she had no company of her own age and hardly a glimpse of the outside world. She was never left alone for a minute, but had to sleep in her mother's bedroom and go everywhere, even up and down stairs, with an attendant holding her hand.

There were rare outings and visits. Victoria liked to go down to Surrey to see Uncle Leopold who was always kind and full of good advice; there was company there and sometimes cousins came on visits from Germany.

Besides her dolls, Victoria was devoted to the dogs and ponies that constantly appear in the diary which she began to keep. A King Charles spaniel called Dash was her favourite: 'I dressed dear sweet little Dash for the second time after dinner in a scarlet jacket and blue trousers'; and there was Rosy the pony: 'We galloped over a green field; Rosy went at an enormous rate—she literally flew . . . I fed dear Rosy who is always so greedy.'

One day, there was the never-to-be-forgotten visit when George IV summoned his niece to Windsor where the child was fascinated by his painted cheeks and old-fashioned wig.

'Give me your little paw!' bellowed the King jovially when she arrived and soon, to Mamma's dismay, she was squeezed into a phaeton between the King and the Duchess of Gloucester and taken for a ride in the Great Park.

They went aboard a barge filled with ladies and gentlemen who were fishing to the strains of a royal band that played from another barge. There were cakes and peaches for tea and music all evening at Royal Lodge. The King beamed at Victoria. 'Come now,' he said. 'What's your favourite tune? What's it to be, hey?'

Innocently, the tired child replied, 'God Save the King,' and the day ended happily for everyone.

At home, things were less comfortable. A deadly feud had developed between Sir John Conroy and Lehzen, in which the Duchess sided with Conroy, and Victoria with her dear governess. The Duchess was furious but she dared not dismiss Lehzen because the King, realising her worth, had recently made her the Baroness Lehzen.

The child's importance grew. Parliament voted her an income suitable for one so near to the throne; the Duke of York died and then George IV himself. The Duke of Clarence became King William IV, a rolling, burbling, seafaring man whose manners were shocking but whose heart was kind enough. Unfortunately, he loathed the Duchess of Kent even more than his brother George had done.

The Duchess made two decisions. First, Victoria must be told of her position as heir to the throne (which Lehzen did by slipping into her history book a piece of paper showing the Royal family-tree) and, second, she must be taken about to view her future kingdom.

Tours were arranged to the West Country, to Wales, the Midlands and the Black Country. Although the Duchess was always there, bursting with self-importance and taking the limelight, it was all a delightful change from the schoolroom. Most of all, Victoria enjoyed sailing in the Solent aboard the King's yacht, though Mamma foolishly insisted that warships and coastal forts should fire royal salutes whenever she herself appeared. The old sailor William IV was very cross about this and he issued a special order forbidding what he called 'all these poppings and bangings'.

But the Duchess continued to annoy her brother-in-law. She had refused to attend his Coronation and now he was convinced that she was deliberately keeping his niece away from the Court. He was very fond of Victoria and gave her a wonderful Ball at St James's Palace on her fourteenth birthday when she was led into supper as the guest of honour between the King and Queen Adelaide.

The Duchess took care that she herself arranged the next birthday dance. When Victoria was seventeen, the King was not present at her Ball in Kensington Palace, but two German cousins were there, one named Ernest and the other Albert. The dancing went on until past three o'clock in the morning and, next day, Victoria noted in her diary, 'Albert is extremely handsome'.

The King was not well but he had made up his mind to live until Victoria was eighteen, because that was the age at which she could ascend the throne without having to have her Mamma as Regent. He invited them to Windsor for a banquet, but the Duchess made difficulties about the date he had chosen. This annoyed him and then, happening to call at Kensington, he found that the Duchess had taken over a suite of seventeen rooms directly against his orders.

Boiling with rage, William went back to Windsor where his guests were arriving. He greeted his niece kindly and then turned to the Duchess and loudly rebuked her in front of the company.

Worse followed. At the banquet, the King rose to make a speech and he soon worked himself into a frenzy of temper about the Duchess, whom he constantly referred to as 'a person now near me'.

While the aristocratic guests, the Queen, the Princess and the white-faced Duchess sat staring at their plates, the King ranted on about the insults he had had to put up with from his sister-in-law; he would endure them no longer; he would not have his authority questioned; he hoped he might be spared a little longer so that 'that person' would never be Regent He would not allow this young lady to be kept away from his Court and so on and on and on.

When this record piece of rudeness was over, the poor Duchess left the room without a word and soon departed from Windsor.

Despite her humiliation, the Duchess could afford to wait. The King could not last much longer and when her daughter was Queen, the daughter whom she had reared so carefully, things would be different. They would see! Mamma would be the Queen Mother with power and influence, for Victoria was an obedient girl and there was good Uncle Leopold to advise them. Leopold was now King of the Belgians, but his letters came across the Channel in a never-ending stream. Victoria said nothing.

By this time, Victoria was enjoying herself. She rode, she danced, she took an increasing interest in music. She seemed to be bursting with life and high spirits; at Brighton, an observer remarked, 'a more homely little being you never beheld . . . she blushes and laughs every instant in so natural a way as to disarm everybody'. But one of her ladies also said, 'a vein of iron runs through her most extraordinary character'.

Truthful and affectionate, Victoria kept her innermost thoughts to herself and sometimes her mouth, so pretty when she smiled, took on an obstinate downward curve. No one, except dear Lehzen, suspected that the tiny Princess—she was barely five feet two inches and used to sigh, 'everyone grows but me'—was a far stronger character than her tactless Mamma.

At last, her eighteenth birthday arrived and the King, too ill to attend the Court Ball, sent her a grand piano as a present with the offer, not to her mother but to herself, of ten thousand pounds a year. The King was content. He had lived long enough to thwart his sister-in-law, 'that nuisance of a woman', and, within a month, he died at Windsor in the early hours of June 20th, 1837.

The Archbishop of Canterbury and the Lord Chamberlain immediately ordered a carriage and drove to Kensington where they arrived at five o'clock in the morning. Apart from a desire to be first with the news, it is not clear why they insisted on waking the Princess at such an hour, but they did so. After they had gained admittance to the Palace, the Duchess was roused and asked to inform her daughter that two visitors wished to speak with her upon a matter of the utmost importance.

With her fair hair loose about her shoulders and a cotton dressing-gown over her night-dress, Victoria went into the room where the gentlemen were waiting, closing the door firmly upon her Mamma. She was, as she wrote in her diary, underlining the word, 'alone'. The Lord Chamberlain knelt, kissed her hand and informed her that she was Queen of England. She took the news calmly and returned to her mother's room to dress.

At breakfast, Baron Stockmar, an earnest friend of Uncle Leopold, arrived with advice on how to carry out her duties. At nine o'clock, Lord Melbourne, the Prime Minister, called to kiss his sovereign's hand and to offer her the declaration which she must read to her first Privy Council. He did this with such polish and fatherly charm that he won Victoria's heart for ever. Then there were letters to write, to Uncle Leopold, to Feodora and to Queen Adelaide. All was done quietly and at half-past eleven, Victoria went downstairs to meet her Council.

The slim short girl took her seat in silence before a gathering of lords, ministers, bishops, generals and two royal uncles. Instead of a shy schoolgirl stumbling over long, unfamiliar words, they beheld a calm young woman who read her speech in a beautifully clear voice.

Then, as they came up one by one to kiss her hand, they were further astonished by her dignity and grace. 'She was perfection,' said one politician and even the hard-bitten old Duke of Wellington declared, 'If she had been my own daughter, I could not have wished that she should do better. Why, she not only filled the chair, she filled the room!'

When the Council was over, Victoria went upstairs to Mamma and Lehzen. To their astonishment, she announced that her first request to them as Queen would be to be left alone for an hour. At the end of the first hour she had ever spent entirely by herself, the Queen gave her second command. Her bed was to be removed from her mother's room and a separate bedroom was to be made ready. Her reign had begun.

It was to be a long reign, the longest in British history. Victoria was to know great happiness and sorrow, for she was to marry her handsome cousin Albert, to have nine children and to lose her husband when she needed him most. Her popularity was to rise, to fall away and to climb again to a peak of loyalty that amounted to reverence. Her country was to grow in power and wealth until she was Sovereign of the greatest Empire in all history and she was to live on into a new century and a changed world.

But on that June day in 1837, Victoria knew nothing of what lay ahead, only that she was Queen and, at long last, triumphantly 'alone'.

More about Victoria (1819–1901)

Soon after her accession, the young Queen went to live at Buckingham Palace and her mother was gently but firmly put into the background. She was upset, but later she and her daughter became firm friends. Lehzen, too, was out of favour for a while but not for long; she retired to Germany but kept up an affectionate correspondence with her former pupil.

In 1840, the Queen married her cousin Prince Albert. It was a happy marriage for Victoria adored her husband, though she was not a sympathetic mother; she did not understand children and actually disliked her eldest son. Albert was serious and far better educated than his wife who, after a brief struggle, allowed him to advise her and play an increasing part in the country's affairs. But he was never popular and only the Queen appreciated his excellent qualities. When he died suddenly in 1861, the Queen was broken-hearted. She went into deep mourning and withdrew so completely from public life that for some years she was very unpopular.

The influence of Disraeli drew her out of retirement and she became ever more respected by her people until at the Jubilee of 1897, there was the greatest outburst of loyal affection that had ever been known in a country where, for three hundred years, the Royal Family had been generally disliked.

The leading statesmen of the reign were Peel, Palmerston, Gladstone and Disraeli, but it was also a period of greatness in literature, science and industry, when Britain's power was at its peak. Victoria herself played a considerable part in politics, though her ministers often found her very difficult and obstinate. Her portraits and photographs usually give her a rather cross expression but, in fact, she smiled often; she had a beautiful speaking voice and a delightful silvery laugh which, to the end of her life, sounded like a young girl's.

The King set himself to inspire unity and the will for victory.

GEORGE VI

'Suddenly at about 2 p.m. a signal was received that the German High Seas Fleet was out and engaging our battle cruisers only forty miles away and that the battle was coming in our direction. Huge excitement. Out at last. Full speed ahead. Sound of "Action"—you can imagine the scene! Out of his bunk leaps "Johnson". Ill? Never felt better! Strong enough to go to his turret and fight a prolonged action? Of course he was, why ever not?'

Thus wrote a naval officer to the Prince of Wales in a letter describing one of the major sea battles of the First World War, the Battle of Jutland in 1916.

'Johnson' was none other than His Royal Highness Prince Albert, second son of King George v and Queen Mary, who had joined the Royal Navy as a midshipman in 1913 and now, at the age of twenty, was serving as a sub-lieutenant in the battleship *Collingwood*.

Although he had chosen, like his father, to make a career in the Navy, Prince Albert suffered from sea-sickness and an obstinate stomach complaint which had transferred him for a time to a hospital ship. He had rejoined his ship but was ill in his bunk when 'Action Stations' rang out. He dashed to his gun turret and remained there until the next day, the first prince in direct line to the throne to see active service since William IV.

Jutland was a confused engagement in which the German fleet severely damaged Admiral Beatty's cruiser squadron, but broke away as the British Grand Fleet came racing up and, under cover of mist and a smoke screen, retired to the safety of the German minefields. *Collingwood* came under heavy attack from enemy torpedo craft and was straddled by salvoes one of which passed just over the ship when Prince Albert was sitting on top of A turret. He saw *Invincible* blown to bits and then *Defence* and *Black Prince* disappear in a welter of smoke and flames.

'We went to "Action Stations" at 4.30 p.m.', he wrote home afterwards, 'and saw the Battle Cruisers in action ahead of us on the starboard bow. . . . we opened fire at 5.37 p.m. on some German light cruisers. The *Collingwood*'s second salvo hit one of them which set her on fire, and sank after two more salvoes were fired into her. We then shifted on to another light cruiser and helped to sink her as well. Our next target was a battle cruiser, we think the *Derfflinger* . . ., and one of the

Collingwood's salvoes hit her abaft the after turret which burst into a fierce flame. After this she turned away from us and disappeared into the mist. By this time it was too dark to fire and we went to Night Defence stations. . . . When I was on top of the turret I never felt any fear of shells or anything else. It seems curious, that all the sense of danger goes. . . .'

Not long after the battle, Prince Albert's stomach pains returned and, although he went to sea again in the battleship *Malaya*, it became clear that he was no longer fit for active service and must be operated on.

Queen Mary noted in her diary:

> *November 28, 1917. It is decided that poor Bertie is to have an operation tomorrow as he does not seem at all well and has constant pain. He is most cheerful about it.*
> *November 29, 1917. Dr. Rigby performed the operation at 10, which was most successful . . . they found the cause of all the trouble he had been having since 1915.*

Thus the Prince's naval career was ended. As a cadet at Dartmouth, a shy highly-strung boy with a bad stammer, he had been next to bottom of his class, much to the dismay of his father, but, by dint of hard work, he had passed out as 'Mr Johnson', a midshipman who cheerfully accepted all the tasks of a 'snotty'—standing watch, handling a picket-boat, coaling ship—and, by seventeen, had learned to take command of older men. His shipmates found him a conscientious good-humoured companion, who never shirked or expected any privileges.

George, Duke of York, was the second son of the jovial Prince of Wales who became King Edward VII and, since it was unlikely that he would come to the throne, the boy was allowed to join the Royal Navy. He loved service life and had risen by merit to the rank of Commander, when his older brother, the Duke of Clarence, died. He was now his father's direct heir and it was therefore decided that he must give up the sea and devote himself to State affairs.

In 1893, George married Princess Mary of Teck and went to live in York Cottage, a gloomy house in the grounds of his father's estate in Sandringham. Far from thinking it ugly, he loved the place and lived there happily for 33 years, a country gentleman who, more than anything, enjoyed bringing up his children, managing the estate and shooting—he was said to be the best shot in England.

There were six children, of whom the first three, Edward, (known in the family as 'David') Albert and Mary, were close to each other in age and therefore great friends. As he was to do all his life, Prince Edward charmed everyone, with his bright eager manner and good looks, while Mary, a sweet pretty child, received her share of attention, but poor Bertie in the middle, a shy nervous boy given to tears and sudden bursts of temper, felt that he was nobody's favourite. He adored his elder brother and followed his lead into all kinds of mischief, for which, somehow, he usually got the blame. On his fifth birthday, his father wrote to him,

'Now that you are five years old, I hope that you will always try and be obedient and do at once what you are told, as you will find it will come much easier to you the sooner you begin.'

The Duke was a great one for obedience. He treated his family as though they were under his command in the Navy; he genuinely loved them but he had to have discipline, punctuality and absolute obedience. His habit of constantly lecturing the children and finding fault with their behaviour created a barrier between him and his sons, so that, in later years, Prince Edward rebelled against his ideas, though Bertie always stood in awe of his father and tried to win his approval. The stammer, which became very marked when he was a small boy, caused him untold embarrassment, especially when he grew older and had to speak in public. Experts were called in and he underwent courses of speech training without much improvement, so that, unlike his brother, he tended to stay in the background and to miss out on overseas tours and the more exciting royal duties.

When he had recovered from his operation, Prince Albert felt that he must find some form of war service, so he decided to join the Air Force. It was not yet known as the R.A.F. and, in January 1918, he was appointed to the Royal Naval Air Service squadron at Cranwell in Lincolnshire, a primitive station of hangars and corrugated-iron huts, where thousands of recruits were being trained.

Here he was put in charge of 2500 boys:

'I am known as the Officer Commanding Boys', he wrote proudly to his father. 'I am going to run them as an entirely separate unit to the remainder of the men. I shall have to punish them myself and grant their requests for leave etc. At present I have not got a proper office. . . . The work is entirely new to me and I find it rather difficult to begin with but I shall get used to it. They live in small huts, 20 boys in each, and these give me the most trouble as they won't keep them clean without my constantly telling them off. . . .'

After the Navy, he found things rather slack and soon earned a reputation as a strict disciplinarian. However, as 'P.A.' to his fellow-officers, he was well liked and his boys earned him high praise when they paraded before the King and Queen, during a visit of inspection.

King George, who praised no-one lightly, must have been pleased with his son's progress, for, in November 1918, when the war had ended, he chose Prince Albert to represent him in Brussels when the King of the Belgians re-entered his capital after years of exile.

Back in the Air Force, the Prince determined not to remain a 'Quirk', or land-based officer, but to learn to fly. His training took place at Croydon and there, on 31st July 1919, he received his wings as a fully qualified pilot, the first, and for many years the only member of the Royal Family to win this distinction.

His instructor found that he possessed the hand and eye of a good games player, for, by this time, Prince Albert had become a first-class horseman and a fine left-handed tennis-player. In 1920, he and his friend, Louis Greig, won the R.A.F. doubles championship and, in 1926, they were good enough to play at Wimbledon.

The world of 1919 was very different from that in which Prince Albert and his brothers and sister had been brought up. The rich would never be so rich again; the right of the Ruling Class to govern the country was being questioned; the Labour Party was growing in strength and discontent became so widespread that riots broke out in several cities. Abroad, the situation was worse, for parts of Europe had been devastated by the war, millions had died and millions more were sick and hungry. The Russian Revolution had been followed by civil war and in central and eastern Europe empires had crumbled and monarchs had lost their thrones.

There was no threat to the monarchy in Britain, but George v felt that his sons must continue to play a useful part in the nation's affairs. The Prince of Wales was despatched on a series of tours through the Empire and Prince Albert and Prince Henry were sent to Trinity College, Cambridge, to complete their education.

In his obstinate way, however, the King laid it down that Prince Albert should not live in college and that one year of study was enough. Thus, although he attended lectures and studied hard, he had little chance to join the light-hearted life of most undergraduates and he left the University without making any lasting friends.

During the next fifteen years, Prince Albert, now the Duke of York, represented the King in the Balkans, Northern Ireland, East Africa, New Zealand and Australia, while at home, he became involved in activities which had rarely concerned royalty.

He had worked with men and boys in the Navy and Air Force and he felt that he must find out more about the lives of ordinary people in an industrial society. So he visited factories, mines and blast-furnaces, asking questions and talking to workers on the shop-floor and, as the first president of the Industrial Welfare Society, he encouraged employers to improve working conditions and provide sickness benefits, pensions and sports facilities.

Another of his schemes was the Duke of York's Camp, to which he invited one hundred public schools and one hundred industrial firms to send two boys each to meet and mix together for a week's camping holiday. His idea was to break down barriers of class, so that by working and playing together boys from completely different backgrounds could get to know one another. After a slow start, the Camp became an established success and was held every year, but one, from 1921 until 1939. The Duke himself always spent a day with his guests, joining in the games, discussions and evening sing-songs, at which 'Underneath the Spreading Chestnut Tree', with actions, was the uproarious highlight.

Two circumstances had changed a shy nervous youth into the mature man who was steadily earning people's respect: his marriage and a cure for his stammer.

In 1923, he married Lady Elizabeth Bowes-Lyon, a gracious high-spirited girl who charmed away his melancholy and gave him the love and encouragement which he so needed. It was a perfect marriage and the King, who took an immense liking to his daughter-in-law wrote in his diary, 'Bertie is a very lucky fellow.'

With their daughters, Princess Elizabeth and Princess Margaret, who were born in 1926 and 1930, the Yorks were made much of in the popular papers and magazines. They seemed to be an ideally happy family, wealthy, of course, but leading unaffected lives, for the Duke had no wish to be a figure in fashionable society. It began to dawn on people that Elizabeth might one day be Queen, for the Prince of Wales was still unmarried and, at the King and Queen's Silver Jubilee in 1935, as the Duke and Duchess drove in procession with their daughters, a voice from the crowed called out:

'There goes the hope of England.'

By this time, Lionel Logue, an Australian speech therapist had practically cured the stammer which had caused the Duke so much distress. He taught him to breathe correctly and gave him self-confidence to overcome the defect; it returned at times when he was tired or anxious, but he knew how to keep it in control.

As he grew old, George V was beset with worries. Unemployment and poverty were rife, India was seething with unrest, Fascist parties had arisen in Italy and Germany, and, in his own family, the Prince of Wales caused him much anxiety. For years, the King had deplored his son's rebellious attitude, his refusal to take advice and his light-hearted almost play-boy, way of life. Now, to the distress of the Royal Family, the Prince was to be seen everywhere with a Mrs Simpson, an attractive American lady who had two husbands living, one, divorced, in America, and Mr Simpson in England. Filled with gloom for the future, the old King muttered to one of his ministers,

'After I am dead, the boy will ruin himself within twelve months!'

George V died at Sandringham and Edward VIII was proclaimed King on 20th January 1936. It seemed to most people that his reign was bound to be a success, for he was popular and far more in touch with modern ideas than his father. But the Prime Minister, Stanley Baldwin, told Mr Attlee that the new King's lack of interest in his duties made him doubtful if he 'would stay the course'.

In the summer of 1936, the King chartered a yacht and took Mrs Simpson with him on a Mediterranean cruise; foreign reporters and photographers followed them everywhere and their friendship made banner headlines in American and continental newspapers. But the British Press remained silent. In the autumn, to Queen Mary's displeasure, Mrs Simpson was invited to Balmoral and, in October, she was granted a divorce at Ipswich.

By this time, His Majesty's ministers were seriously concerned, for, if the King meant to marry Mrs Simpson, she would be Queen and would be crowned with him in Westminster Abbey. But he was Head of the Church of England, which, in 1936, held that Christian marriage lasted for life. The Prime Minister consulted the leading politicians, the trade unions, the Archbishop of Canterbury and the Dominion Prime Ministers. They all gave the same answer: as the Australian High Commissioner told Mr Baldwin,

'If there is any question of marriage, the King will have to go.'

For his part, Edward VIII was equally firm, turning a deaf ear to the pleadings of Queen Mary and his brothers:

'I have looked at it from all sides,' he said, 'And I mean to abdicate and marry Mrs Simpson.'

On 10th December 1936, the Duke of York, silent and almost sick with anxiety and regret, watched his brother calmly sign the documents of Abdication:

'It was a dreadful moment and one never to be forgotten. . . .' he wrote afterwards, 'I later went to London where I found a large crowd outside my house cheering madly. I was overwhelmed.'

The new King, who took the name of George VI, began his reign in a mood close to despair.

'Dickie, this is absolutely terrible,' he said to his cousin, Lord Mountbatten, 'I never wanted this to happen; I'm quite unprepared for it. David has been trained for this all his life. I've never seen a state paper; I'm only a naval officer, it's the only thing I know about.'

However, the shy man who had never wished to be in the limelight, had two qualities that were to stand him and the Commonwealth in good stead during the next sixteen years: courage, as he had shown at Jutland, and a sense of duty that never failed him or his country.

The first two years of George VI's reign were the period of appeasement, that is, when the British Government, led by Prime Minister Neville Chamberlain, tried to come to friendly terms with Germany. Attempts were made to satisfy old grievances and nothing was done, apart from mild protests, to oppose Hitler's aggressive policy and obvious preparations for war.

Like the vast majority of his people, George VI dreaded the thought of war and air bombardment of cities, so he supported Chamberlain in his efforts for peace, and, with the Queen, made a state visit to Paris in May 1938 to demonstrate to the world the friendship between France and Britain.

Within a year, Hitler had broken his promises made at Munich and had sent troops to occupy Czechoslovakia; this meant that war was certain and, in the few months that remained up until September 1939, Britain was engaged in frantic attempts to find allies and to rebuild her long-neglected armed forces. During this period, the King and Queen visited Canada and the United States, where they were entertained at Washington by the President, Franklin D. Roosevelt.

The tour was a great success and, years later, Mrs Roosevelt wrote:

'My husband invited them to Washington largely because, believing that we might all soon be engaged in a life and death struggle, in which Britain would be our first line of defence, he hoped that the visit would create a bond of friendship between the two countries.'

The war was indeed a life and death struggle in which Britain came close to total defeat and the British people endured bombing, food rationing, the blackout and all kinds of restrictions, grief and anxiety for five and a half years.

From his broadcast to the nation on the first night of the war, the King set himself to inspire unity and the will for victory, no matter what the cost, and to encourage, advise and, at times, to warn his ministers and senior commanders. During the early months, he was constantly with the Services, visiting the Fleet, inspecting army units in France, the Home Guard on remote stations and the R.A.F. squadrons on their airfields during the Battle of Britain; but, when the Blitz fell upon London and many of Britain's towns and cities, he and the Queen were there, picking their way through smoke and rubble, to comfort and, by their presence, to share the horror and shock of those who had lost their homes and, all too often, a wife, a husband or a child.

The King himself lost his brother, the Duke of Kent, who was killed flying with the R.A.F. Buckingham Palace was twice bombed in September, once when the King was at Windsor visiting his daughters, and, on a second occasion, when he and the Queen were severely shaken. The Queen said afterwards:

'I'm glad we've been bombed: it makes me feel I can look the East End in the face . . . The destruction is so awful and the people so wonderful—they *deserve* a better world.'

Throughout the war, King George worked closely with his Prime Minister, Winston Churchill. In place of formal audiences, they met on Tuesdays for lunch to talk about the situation and, while the King had no control over decisions, Churchill valued his opinion and judgement. He was trusted with the innermost secrets of war, such as the plan for the Normandy landings and the development of the atomic bomb. As the tide turned and victories took the place of defeats, he was able to visit the Eighth Army in North Africa and the invasion troops on the beaches. Both he and Churchill had wanted to be present at the D-Day landings, watching from the deck of a cruiser and it was only with difficulty that their advisers persuaded them not to go.

Victory came at last in May 1945 and it was a tired King who appeared on the balcony of Buckingham Palace, to wave to the crowds, with the Queen, Mr Churchill and the two princesses. His health had never been good and in the six years that remained to him, he kept up his rigorous attention to duty, concerning himself with home affairs, foreign policy and the Commonwealth. Towards Mr Attlee, whose Labour government was introducing sweeping changes, his attitude was at first rather distant but they later came to like and respect one another.

In 1949, George VI underwent a major operation; it appeared to be successful and after recuperating in Scotland, he was able to go shooting again, though he had to give up hill-walking. But he became increasingly frail and, in 1951, had to be operated on again, this time for the removal of a lung. Yet he rallied and, in January 1952, insisted on going to London Airport to stand in a bitter wind to wave goodbye to Princess Elizabeth and Prince Philip as they left for East Africa. He returned to Sandringham and on February 5th felt well enough to go out shooting hares. He died that night in his sleep and, out in Kenya, at a game-reserve, his daughter learned that she was Queen Elizabeth II.

More about George VI (1895–1952)

Prince Albert was born at York Cottage, Sandringham, and named after the Prince Consort, which greatly pleased Queen Victoria, the baby's great-grandmother. She died when he was six and was succeeded by Edward VII, a benevolent grandfather who enjoyed spoiling the York children (when their father was absent!).

They were Edward ('David'), Albert, Mary (who married Viscount Lascelles), Henry, Duke of Gloucester, George, Duke of Kent and John, who died at the age of 14 years. Their father, the martinet, George V, reigned from 1910 until his death in 1936, the year in which Edward VIII abdicated in order to marry Mrs Simpson. Thus, unexpectedly, 'Bertie' came to the throne as King George VI.

INDEX

Bold figures refer to colour plates